BREAKING BREAD

BREAKING BREAD

ESSAYS FROM NEW ENGLAND
ON FOOD, HUNGER, AND FAMILY

A COLLECTION OF ESSAYS TO RAISE
FUNDS FOR THE NONPROFIT BLUE ANGEL

Edited by
Deborah Joy Corey and Debra Spark

BEACON PRESS
BOSTON

BEACON PRESS
Boston, Massachusetts
www.beacon.org

Beacon Press books
are published under the auspices of
the Unitarian Universalist Association of Congregations.

25 24 23 22   8 7 6 5 4 3 2 1

This book is printed on acid-free paper that meets the uncoated paper
ANSI/NISO specifications for permanence as revised in 1992.

Text design and composition by Kim Arney

Library of Congress Cataloging in Publication Data is available for this title.
Library of Congress Control Number: 2022005448
Hardcover ISBN: 978-08070-1086-0
Ebook ISBN: 978-08070-1089-1

*For Karen
and Cyndy
and all our angels*

Contents

PREFACE
Deborah Joy Corey

A FEW YEARS AGO, I was hearing more about hunger increasing in Maine, and so I began to do some research, thinking that I would write an essay. I visited nearby food pantries and shelters. One shelter director said that her pantry rarely receives fresh vegetables or jams and jellies or brand-name peanut butter. She also told me that many people she serves do not have happy food memories. Some of the children have never experienced home cooking. Their appetites are driven by growling bellies, not the smell of a roasting chicken, or a simmering stew, or chocolate chip cookies baking when they arrive home from school.

I also talked to local church and community leaders, who told me that members of my own village often did not have enough food. All of them, with the exception of a few who are elderly or chronically ill, have jobs and work hard. Upon learning this, what had started as a research mission became a mandate to help.

In February of 2019, I asked Paul and Dixie Gray, leaders at the church that I attend, if I could use an empty space on church property to build a garden. The space had once been a playground for a daycare, and that seemed to ordain it for growing vegetables for local families. The Grays were immediately supportive and have remained so.

MARCH OF 2019 was a cold month. On the first day, my beloved niece Karen died suddenly of an aneurysm. She had the most beautiful blue eyes. She was a caring mother, an experienced gardener, and a wonderful cook. Each morning when I woke, the frost had made beautiful and intricate angel wings on my bedroom window. For many mornings after her death,

I studied the frozen angel wings, the rising sun shining through them and making them gleam as they melted away. One night, I dreamt of an angel with mighty blue wings the color of Karen's eyes.

This dream sustained me while forming Blue Angel. I began to talk to local farms to see if they might help provide fresh produce for families. Amanda Provencher of King Hill Farm was the first on board, and others followed.

Later, I asked my community to donate from their home gardens, and boy, have they delivered! Others have given financially, some water and weed the church garden, some bake bread and cakes and cookies. Village chefs make soup and stews, and the local markets and restaurants give—all leaving their donations on my porch. By the grace of those blue wings, it continues.

Since the spring of 2019, Blue Angel has been making weekly deliveries of healthy food to nearby homes. From porch to porch, it goes. Often, we have extras that we give to local daycares and food pantries. At a shelter in Orland, Maine, we have set up a free summer vegetable stand. Some of the families that we help now plant their own gardens and give back to Blue Angel. Our youngest gardener is seven years old. Her name is Fiona.

THE OFTEN-USED PHRASE *food insecure* seems to soften the crisis of hunger that I have witnessed. *Ravenous. Starving. I could eat a horse and chase the rider*—these are the things that I say at the first twinge of hunger. I never say, "I feel a little food insecure." The low impact of this language is dangerous. It provides comfort to the wrong people, allowing the fortunate to maintain an illusion that hunger in our community is a mere inconvenience, rather than an immediate crisis.

The fact that many do not have fond food memories has stayed with me, making me examine my own food memories and wonder about those of others. What if we were to share our memories with one another, the good and the bad? What if we did something to start a broader conversation? Could sharing our stories be the catalyst to change, as it so often is? And, so, I asked my writing community to take the lead by submitting essays about their food memories.

The generous response was so overwhelming that I soon knew I needed a coeditor. I partnered with an old friend, Debra Spark. Debra and I met many years ago when we were both young writers living in Boston. I am so grateful to her and to all the writers who have shared their work. By offering their stories regarding their food heritage, they are breaking bread through story, and they are supporting Blue Angel's mission. From the bottom of my heart, I thank them.

www.blueangelme.org

THE RHUBARB ROUTE
Wesley McNair

On a spring evening in between the black fly season
and the first mosquitoes, as the red stems lift
their broad leaves like scores of tilted umbrellas,
I call them on the telephone of my mind and drive
bagfuls of rhubarb down through the town, past
the white revenants of the Grange Hall and the closed
library, past the house lots and the treeless modulars
where they have no use for rhubarb, turning at last into
a wide driveway while little Herman, alive as anyone,
comes out of his old farmhouse with his chesty walk
to take two bags inside to Faye, enough for a whole
year of pies and red-Jell-O cobblers, then drive the back
way along the river, by the oaks and sumacs gathering
the shadows of twilight, to swing in beside the dead
school bus of True's cowless farm and see old Billy,
before his legs gave out, who loved rhubarb almost
as much as his long-lost mother, take the biggest bag
of it into his arms and carry it up the steps of his porch,
leaning on the rail to wave goodbye. Goodbye to Billy,
goodbye to little Herman, goodbye to the Gagnons,
who laugh in the deepening dusk about eating sticks
of rhubarb right from the patch as kids, goodbye
to my old neighbor Ethlyn in the house on the corner,
empty for two years, who all the same calls out
Hello from somewhere inside when I knock, *Hello,
I'm here*, and suddenly she is here next to me behind
the screen, smiling because I've remembered her again
on this spring evening with fresh rhubarb, which
she holds up to her face, breathing it in with a long
breath before she turns and goes back into the dark.

PART I

TASTE AND DISTASTE

THE ZEN OF FIDDLEHEADS
Cathie Pelletier

F OR THREE OR four weeks each spring, a small green miracle appears
along New England's shady riverbanks, brooks, and damp marshes. In
its first few days of life, before it has time to unfurl into the ostrich fern
it really is, it looks like the scroll on the tip of a fiddle. Botanists call it
Matteuccia struthiopteris, but we northern Mainers know it as the humble
fiddlehead. It is born swaddled in a brown papery chaff carried over from
the previous autumn. With southern Maine being so tourist-centric in the
summers, fancy recipes using fiddleheads have made their way into print
over the years. There are quiches and omelets, Gruyère tarts and sauces,
saffron soups and edamame salads. Some cookbooks have fiddleheads in
league with *quenelles de brochet* or lemon rosemary risottos. We locals are
often saddened to see photographs of our beloved fern cuddled up to a red
lobster or lounging next to glazed shrimp.

We are rivers and lakes people this far north. The fiddlehead looks best
when lying next to brook trout and biscuits. So ignore those dishes that use
fancy words. Take it from a purist who was raised with fiddleheads growing a stone's throw from the kitchen stove. You pick them in the spring
when they are still unfurled, two or three inches high. Otherwise, within
a month, the fronds will be a yard tall and swaying in the breeze like can-
can dancers. I usually take a pan or a basket. But if I happen upon some
while walking, I just remove my jacket and fill the inside. We never use the
word "harvest." We say, "I picked a mess of fiddleheads today." Rinse away
the chaff and any dirt and boil them with potatoes. Some people throw in
a chunk of salt pork. When they are cooked, cover them in butter (unless
you're a vegan like me) and sprinkle them with salt. But think of the riverbanks and brooks and marshes as you eat. Savor the smell of moist earth.

DURING THE YEARS I was growing up in Allagash, my brother Vernon was the one who picked fiddleheads for the family. The rest of us weren't interested, or we couldn't tolerate the blackflies. Vernon seemed oblivious to them as they swarmed around his head. Many of you know the black-fly, from the family *Simuliidae*. They prefer those same peaty areas where fiddleheads thrive. The female feeds on the blood of mammals, including humans, for the protein she needs to lay her eggs. Thoreau was right when he wrote in *The Maine Woods* that blackflies are "more formidable than wolves to the white man." This was because Joe Polis, his Penobscot guide, wasn't deterred in the least by them. Vernon was our family's Joe Polis for many years when it came to picking fiddleheads.

I was twenty-three when I left Maine and moved to the South, away from those pesky northern blackflies. That next spring, come fiddlehead season, I received a box from my mother. Inside was a freezer bag stuffed with fresh fiddleheads, all nicely cleaned. It became a yearly ritual. Her note would say something like, "Vernon's been picking fiddleheads." Or, "I put in a jar of mustard pickles since there was room in the box." When my niece moved to Tennessee some years later, she also began getting a box each spring. When mine arrived, I'd call her to ask, "Did you get your fiddleheads yet?"

I wonder how many pots of fiddleheads and potatoes Mama cooked for our family over the years. I wonder how many jars she canned for the long winters. I came back to be with her so she could die at home, in this house where she gave birth to me. We buried her in the spring of 2001, just as the first fiddlehead nubs were pushing up from the earth. She was first to go into the family graveyard, near the riverbank where wild chokecher-ries grow. Afterwards, still stunned from our loss, Vernon said he was going for a canoe ride. "Do you want to come?" he asked. "We can pick some fiddleheads." He brought with him four plastic pails that he threw into the canoe. I sat in the bow as we motored upriver. Ducks scattered ahead of us and deer watched from the shorelines. Near a cluster of hazelnut bushes growing on the riverbank, my brother pointed out an indentation. "There used to be a homestead there once," he said. "The old Casey Place. It's been gone for years."

At Aegan Island, where grass grows tall on soil that is always moist and shady in the spring, Vernon pulled the canoe to shore. "This is my best spot for fiddleheads," he said, as if it were a secret that could only be shared on such an important day in our lives. We picked yards apart, saying nothing as we leaned over our pails, hearing only the river and the wind. Once, when I stood to shoo blackflies and take a drink of water, I heard him say, "There's an eagle." As I looked to the corner of sky where he had pointed, to the magnificent wingspan and solid white head, I knew then that nature would save me. And that I would pick fiddleheads for the rest of my life.

On our way home, we rode away from a setting sun with full pails of fiddleheads to be given in "messes" to family and friends. The canoe followed channels in the river well-known to our ancestors, those first settlers of Allagash. *Our tiny places on earth belong to us for such a short time,* I thought, as we again passed the spot where the old Casey Place once stood. The ache I felt was in knowing that I'd never again get fiddleheads in the mail from my mother. It was just one small marker of the many ways I would miss her.

Later that night, suitcase packed for my return to Tennessee, I went down to the basement where Mama had kept so many treasures. That cellar had been dug by my father with a team of horses when he built the house in 1948. There was the lantern Mama dusted off and filled with kerosene each time our electricity went out. A yellow Post-it with her handwriting clung to the handle. "Lantern works fine," the note told anyone who might need to know, in case she wasn't there. Strings of Christmas lights hung from nails along the wall, their bulbs remembering the glisten and sparkle of yuletides past. She had always found nooks and crannies in that basement to hide Christmas presents where the best little detectives could never find them. Lined up neatly on a wooden shelf were a dozen Mason jars filled with canned goods. A few held the mustard pickles that I loved. Others had beets and yellow beans grown in her last garden, as well as cranberry jam, made from berries that still grow along our fields and roadsides. But on a bottom shelf, dust coating the lid, was the last jar of fiddleheads.

THE FOLLOWING SPRING, and a year after losing my mother, I was sweeping my patio in Tennessee when a UPS truck rolled up to my door. I knew instantly what was in the box the driver carried as he came up the walk. After all, it was springtime in northern Maine and the riverbank near the old Casey Place would be moist and shady. On the return label was my brother's name and address. Inside, pinned to a freezer bag of fresh fiddleheads, was a note. "You'll have to clean them yourself. I'm not Mama."

A DECADE AFTER my mother died, I came home to be with my aging father. I packed my life into boxes and moved with my husband back to Allagash, to the family homestead, to this house built on memory. These days, reacquainted with the river, I prefer to pick fiddleheads alone. You can smell the past at times like that, the earth alive again from winter. The calls of yellow-breasted chats and song sparrows echo along the banks, and from the hardwood ridge, the pileated woodpecker. Trilliums and trout lilies are up, and the first marsh marigolds are eager yellow buds. Sensing my respiration, the blackflies surround me by the hundreds. Swarms of them orbit my head and spatter my white shirt. I no longer notice them. I breathe slowly to expel as little carbon dioxide as I can. As if meditating, I concentrate on the miracle of the ostrich fern, on the miracle of families, on the miracle of life and death that will unfurl, perpetually, for each generation. It's a lesson I learned late in my life, thanks to the Zen of fiddleheads.

BEANS
Richard Russo

A L's BARBER SHOP, circa 1957. Upstate New York mill town. The sign in the window says "Haircuts. No Waiting." I'm a boy and my father doesn't live with my mother and me, so when I need a haircut, it's my grandfather who takes me. The "No Waiting" sign troubles me. Every time we go to Al's, the chair is occupied, so we go inside and sit down and wait until it's our turn. I keep expecting the police to come in and point to the sign and tell us we're not allowed to wait. We should stand outside in the cold until the chair is unoccupied. Somehow, time after time, we get away with this clear violation of the rules. Then one day *I understand* and this, in a nutshell, is my life as a boy in our small town: I don't understand until, suddenly, I do. I learn not to ask questions, because, in the fullness of time, all will be revealed.

Eventually, I'm allowed to go to Al's without my grandfather. Al is Italian, as in, from the old country. Not like my absent father, who's American and, I'm told, a war hero. (That he could be both a war hero and absent is another thing that confuses me, but I have faith that one day I will understand.) Al is a talker. He likes to make conversation, even with boys my age. "What are you having for dinner tonight?" he wants to know as he snips. I tell him I'm not sure. My mother works at GE in Schenectady, so whatever my grandmother is fixing. Pork chops? Chicken noodle soup? I offer him a range of possibilities. Al invariably says he and his wife will be having pasta fagioli. Every single time he says this, what I always hear is *pasta fah-zool*.

When I mention this exotic dish to my mother, she tells me I wouldn't like it. She explains that it's foreign, immigrant food made from cheap ingredients, like macaroni and beans and olive oil. Americans don't eat food of this sort. They eat meat and cook with butter, not oil. Confused, I tell her that Al is always nice to me and he seems to look forward to his pasta fah-zool. My mother admits that, yes, he is a nice man, but that he's not like us, which confuses me even more because my absent father is also Italian. And what am I to do with the other obvious similarities between Al and our own family? Each year, as fall segues into winter, my grandfather rubs his hands with glee, anticipating the return of his favorite meal: baked beans and brown bread, both from the can. Not Campbell's, which does offer canned beans, but the far superior B&M Brick Oven brand. They remind my grandfather of Vermont, where he's from. He tells me the reason we don't eat them all year round is that it's too hot in the summer. The oven would overheat our small kitchen. In winter, though, if he had his way, we'd eat them every single night. Though I've never known my grandfather to lie to me, I suspect that this is not entirely true, because who would want to eat the same thing every night? Also, while baked-bean season does dovetail nicely with colder weather, when a warm kitchen is comforting, it also coincides, in our town, with the men who work at the tanneries and glove shops getting laid off and going on unemployment until spring. In anticipation of this annual recurrence, my grandmother dutifully stocks the pantry with canned beans—green, waxed, B&M baked—throughout the summer. Beans are inexpensive, and they get us through the winter until my grandfather has a regular paycheck again. So, I suspect that Al and my grandfather are more alike than my mother is willing to admit: they've both decided to love what they can afford. So, what's really wrong with pasta fah-zool? Maybe in time I will understand.

Now, fast-forward thirty years. (That should be time enough.) My wife and I now live in Maine, where I teach and write. We've rented a small apartment in Venice, Italy, for two weeks. We hear that a couple we're friends with on the coast of Maine, both teachers, will be shepherding a group of high school students around the city, so we make plans, well ahead of their arrival, to have lunch at a favorite restaurant of theirs and ours, Ristorante Alla Madonna. The night before, I feel like I'm coming down with something and, sure enough, the next morning I wake up with a sore throat. By lunchtime, that throat is actually closing. I'd hoped to order my favorite dish, spaghetti with squid ink and cuttlefish, but by the time we arrive at the restaurant, I know that I'll never be able to swallow the cuttlefish, which resembles calamari rings. In fact, I'm not sure I'll be able to eat anything solid, so when we're seated, I scour the menu for soups, and there it is: pasta fagioli. When it comes, I begin to feel relief even before the first spoonful reaches my lips. The soup's aroma isn't just rich; it's heady, and that first spoonful glides down my ruined esophagus like warm silk. Does my throat actually begin to open? I don't know. Probably not. But I remember Al all those years ago trying to sell me on the merits of his wife's pasta fah-zool, as well as my mother tenaciously trying to dissuade me. She, I realize with shame, had triumphed. In the forty years since Al recommended it, I've probably eaten every other Italian dish under the sun: calf's liver, scungilli, various sweetbreads and viscera, even tripe. But until that day, I avoided pasta fagioli because my mother told me—and I believed her—that I wouldn't like it, that people who ate such food were not like us.

These days, I'm an adventurous eater, not at all averse to sucking the brains out of a prawn. And much of what confused me as a boy has, in fact, been made clear. At seventy-two, I still mostly adhere to my old conviction that what baffles me today will become clear tomorrow. I now understand how a man can be a war hero and also largely absent from his own son's life. In many respects, my stubborn faith that I'll eventually get to the bottom of things is fundamental to my being a novelist, because every time I start a new book, what I *don't* know dwarfs the little I do know. And yet I suspect that maybe I need to start asking more questions. Time, after all, is running out, and while it may be true that answers have a way of presenting themselves, even to unasked questions, too much of importance remains shrouded in mystery and paradox. Like this: I love good food and am excited by new dining experiences, many of which are expensive. It's no accident that the best of what life has to offer is seldom cheap. But I'm also suspicious of anything fussy or that needlessly (to my mind) pushes the boundaries of expense. I'd like to think that this is not because I'm cheap. In fact, my wife and I spend, I fear, far too much money on food. But I won't order a sixty-dollar steak, even if someone else is paying for it, because there isn't enough Béarnaise sauce to mask the taste of shame that eating a sixty-dollar steak would occasion. Indeed, that shame would yank me right out of the fancy restaurant, as well as the present moment, and plop me back down again in my grandmother's kitchen, the pantry of which was full of what the people I loved as a boy could afford. What my grandfather and Al were both trying to teach me, it seems, was to love what you're given by the people who mean the most to you. If it's the best they have to offer—and it was—then there's nothing better. There's mystery in that. And maybe wisdom.

EXACTLY LIKE PIZZA
Phuc Tran

CARLISLE, PA. SEPTEMBER 1983.

Pizza Hut called to me. Trapped inside our Ford LTD, I smelled baked cheese and dough and spices even from across the intersection.

"Why can't we go out to Pizza Hut? Or at least order pizza from Domino's?" my younger brother, Lou, and I pleaded with our parents.

"We can just make pizza at home. It's the same thing: what I make and what we can buy. It's the same ingredients. Don't worry. It will taste *exactly* like Pizza Hut. You'll see!"

My mother was confident, and we didn't want to argue the point again as we had done dozens of times before. I understood her deflection—a deflection informed by our meager finances. In the eight years since our arrival in Carlisle from Sài Gòn, my parents had learned English and its idioms like "working around the clock." (No one told them that it was metaphorical.) They'd earned their GEDs, rescued my father's parents and siblings from a refugee camp, and squeezed a dime's worth of goods from every nickel earned. So who were we to ask for Pizza Hut? Why spend money on pizza that we could make at home for a fraction of the cost?

Back at our apartment's cramped kitchenette, my mother made the pizza—she who could create a dazzling array of *bún bò Huế* and *bánh xèo* and *canh chua*. American pizza, with only three ingredients, seemed so basic to her. She cheerfully spread ketchup on sliced white bread, unwrapped a single slice of white Kraft American cheese and placed it on top of the bread. She lay the whole assemblage in the toaster oven, and as it heated up and melted, it turned into a funeral pyre, immolating what I understood of pizza. The American cheese, because of the cold ketchup, was slightly

9

burned at the edges while remaining cool and gelatinous in the middle. The bread was toasted hard at the edges but soggy elsewhere. Truly a feat of kitchen magic to serve something both cold and burnt.

The pizza [sic] was plated and laid before us. My father praised the gooey squares. "Oh, good job! It looks just like pizza!"

My mother beamed at me and Lou, nudging us toward our plates. "See? It's exactly like pizza! I told you!" She was so triumphant that my brother and I kept silent. The fact that she had described her pizza as "exactly like pizza" was not lost on me, and I suspected that even Lou, a precocious second grader, knew the difference between pizza and the open-faced, ketchup-cheese-toast that was growing cold before us.

We had eaten real pizza at Pizza Hut.* Thanks to other kids' birthday parties, we had eaten pizza from Domino's. We knew that our homemade pizza [sic] was not real pizza. We couldn't unlearn what we had learned. I choked down my reluctance to eat my slice of exactly-like-pizza and picked it up.

FOR OUR ENTIRE childhood, my mother bought different brands of ketchup and American cheese in an effort to perfect the combination for her pizza, and every time, the results were the same: melted American cheese over ketchup on toast. It was not medieval alchemy. We were not asking her to turn lead into gold (though we might as well have thrown that into the request). We were asking her to make a pizza at home that tasted right, and cheese over ketchup on toast was not pizza.

WHO COULD HAVE explained to her that there were dozens of different types of cheeses and that pizza used a combination of cheeses? Vietnamese didn't even have a word for cheese—the word is just *fromage*, borrowed from French. I wouldn't actually learn the names and flavors of different cheeses until I was in college. The three cheeses we knew were Swiss, American, and cheddar, and, as a pledge of our allegiance, we *always* chose American. How was my mother supposed to know that, in the vast aisle for tomato products, ketchup was not pizza sauce, which was not marinara sauce, which was not crushed tomatoes, which was not stewed tomatoes,

---

* Obviously, this was not the platonic ideal of pizza either, but it's what I knew in 1983.

which was not tomato paste? She didn't know to ask, having assumed that all tomato products were the same, based on the pictures on the labels.

Homemade pizza it was.

Lou and I ate the pizza [sic], forcing it down. My mother glowed, proud that she had, indeed, made something that was just like pizza.

PORTLAND, ME. NOVEMBER 2020.

It's Sunday night, our weekly family movie night, and we're all discussing where to order pizza before we start the movie. My wife and I make several suggestions, because it's Portland and there's a long list of pizzerias that range from Milanese style, Sicilian slab, New York thin crust, and modern variations of the traditional pizza.

My daughters, seven and ten years old, are unanimous in their praise. "DOMINO'S! WE LOVE DOMINO'S! THEY MAKE THE BEST PIZZA!"

I look sideways at my wife, who is stifling her disapproval by avoiding eye contact with any of us. A back-and-forth about the pros and cons of all the pizza options ensues. My wife and I try to convince the girls that a local pizzeria will be better for all of us; we avoid telling them that their pizza tastes are, well, awful. They grumble, but our family is not a democracy so there's no voting. We are a benevolent dictatorship, and we placate—if not suppress—the small, girlish rabble with the promise of some chocolatey dessert.

In part, we don't tell them that their taste in pizza is terrible because it would be an admission that we ourselves are to blame for nurturing their terrible taste in pizza. As I reject Domino's, I even say something about not wanting to support them because of their philanthropy, politicizing what should be a simple decision about where to order dinner.

But if we're just talking about good pizza . . . *really*? Domino's is their choice? I chalk it up to youthful palates and aggressive advertising and their friend group. (I never liked that one girl anyway—she's probably the one who told them about Domino's.)

Our daughters finally yield, and we order the Milano-style pizza, but they still declare that Domino's is the best, and they can't fathom why we wouldn't want the best pizza. The Milano-style pizza seems strange to them—the cheese is not shredded but laid out in artful, large slices of fresh mozzarella. There are whole basil leaves on top. Sometimes, the pizza is not even cut into triangular slices but squares. And it's not even called a cheese pizza, but a *Margherita*.

We sprawl in front of the TV, slices warm on our plates. They're delicious, of course, and I'm hopeful that someday the metaphorical oven light will shine its light on my daughters, that someday they'll see just how much better this is than Domino's. I want them to know that it *is* better—but I also see the simple pleasure that radiates from their innocence.

I don't say anything to my girls about Domino's—I never have—and I let them have their joy just as I let my mother have hers. Despite all the ways that I've changed, I can feel in these moments the contours of that ten-year-old boy who ate his mother's cheese-and-ketchup toast concoction in silence.

And in my present silence, I see how pure their guiltless, guileless joy is. Who am I to steal it?

A MESS OF PEAS
Kimberly Ridley

I N A PHOTO THAT I TOOK of him more than thirty years ago, my father watches over me from his pea patch. The peas are blooming, and he is in his prime: burly in a navy-blue baseball cap, green polo shirt, and jeans, his arms as brown as the ground he works. His expression is serious, unusual for a cheerful man who loved to joke around and sing Willie Nelson tunes, a man whose standard response to "How are you?" was "If I was any better, I couldn't stand it."

This was especially true when he had his hands in the dirt, as he did every spring and summer afternoon after filling potholes and digging ditches all day for the Maine State Highway Department. Peas were the first seeds he planted after the interminable winter. If you want peas on the Fourth of July, plant them on Patriots' Day in April, he always said, when the maples bloom and the first wood thrushes return to southern Maine.

I don't remember the first time I helped my father plant peas, but I was surely young, maybe six or seven. Following along behind him, I mimicked his gestures, strewing wrinkled pellets into shallow furrows, then gently tamping soil over them with my small, bare hands, my fingers stinging with cold. I never grew into the passionate gardener my father was, but something else took root.

After the peas bloomed in June, we kept a close watch on the pods. One day, they were flat, the next, swelling with tiny peas, which could get away from you fast and grow big and mealy, the sugars turning to starch. We picked the first peas when the pods yielded to a gentle squeeze, and the peas inside were the size of a baby's first teeth. This we did with two hands, one to hold the vine, the other to gently pluck the pods.

"That's a nice mess of peas," my father would say after we filled a basket.

Preparing peas became a ritual. We fetched a pot and sat at the round oak table on the screened porch, where my father showed me the secret to shelling them: Gently press the curved end of the pod with your thumb until it pops open. Turn the pod with the pointed end facing down and run your thumb along the inside so the peas plink into the pot. There was no rushing this, yet with time, my fingers grew nimble and efficient. The knowledge embedded itself in my hands.

After we filled the pot with green pearls, we covered them with water, boiled them for one minute, then drained and served them in a white china bowl with at least two tablespoons of butter and a sprinkling of salt and pepper. Our family feasted on steaming bowls of peas. That first mouthful. Oh! Here was something that couldn't be bought. Something worth the wait: tiny, tender orbs of green sweetness, the essence of early summer.

We gorged on peas from my father's garden night after night until we'd had our fill. It was an unspoken rule that freezing peas was a crime and canning them a sacrilege. It was understood that peas from the garden were only to be eaten fresh. My father always grew more than we could eat, so he shared them, delivering messes of fresh peas to family and friends.

This was the way he grew up, on a subsistence farm in Springvale, a mile down the road from the little Cape that he and my mother bought to raise my brother and me. We often walked to my dad's old home on summer evenings, and I pestered him for stories. I loved asking him for tiny details, like what his family had for supper in the winter. He told me most of it was from the root cellar, and all of it cooked by my grandmother on the kitchen woodstove: red flannel hash, biscuits with salt pork gravy, apple crisp, or cake for "afters."

"Wasn't it hard to live like that?" I asked my father one evening. I told him I couldn't imagine growing and preserving most of my own food, cutting firewood by hand, and living without electricity and running water.

"What we didn't get done one day, we did the next," he said, laughing. "We never hurried." He paused. "And we always had time."

In all of his nearly eighty-five years, I never recall seeing my father hurry.

The photo of my father in his pea patch sits on my desk in a silver frame. I study his serious expression and wonder what he was thinking that day. As much as I loved him and his stories, he was also a mystery to me, as we humans are to each other, even among beloveds. For years, I was embarrassed when my city friends asked what my father did for a living. I couldn't understand how he could be content with so little and live nearly all of his life on one small patch of ground in Maine. I have always wanted more of everything, and I'm antsy and seldom content.

This will be my tenth year without my father. I'm a haphazard gardener, but my husband, Tom, and I always plant peas on Patriots' Day in our own garden in Brooklin nearly four hours north of my childhood home. On a cool evening in early July, we gather the fragile harvest, filling a basket with perfect pods. We sit on the deck together and shell peas. A hermit thrush sings and the late afternoon sun flashes through the spruce woods. We talk about my father, how much we loved him. After preparing the peas, I pour them into two blue bowls. We eat them slowly. The buttery sweetness bursts in my mouth. I close my eyes. I have time.

ELEPHANT EARS
Lily King

I DIDN'T BAKE WITH my mother. She was a good cook and made all kinds of yummy desserts—lemon meringue pies, bittersweet chocolate mousse, paper-thin sugar cookies, a bûche de Noël every Christmas—but I was never her helper in the kitchen. I knew to stay away. One of my earliest memories is of her whacking my hand with a wooden spoon when I'd tried to stick a finger into the bowl.

The first thing I learned to bake was chocolate chip cookies, something my mother never made. Most likely, it was my best friend, Becky, who showed me the recipe, which was in a spiral-bound, locally published book called *Essex County Cooks*. My mother and her contemporaries had all contributed recipes, and every house I knew seemed to have both volumes, one green and one red, though my mother had long moved on to Julia Child. The cookie recipe was in the green book. The story was that a few years earlier some kids who lived down the hill from me and Becky had meant to make the standard Toll House recipe from the back of the Nestlé chocolate chip bag but either accidentally or deliberately messed it up. They used less flour and more vanilla. They added a tiny ¼ teaspoon of water. They melted the butter instead of waiting for it to become room temperature, and they cooked the cookies at a higher heat—425—for a mere 4–5 minutes. What came out was a tray of larger, thinner cookies that had to be removed with a surgeon's precision and cooled for a few minutes before you could put them in your mouth where they burst into a buttery, salty, chocolaty swirl of perfection. They transcended debates of crispy or chewy. They were both at the same time. They were manna. The kids called them Elephant Ears, and children in my hometown are probably making batches of them still. Soon our copy of the green cook-book fell open to that page, which grew translucent from smears of spilled melted butter, and crunchy from the grains of white and brown sugar that got stuck in the grease.

Most weekends and all summer, Becky and I made batches of Ele-phant Ears. We were in third grade, fourth grade, fifth grade. We'd be in my kitchen on Proctor Street or her kitchen on Beach Street. Someone would be stirring and someone would be calling WRKO to ask them to play "Rock Me Gently," our favorite song ever. Once, we wrote our own song made up of all the swear words we knew: "Fuck, shit, dammit all/We want to ditch it all/So we won't become a bitch's ass." There were more verses, but I will spare you. We wrote out the whole song twice, a copy for each of us. We can still sing every word on command. (Becky and I fell out of touch for twenty years then ended up in Maine, with no planning or communication, three miles apart, and took up our friendship right where it left off.)

Fifth-grade summer we both got boyfriends who were best friends, and they gave us matching engagement rings from Foster's Gifts downtown. We made cookies and met them on the rocks at the end of the beach. Halfway through that summer, I left town with my mother. She'd filed for divorce, and I couldn't tell anyone we were leaving, not even Becky. When we came back before school started again, my mom and I moved into an apartment near the gift shop. I called up Becky, and she rode her bike down and said it was cool. She said all the lights on either side of the mirror in the bathroom were like the dressing room of a movie star. We made cookies there and not at my old house where my father was living with his girlfriend and her kids. That kitchen was hers now, and she made brownies. I didn't feel com-fortable rummaging through the cabinets for an old package of chips. And she'd moved the table where we always mixed up the batter into another room. There were armchairs now, in the kitchen, and that was where she and my father did a lot of their drinking and their fighting. They liked an audience for all that they said and did to each other. I didn't invite friends over when I went there on weekends.

I LEFT THE COUNTRY as soon as I finished college. I found a job in Paris cooking for three kids whose parents both worked. They walked home from school every day for lunch. I made them a snack when they returned

in the afternoon, helped them with their homework, and made them dinner. Within days, I was on a hunt for baking soda. It wasn't in my dictionary,
the Internet hadn't been invented yet, and the grocer had no idea what I
was talking about. I finally found it, *bicarbonate de soude*, at a pharmacy. A
few years later, when I lived in Spain, I was able to find *bicarbonate sodico*
faster. I made Elephant Ears in Vermont, New York, California, and back in
Massachusetts. I made them for my boss at the bookstore in California and
my coworkers at the restaurant in Vermont, and our guests when I worked
at an inn on an island in Penobscot Bay.

I BEGAN BAKING the cookies with my children as soon as they could
sit cross-legged on the wooden island in our kitchen in Yarmouth, Maine.
There were negotiations: who would crank the sifter first, who would
crack the egg, and who would stir it in. When the brown sugar came out,
each girl could have just a "smoodge," our word for a small pinch straight
from the box. These cookies went to school for bake sales and birthdays,
to neighbors for celebrations and condolences, to Santa every December
24th. They weren't called Elephant Ears or Toll House or even chocolate
chip. They were just cookies. We rarely made any other kind.

A girl named Emily lived across the street, and for many years she came
over on weekends and summer days to play with the girls. She was a few
years older than they were, an only child, and she liked playing oldest sister
to them.

The summer Emily turned eleven, my daughters were eight and six. I
remember a rainy afternoon baking cookies with the three of them. I had
to go to the bathroom, and while I was washing my hands and hearing
their happy baking chatter from the kitchen, I realized that Emily was now
the same age I was when my parents split and I started shuttling back and
forth between the apartment and my old house, and my father started revealing this other side of himself with his new partner. I was seeing a therapist then for these memories, for the exposure to the drinking, the rage,
the sexual language and behaviors most parents try to protect their children
from. I didn't know that at the time, didn't understand how abnormal it
was, didn't feel particularly young—I was the oldest of the four of us kids
in my father's new family. The therapist was trying to get me to see how
aberrant it was and to connect with that younger self, to feel what she'd
numbed herself against and to give that eleven-year-old girl the love and
protection she needed. I thought it was a silly and futile exercise. But when

I stood there in that bathroom washing my hands, I finally understood that I had been *Emily's* age, this young girl who wore braids like I had and played dress-up and still rode the least scary ride at the carnival.

They were calling to me from the kitchen: Is it a half or a fourth of a teaspoon of water? But I was crying too hard to answer right away.

I DIDN'T BRING much stuff with me from childhood into adulthood. My parents had several marriages each, moved in and out of houses, didn't save our things. I don't have many memories either, not normal, everyday memories. Whole years are blank. It's like my mind wasn't imprinting, the recorder was off. This recipe, the memory of these cookies, is one of the few things that made it out with me.

My kids are nineteen and twenty-one now. They came home, like all college students, in March of 2020 to finish out the year online. The cookies get made at night now. We turn on a show, and Eloise says, "I'm making cookies," and we get our smoodges and soon the warm cookies are bending over our fingers, and then they are melting in our mouths, the butter, sugars, and chocolate all whorled together then washed down with cold milk.

KENTUCKY BREAD
Roxana Robinson

Pine mountain is in the southeastern corner of Kentucky. It's a steep, densely forested region, remote and beautiful. Early settlers there led hardscrabble lives, clearing wooded slopes, plowing sloping hillsides, building cabins up in the hollows. The land was slant and challenging. It resisted farming, but it was generous in other ways: lush with plant life, vivid with animals, lavish with views.

The isolated life of the mountaineers meant a paucity of education, and schools were few and far between. The children who lived "back in the hollers" were a long way from any classroom, and many of them never reached one at all. Troubled by this, in 1913, a farmer named William Creech founded a school. He was a large-hearted man, and he had a vision. "I have heart and craving that our people may grow better," he wrote. "I have deeded my land to the Pine Mountain Settlement School. . . . Hoping it may make bright and intelligent people, after I'm dead and gone." Creech donated several hundred acres to the school—rich green bottomland at the foot of Pine Mountain, down in the narrow valley where Isaac's Run meets Shell Run to form Greasy Creek.

Pine Mountain was a boarding school. It taught academic subjects, but Creech wanted to preserve the regional crafts and culture, so the girls learned baking, quilting, and weaving, as well as Shakespeare, and the boys, farming, carving, and woodworking. The students worked at the school farm, which produced all the food. It had a dairy herd, chickens and pigs, oxen and mules. The early settlers had come from England and Scotland, and their traditions—the old songs, ballads, dances, and festivals—were honored. May Day was a great celebration in that green bottomland along the winding creek.

Pine Mountain was where I was born, though it's not where my family was from.

MY FATHER WAS FROM NEW YORK. He went to boarding school in New England and then on to Harvard, where he trained to be a lawyer, like his father. My mother grew up outside Philadelphia, where her father, too, was a lawyer. She went to a private school and then Vassar. When my parents married in 1935, they moved to an apartment in Murray Hill. It seemed like the start of a conventional, decorous, and affluent life, but things took a sharp left turn.

My father didn't find much satisfaction in the practice of corporate law, much to his father's disappointment. My father felt stifled and was troubled by an absence of ideals and altruism. A bit like William Creech, my father had a heart and a craving to help people. So, he changed everything; he left law for education. He left the Episcopalian Church for the Society of Friends. He left New York City for the hinterlands.

Who's to say what drives the shifts and turns of a family's narrative? As I look back, my family's history is so familiar to me that these moves seem inevitable, entirely normal and predictable. Of course, my father left the law. It's so obvious, now, that he wouldn't have been happy there. Of course, we all went to Pine Mountain, which is so central to our history. Of course, we left Kentucky later and moved finally to Pennsylvania, where my parents spent the rest of their lives and where I grew up. How else could it have been?

At the time, though, it must have been a tremendous adventure for my parents—exciting but perilous, there was no turning back—as they walked forward into the rest of their lives, which still lay hidden before them.

My mother embraced the venture. She shared my father's ideals, and she left the Presbyterian church to become a Quaker. She left her friends, family, and the life she'd known, moving to a remote mountain community. This was during World War II, when transportation was difficult and communication limited. Our family lived in a log cabin, with a sleeping loft for the children, reached by a ladder. The only traffic on the dirt roads was from carts and sledges, pulled by mules and oxen. In some ways the life was primitive, but Pine Mountain offered one great luxury: three hot meals a day. Everyone at the school ate in the communal dining room at Big Log. So, my mother did not have to cook, which was a good thing, since she had never learned how.

My mother's family lived in a (big) pleasant house on the Main Line, outside Philadelphia. They had a cook and a maid. On Sunday evenings, the cook was off, my grandmother would say brightly to her children, "Now dears, we're having a special treat for supper: graham crackers and milk!" This happened every week. In our own family, when I was growing up, whenever my mother's invention or larder was empty, we had the same meal, which I loved.

Every family has its own culinary traditions, its own peculiarly idiosyncratic attitudes toward food. Every family thinks its own attitudes are the norm. It's not until you're older that you realize that everyone else doesn't eat the way you do.

MY GRANDPARENTS WERE married in 1899. I still have my grandmother's recipe box, with her collection of recipes, which was started before they married and continued for decades. It's full of carefully handwritten entries like "Mrs. Louis Searle's Orange Cake." These are replete with detailed instructions about stirring and baking, but I don't think my grandmother actually made the dishes. I think she and her friends traded recipes and then they gave them to their cooks. I think they were proud and proprietary about what came from their kitchens but didn't produce it themselves.

THIS CULINARY DEFICIENCY isn't limited to my own family. It seems to be tribal. We WASPs aren't famous for our cuisine. But we've always eaten; we've made meals for centuries. It's just that our food seems to be a bit dull, a bit limited in scope and invention, though it's healthy and nourishing. Our meals are more like obligations than celebrations.

Since everything comes from somewhere, where does *this* cuisine come from, and where do we get our feelings about food?

SEVERAL YEARS AGO, I went to Scandinavia for the first time, and I was amazed by how familiar it seemed: the whole region produced a deep cultural resonance. For a WASP from the Northeast, it seemed like an Ur-summer community, the one on which all the others are modeled. The shingle-style architecture, mountains, and rocky shorelines, beautiful but challenging terrain; everyone dying to get out onto the water; yellow rain slickers; a cold, uncertain climate; a bleak religion; deep personal reserve; an unflinching dedication to principle, an inclination toward austerity; sternness and implacable judgment. I felt I had arrived at my mythic ancestral homeland, though no one in my family is from Scandinavia, and my ancestors are mostly from England, Scotland, and Ireland.

This tribal affinity was reinforced recently, when I read *Independent People* by the Icelandic author Halldór Laxness, the 1955 Nobel Prize winner. His characters were so eerily familiar I thought we'd been separated at birth. And in a way, we had been: the Vikings had a profound effect on the culture of the British Isles, raiding and settling for several hundred years before the Normans (who were actually "Norsemen") arrived in 1066. It was the Vikings who predominated, culturally and genetically. WASPs are said to have originated in the British Isles, but really we go straight back to Scandinavia. Reserve, austerity, asceticism, a certain Northern tendency toward pessimism: for a New Englander with a long Puritan tradition, all this was familiar.

Physically, too, we seemed related: the long bones, the fair skin, the blue eyes, and linguistically, there were a surprising number of shared words. *Brod* for bread, *bageri* for bakery. The relationship to food seemed familiar as well, a Spartan self-denial about it, something very practical under the circumstances. The Scandinavian growing season is short, the climate is hard and the terrain largely difficult. Nature is not reliably bountiful, and meals reflect this. A slice of good brown bread, a chunk of hard cheese, a few berries, and a swig of cold water might easily be lunch. This was an attitude I knew very well.

In our family, meals were never the gorgeous celebrations that seem to occur daily in a Mediterranean household. For us, eating was always marginal, a digressive aside, an afterthought. *Oh, right, lunch!* Bread and cheese and a swig of water was perfectly acceptable. We'd have been thrilled by berries. My mother didn't much enjoy cooking and had no hired help at all. There were five of us children, and meals were haphazard and makeshift, scrambled together at the last minute or not at all. It was always an agreeable surprise to discover that food had been somehow found and made into a meal. *Oh, dinner!* Or not, we didn't much care, really. If you asked my father, at night, what he'd had for lunch, he wouldn't be able to remember if he'd *had* lunch. This attitude has been passed down in my DNA: when I'm alone, I often forget to have a meal. When I'm working, I have the same lunch every day for months.

It's not that I don't like food. I do. I just don't like making a fuss over it. I like good, simple food that takes moments to prepare. My working lunch is minimalist in the extreme: two slices of good bread, with good cheese and good butter, harking right back to the Nordic landscape of Scandinavia.

⌒

OUR FAMILY VOYAGE ended in Bucks County, Pennsylvania. There my
father became the head of a Friends School, and there he lived for the rest
of his life. We moved on, but we kept Pine Mountain with us, and our stay
there is at the heart of our family history.

Pine Mountain was our family's great adventure. It was where we lived
for a time at a vital confluence of ideals and hardship, of education and
tradition. It was a foray into a splendid, challenging landscape that we've
never forgotten. Those braided memories twine through our shared consciousness. The life there—the wild countryside, the mountain people, the
ballads, and the country dances—is still part of us. It's in all our stories. It's
where my older brother learned to love the woods. It's where my older
sister learned to quilt. It's where my second brother was chased by a pig.
And it's where I was born, delivered by Doctor Elizabeth, in the two-room
school infirmary. It's where we learned the songs that we still sing, whenever we're together. "Sourwood Mountain," "Lord Lovel," "Barbry Allen":
they remind us of that beautiful green valley, along the winding creek. And
it's where my mother learned to bake bread.

My mother's recipe for whole wheat bread is from Pine Mountain. I
don't know who taught it to her, but the mountain settlers of Kentucky
were originally from Scotland and England, as ours were. Four hundred
years ago, our ancestors were all in the British Isles, and four hundred years
before that, they were probably in Denmark, getting ready for a savage raid
on the Scottish coast. Our history—and the lineage of this bread—goes
back a long way.

I think of this Kentucky bread as part of my culinary heritage, even if
it doesn't come from my grandmother. My mother gave it to me, and I've
given it to my daughter. My mother wrote the recipe down by hand, and
she baked it herself. She cherished this recipe, and I do, and so does my
daughter. How else is a family recipe defined?

I've baked this bread for years. It's the best and simplest bread recipe I
know. Oddly, this bread doesn't much like being baked in a city, and I could
never make it happy in New York. But in country kitchens the recipe has
never disappointed me, though many times I've disappointed it. I've set the
bread to rise and then forgotten it and left it in the oven. I've run out of
time and cut the rising short. I've forgotten the salt, I've run out of wheat
or white flour, I've used the wrong proportions—but Kentucky bread is

always forgiving, which is just what you'd hope for from your family. It's very happy being baked in Maine, where for thirty years I spent my summers and, for twenty years, part of my winters.

The loaves come out firm and solid, brown and crusty outside, nicely hollow within when you knock on them, and smelling like heaven.

ODE TO THE PB&J

Kate Christensen

NOTHING SATISFIES REAL hunger like peanut butter. It doesn't much matter what kind you use, creamy or crunchy, smooth or chunky, salted, roasted, pure ground peanuts, or a commercial brand with oils and sugars added. Peanut butter is a divine substance of umami and fat. It's sticky without being overly sweet, hits your mouth like a luxurious taste bomb, and it fills you up straightaway. A glob of peanut butter on a spoon straight from the jar is a snack in itself that you can also share with your dogs, who will make hilarious goofball faces while they happily gum it against the roofs of their mouths. Smear it thickly on crisp apple slices, and you have a plateful to take to bed with a book to crunch in solitude while you read.

But spread a wad of peanut butter on two slices of bread (or, better yet, hot toast) with a dollop of jam or jelly, and you have a classic three-ingredient dish of peerless perfection, an alchemy of texture and taste. Aside from the delicious combination of bread and fat and fruit, you're awash in childhood memories, the smell of the inside of your Partridge Family lunchbox in the school cafeteria in third grade, when a PB&J always meant Laura Scudder's Nutty and Smucker's strawberry jam on honey wheat-berry bread.

There's nothing better or more satisfying than a PB&J for that stomach-growling hunger that comes from playing outside all afternoon, from running around town doing errands with no time for a bite, from a hard hike up an Acadian mountain. It's the best, most versatile answer to the urgent need to eat something quick and solid. The beauty of this sandwich stretches as far as the eye can see, to the horizon of satiation and over it to contentment. It's savory and nutty, it's sweet and fruity, it's starchy and bready, it's filling and cheap, it's portable and easy to make, it's shelf-stable, and it can be eaten at any time of day, in any season or mood. It's a good source of protein and carbs, as well as vegan and vegetarian, and, if you use the right bread, dairy- and gluten-free. Unless you have food allergies—in which case, I apologize to you and hope you read no further than the title—the PB&J is a food for all ages, classes, races, nationalities, creeds, and orientations.

It can be devoured in private or shared with friends—or "here, take half," traded for someone else's half of turkey-and-Swiss on white with mayo, or ham-and-cheddar on rye, or hummus-and-pita with cucumber slices. It's a budget-friendly sandwich for lean times whose ingredients can be found at any Dollar Store, gas station mini-mart, or 7-Eleven. Buy a loaf of enriched wheat bread, a jar of Skippy, and a jar of generic jelly or jam, and you're out of there with a week's worth of lunches for not much more than the cost of one lunch at McDonald's.

Or you can go upscale with a Whole Foods bakery boule, fresh-ground organic roasted salted peanuts, and Tuscan artisanal jam, but I guarantee your PB&J won't taste better or satisfy the palate any more than the sandwich from the mini-mart. The beauty of the PB&J is that you can't improve on it. You can't fuck it up. There's never a time when you're not in the mood for one: breakfast, second breakfast, lunch, after-workout pick-me-up, dinner on the run, midnight snack. The PB&J is the unsung, underrated food of true democracy.

THE COMFORT OF THE KNISH
Melissa Senate

G RADUALLY AND THEN SUDDENLY, as the famous quote goes, I'm
on my own, my wedding ring and engagement ring under a bunch
of papers in the top drawer of my desk. I'm forty (this is years ago now)
with an about-to-turn-four-year-old son named Max, and he's confused
about the two houses, why his father doesn't live here. He's full of questions, and so am I.

One thing is an enormous help during this ridiculously painful time:
We live in Maine, and Maine in June is spectacular. Five minutes in any
direction from our new apartment in a three-family house is a body of
water, a river, a lake, the Casco Bay, the Atlantic Ocean. There are lobster
boats and clamdiggers to watch, kayakers to wave to. We swim in calm
waters and big waves, go inner-tubing, study the periwinkles making tiny
bubbles under the sand, and collect shells. I take my son for walks along
Main Street in our small coastal town and look at the plaques to the side of
the painted front doors of the clapboard New Englanders: Captain Sewall's
House 1872, Mamie Smith's House 1887. I wonder about the history, the
generations, note the huge blue hydrangea bushes in every front yard and
the dogs, big and small, napping in the sun, chasing their tails, protected
by Invisible Fence. A corner store a block away from our house has an ice
cream window, and every day after dinner, my son and I stop there, coffee
chip for me, Moose Tracks (for the name alone) for Max.

What the town doesn't have is a kosher deli. With its less than 1 percent Jewish population, Maine doesn't have a single kosher-style restaurant. Three years earlier, we had moved from New York City, where there's
a knish cart vendor on every corner. The kosher deli is to New York City
what the lobster shack is to Maine. I'm not kosher, but I don't eat shellfish.

My comfort food is the food of my childhood. My grandmother's home-made challah with its six braids and shiny top. Corned beef with mustard on rye, a fat sour pickle on the side. Whitefish salad and cream soda. And my favorite: knishes. I know people now, here in my adopted state of Maine, who have no idea what a knish *is*. I explain the most basic one, the kind they might get while visiting New York City, walking through Times Square or at the Central Park entrances where food cart vendors congregate: a square-shaped (though sometimes round), fried (though sometimes baked), rough-textured dough shell filled with pillowy-yet-dense-at-the-same-time mashed potatoes, seasoned with onion, salt, and a little pepper.

At a kosher deli or a knish cart, the guy (it's always a guy) will slit the top and squirt in mustard. You unpeel the tin foil halfway down and eat it like a hot dog on the street. Instant comfort. You eat a knish and you're reminded of Shabbos dinners when your grandmother was still alive. But that's in New York City, where you came from, where you left to start a brand-new adventure with your husband and toddler. And now you're go-ing through a divorce and want a knish every day, twice a day sometimes. And you can't get one.

Max's favorite food are French fries. So when I ask him if he wants to help me make a French fry–like food, he's all in. The problem is that I'm a terrible, impatient cook, and even when I follow a recipe to a T, it comes out wrong. But I'm going to try, because I want and need a knish to make me feel, for the bit of time it takes to hold and behold and consume, that everything is okay, that everything is familiar.

I Google knishes and lots of varieties come up, round and soft-baked with their short-crust or phyllo-dough exterior. But what I want is the gold standard, in my opinion, the street-cart knish, made famous by Jewish immigrants in the early 1900s on the Lower East Side of Manhattan and on boardwalks, like at Coney Island, where my parents met, despite both being from the Bronx, when my mother was still in high school, my father fresh back from the Marines. (They are long-divorced but that is another story.) I consult my mother, who's also not a cook and has never made a knish from scratch. She lives in New Jersey, also home to the kosher deli, so there's no need to. "Just order some from Katz's or Russ and Daughters or Zabar's and stick them in the freezer and be done with it," my mother suggests. I *could*, but getting the delivery from the famed appetizing delis will make me homesick, will make me cry, will make me want to go home, and Maine is home now. My son's father (also a New Yorker) is here and not budging, and for my son's sake, that means I'm not either.

Max likes to say the word *knish*—it makes him laugh. I assume knish is Yiddish, but it turns out it's not entirely (many Yiddish words themselves are not entirely Yiddish, of course), and I find this from chef Arthur Schwartz on the cooking website Cookstr: "Whatever their origin the word itself is related to the Italian word gnocchi, the Austrian word knoedle, and the Yiddish word knaidlach, all of which are kinds of dumplings. (Some sketchy etymological research on this produced the word 'lump' as the meaning of the 'gn' and 'kn' root.) The New York City knish is a kind of dumpling, too—a baked dumpling, much as people call apples baked in pastry apple dumplings. It is stuffed pastry."

"Kuh-NISH!" my son says and giggles, holding his long wooden spoon, which he likes to carry even when we're not making something. We're at the table in the kitchen of our apartment, an unexpectedly beautiful kitchen, I should note, which also helps when you're going through a divorce and stress-eating buttered sourdough toast and bowls of Apple Cinnamon Cheerios at 2 a.m. The kitchen is remarkably big enough that one of my first post-separation purchases, a round white wood pedestal dining table from an antique/thrift shop, is in the center, like an island, on a not-new kilim rug. The cabinets are a distressed painted-wood turquoise, the entire wall behind the stove a glittering backsplash of colorful small tiles, the floor wide-planked pumpkin pine. My landlord is a South American designer who has settled in Maine to make wedding dresses in her studio, which is separated from my kitchen by an internal door. I might not like to cook, but I like this kitchen.

My son is sitting on his legs, ready to assist. I've found a recipe with a photo that looks like the street-cart knish I crave. The ingredients, laid out on the table, are so simple. Russet potatoes, a large white onion, a few eggs, flour, salt, pepper, oil, and water. We make the dough, Max liking the idea that the dough has to rest. "The dough is taking a nap, Mommy!" he says, bringing his face close to it after we get it in plastic wrap. "Night, night, dough!" An hour later, I show him how to tell the dough is ready because it's elastic and stretches easily. (Another comforting thing is sounding like a brilliant expert to an almost-four-year-old when you're just reading from the recipe you found online.) We plop in the thick, mashed potatoes, fragrant with onion, and cover the potato mixture completely with the dough, making a square the size of an average sandwich. I have a big pot with oil on the stove, and I get out the special metal colander I bought to hold the knishes in the oil. We wait until they turn golden brown and then lay the knishes to rest on a paper-towel-covered plate. We've made two, one for each of us. If they're good, we'll make more. If they're not great, I'll try a different recipe, a thicker dough, more onion. We'll see.

But like French fries, like any potato dish, it's almost impossible to get wrong. The knishes are delicious. Max takes a bit of his with mustard and wrinkles his face in horror, so I cut that part away, and he gobbles up the rest. No surprise there. He's a Mainer now, he'll grow up in Maine, but he was born in New York City, and generations of his family come from the boroughs, where knishes were like Goldfish crackers for kids. Of course, he loves knishes.

I eat my knish, an *ahh* forming in my chest. I cry, as expected, moving to the sink so Max can't see. But it's a good cry, a cathartic cry. A little bit of home in my new home.

As I write this, fifteen years later, I don't need knishes the way I once did. Somewhere along the way, at around year ten or eleven of living in this beautiful, wild, rugged state, Maine became home in both head and heart (though I still don't eat shellfish). Max is now a freshman in college—five hours away. Sometimes, when my empty nest makes me wistful and I need a little comfort food, I can actually find a knish (and very unusual varieties) at the new "knishery" just twenty minutes away. Yes: a place in Maine devoted to the knish! I can also usually find knishes at the Whole Foods in Portland, just ten minutes down the road. Of course, they're not the same as the knishes of my childhood, but that *ahh* in my chest always is.

HOW TO EAT A LOBSTER
Jenny Bicks

PUT THE CALL OUT. Because the dappled Penobscot Bay is gleaming and the winds are blowing lightly across from Smith Cove, and it is a shame if you are not out on the water. Bring a lobster cracker and a napkin if you want. Not a fancy napkin. Make it an old white paper one that you saved from the bottom of a brown bag last summer. The cracker is important because the lobsters can be hard in late August and will take more than the light twist of a wrist to open the shells and reveal the glistening meat. Someone will call Miles out on the Penobscot Road and pick up the pound and a quarters, and someone else will borrow a skiff with an engine. Check the gas level in the tank because getting to Pond Island is no easy feat. Once we ran out of gas on our way into the harbor and ran up on the sand bar. The man who lived above the bar came down from his woods and banged a pot at us and called us trespassers.

And we are, as is he. The people who lived on Pond Island long before any of us came upon it? They too ate their meals on the warm rocks. They opened their catch with round rocks that the sea gave to them. And if you are lucky, you too will find a warm rock and round stone that will crack open your meal, and maybe you won't need your cracker at all. The sea gives treasures, if you look.

When you get to the island, dig a hole in the sand. As you dig, the sand will become darker, wetter, less forgiving. Do not give up. When a young child or a small dog can stand inside the hole, remove the child or the dog and line the hole with rocks. Then make your fire and layer on your burlap and seaweed. And then your lobster, still cold and ocean green, and then again, your seaweed and cloth. Send the children into the pond to find clams with their toes; to pull them up, muddy, rough, and heavy with muscle. They will use their T-shirts as slings, filling their fronts until their shirts are streaked black and weighted to their knees.

Lay the clams on the burlap. Now you must wait. This is the time for walking and exploring along the trails and through the marsh. Grab a sea peapod off its spindly vine and gently open it with your thumbs along its seam. Inside will be tiny, perfectly formed peas, three or four, the color of the water by the rocks near Holbrook Island. Eat one. It is sweet, giving, the taste of spring.

Back at the beach, the seaweed smolders under the burlap, but there is still more time. Open a beer, its glass still perspiring from the ice chest, and let the bubbly coolness linger on your tongue. Share the potato chips you bought at the market. The ones you have eaten all your life, not the fancy ones from away. The ones that have oil that slicks your fingers and an overabundance of salt.

The sun and the beer lay you open, and you begin to tell your stories. Not new ones. The ones you all know by heart and repeat anyway. The time the old ladies crested the hill at Battle Avenue in their golf cart and you almost had a heart attack, because you thought one of them had died the previous spring. The campouts on islands like this one, where you shared first kisses and first beers. The angry man with the pot and his righteous ownership of land that belongs to no one and to everyone.

Stories were told on this beach before. If you are lucky, stories will be told of you here after you are gone. About how you would only use old napkins and how once a group of shocked teenagers saw you on the town dock, in a wheelchair but very alive, when they thought you had died the year before.

And then the call goes out. Dogs and children gather near the pit. It is time. Hands gently peel back the blackened burlap and shovels dig into the steaming seaweed.

Find your warm granite rock and your round stone.

Marvel at your fortune.

Eat the lobster.

SWEET AND SOUR
Kathy Gunst

1966. We piled in to the blue and brown station wagon, with its plaid stripe across the middle for the weekly Sunday trip to the deli with my father—one of the few domestic chores he willingly took on. My mother had a few hours off to lie in bed in her thick, pink terrycloth robe, read her latest novel, and listen to the quiet. No squabbling children. No demands.

Sunday mornings meant picking up orange juice and bagels and cream cheese and sometimes, if we were really lucky, smoked salmon. No one in the family loved salmon as much as I did: the salty, buttery, paper-thin slices of orange-pink fish piled on top of scallion-studded cream cheese and doughy bagel rounds.

Sunday was also the day we received our allowance. My younger brothers grabbed their fifty cents, dashed out of the car and into the Toy and Party Shop next to the deli to spend their two quarters on penny candy. In those days, most penny candy actually cost a penny, which meant that fifty cents went a long way.

I headed to the deli with my father. While he ordered the Sunday breakfast, along with a week's worth of sliced ham, Swiss cheese, and maybe roast beef for sandwiches and his late-night snacks, I shopped around, looking for the best way to spend my allowance.

The Heathcote Deli had sawdust-strewn floors and, toward the back of the narrow shop, two tall barrels of dill and half-sour pickles. With my quarters neatly tucked into the coin pocket of my pink patent-leather Barbie wallet, I weighed my options. I could choose two pickles—one dill and one half-sour, each a quarter—or one pickle and a generous handful of coffee-flavored hard candies. I wasn't really allowed to drink coffee, but the jolt of caffeine and sugar made my ten-year-old self feel dangerous and sophisticated.

My father's order was almost ready when the man everyone called Fat Al peered over the glass counter and asked, "And what can I get for you, young lady?" I ordered the pickles.

Fat Al came out from behind the counter and lifted the tongs resting on the side of the barrel. "Go ahead, Sweetie, and show me which ones you want," he said. I appreciated his kind indulgence, and I took my time, studying the weight and heft of each pickle, avoiding the ones with bumps and wrinkles, and eventually choosing two perfect pickles. He wrapped the dill and put the half-sour in its own wax paper bag. When I handed him my coins, he slipped a coffee candy into my hand and winked.

By the time we met up with my brothers, they had eaten nearly half their candy. Their sugary frenzy was deafening. "Dad, Dad, let's go play mini-golf." "Dad, Dad, Dad, let's go swimming!" Being the oldest, I got to ride shotgun. I carefully opened the dill pickle bag and the car was overtaken by vinegar, acid, and herbs. "Gross!" my brothers protested. "Open the windows! I'm gonna puke."

That was my cue to take the first bite of the pickle, the snap and crunch audible. I inhaled the deliciousness of sour, the amazing way a plain old cucumber can be transformed. My brothers tried to wave away the smell, dramatically fanning their hands in front of their noses. "Ugh! Gross! Get me outta here!"

They eventually settled in and chewed on peanut butter and molasses-filled Mary Janes and nutty Bit-O-Honey bars. The sickly-sweet scent of ersatz red cherry was released as they gobbled up Swedish Fish. Licorice sticks and pink Bazooka bubble gum came next. The car filled with sweet and sour.

MY TEN-YEAR-OLD SELF had no idea that one day, only a decade or so later, I would become a food journalist, eventually authoring sixteen cookbooks and becoming the "Resident Chef" for National Public Radio's *Here and Now*. My hunger to try new flavors, to choose a fermented vegetable over the lure of childhood candy, seems like some kind of portent. I now understand that even as a child I saw food as a way to distinguish myself from the rest of the family.

My mother loved to eat, but she deeply resented cooking dinner for her family each night. It's not that she was such a terrible cook. In fact, the memory of her meatloaf smothered in Lipton's Onion Soup mix and her Twice-Baked Potatoes, her dinner party go-to, stuffed with sour cream and grated orange cheese and sprinkled with paprika, still makes me swoon. But back then, each night she put dinner on the table in a perfunctory way that let us know that mealtime was not a cherished activity. Our dinners averaged a total of ten minutes. My mother couldn't wait to clean up and be done with it. There was no lingering. No enjoying around the table. And, most definitely, no joy or appreciation at the food placed in front of us.

I have often wondered what my mother would have rather done. Being a housewife in the '60s, with three young kids and a husband who came home from his job in New York City well past the children's dinner hour, couldn't have been fun. Her mother, a wealthy New York City woman, never cooked. Was it that no one had taught my mother how to prepare food and enjoy it? Or was it that she longed for a life filled with her child-hood passion for musical theater?

Still, for some reason, at a very young age, I saw mealtime, and the ritual of sharing food, as a possible key to understanding things about the world. So when friends invited me for dinner and a sleepover, I took in the food, the banter, and the lingering at their tables as if I were a cultural anthropol-ogist. I was hungry to learn about why people ate what they ate. To learn how they cooked a tuna noodle casserole or matzah ball soup. What it said about who they were. What it might teach me about who I was.

I started throwing family dinner parties around the age of twelve. I would go to the Hallmark store and spend my allowance on paper plates and matching paper streamers. I would mash egg yolks with mayonnaise and my mother's paprika and scoop them into the hollow of the cooked egg whites. I learned to make ice cream pies—layering vanilla ice cream on top of a dark chocolate pre-made grocery-store crust—and would surprise my mother with these meals. I think I was filling in gaps, emotional holes. But the more I cooked and created colorful tables, and served my family and later on my friends, the better I felt.

I still adore pickles. Each summer, I grow cucumbers, peppers, green beans, and onions in my Maine garden, making sure to grow extras to fer-ment. I experiment with flavors: my beans are now pickled with turmeric and cumin seeds, mustard seeds, and fiery chili peppers. But I still love nothing more than a crisp half-sour pickle, for its crunch and acidity, but also for the memories.

KOFTA STORIES
Reza Jalali

YOU NEVER KNEW if kofta would hold together after it was cooked. Sometimes the large stuffed meatball did just fine, but when women in Kurdistan found the time to sit together to gossip and chew on roasted pumpkin seeds, they often shared stories of kofta disasters. This was before the age of satellite dishes and television, when they watched Turkish-produced soap operas while peeling the skins off eggplants and cleaning rice.

My mother and the women in my extended family shared a secret: the way to make round balls of ground beef, mixed with the right amount of grains and perfumed with herbs, stay intact and whole, even after being simmered in a thick and bubbling tomato-onion-based sauce. Unfortunately, once my mother died, she took the secret of making good kofta with her. I was not with her during her final days, but living in exile, in Maine, some seven thousand miles away from Kurdistan. Indecent governments and hostile borders stood between my mother, with all her fantastic stories and secrets, and me.

With her gone, I was left with many worries. Among them: if I were to try to make kofta, would they stay whole or break apart once cooked? Taste was a whole different issue. Those of us who have lived in exile for a long time have lost the ability to taste and smell as we once did. Perhaps we left such senses at an airport transit hall, like a misplaced piece of luggage, on our way to America. Perhaps subconsciously we thought such senses burdensome as they'd only remind us of home.

Newcomers tend to complain, whenever they find a sympathetic pair of ears, about how tasteless the tomatoes are in America, compared to those found at home, or how the roses at Trader Joe's are pretty but lack aroma, and so on.

When I go for walks, I fantasize about cooking kofta. In my head, I mix the ingredients and knead them before shaping them into balls and placing a pitted dried plum inside. Then I insert the stuffed balls, gently, into a pot, as if bathing a newborn baby in a kitchen sink. In my imagination, I wait before I fish out the intact kofta, looking glorious, to rest on a plate, with aromatic steam rising to the heavens above. Still walking, with my heart racing, I wet my lips and promise to risk it all and make the dish soon.

MY MOTHER'S KOFTA STORIES were wild and put together in the same way her plump hands shaped the koftas—with magic and mystery. She claimed that she had seen koftas prepared for rich families' wedding receptions, koftas large enough to contain a fully cooked whole chicken hidden inside. Rumor had it, she added, that the chicken had a peeled hard-boiled egg placed in *its* guts.

When my mother made koftas, she looked like a dazed dervish high on hashish. Though her eyes were closed, her hands acted skillfully. I would watch her lips moving soundlessly as she reached out for walnuts, plums, raisins, barberry, and dried herbs. I imagined she was talking to her ancestors as she sprinkled the combination with saffron and pinches of ground cinnamon.

Some days, she would ask me to run to stores owned by men with sad eyes who sold grains and herbs, whose names I had yet to learn. At one store, I picked up herbs and spices, on credit. I found dried flowers, oils, and other items inside large clay containers, metal drums, and gunny sacks. The sharp smell of turmeric powder mixed with cumin tickled my nose. The storekeeper, his face wrinkled by age, knew me by name. I stood, shifting my weight from one foot to another, nervous about taking too long to return home. I tried my best to wait patiently as the storekeeper found the right container and poured a few fistfuls of the dried herbs he had blended specially for our family.

As the years went by, my mother upped her kofta stories. As her age increased, so did the size of the koftas. The stuffing changed dramatically too. She insisted she knew of a woman, a cook known across Kurdistan for her culinary skills as well as her rare talent to speak to jinn, who made koftas in a king's kitchen that were so large that a whole lamb was stuffed inside. Before being placed inside the kofta, the baby lamb itself had been stuffed with a chicken. My mother said a whole pomegranate had probably been placed inside the chicken too. With her eyes closed, so as to conjure the magical kofta, she added that the kofta had been cooked inside a pot so large that a man could comfortably sit inside it. To top it all, the sauce had been made with the juices of seven fruits—apricots, figs, pears, dates, peaches, plums, and sour cherries. The king was so impressed with the result that he gifted the cook a bag full of gold coins, so heavy that a donkey had to carry it to her house.

WHEN I WAS IN COLLEGE IN INDIA, frequent general strikes, called by one political party or another, caused universities to suspend classes for weeks or even months at a time. With no classes, we sat up all night, playing cards, talking politics, and making up conspiracy theories. Once I shared the story of the kofta, made by the famous cook, stuffed with a lamb. I didn't stop there and, in honor of my mother's style of storytelling, upped the ante and added a cooked goat to the stuffing. This delighted my friends. I told the story, again and again, each time adding more fantastic and unreal details. I may not have inherited the gift of making koftas that stood the test of time by staying whole, but I could tell kofta stories that were as wild as my mother's.

And that's my inheritance: my mother's storytelling skills. As for the actual sweet and sour taste of the koftas she made, I treasure them in memory.

WICKED GOOD SCALLOPS
Nancy Harmon Jenkins

T HERE'S A PHRASE Mainers use when they really-really like something: "Wicked good," they say. Maine sea scallops, harvested from the cold, clean waters in the state's deep bays and around widely scattered islands, are truly wicked good. In the short winter season, they are brought in by dayboat fishermen, who forage only within three miles of shore, leaving port before dawn and returning in the early afternoon with up to fifteen gallons, the permitted harvest, of fresh shucked scallops. (A gallon of scallops weighs around nine pounds, and the catch is closely regulated.)

What makes Maine sea scallops so desirable is both texture and flavor. That requires a brief lesson in physiology. The part of the scallop we consume is the adductor muscle, which connects the two shells of this bivalve. Most bivalves—clams, mussels, and the like—are immobile, sitting in one place throughout their entire life cycle, patiently waiting for food to float by. But scallops are unusual in that they actually swim, clapping their shells together to propel themselves away from predators as their adductor muscle grows into a meaty chunk, as tender and tasty as filet mignon. As for the flavor, Maine sea scallops have a distinctive sweet nuttiness that experts say comes from the cold salt waters in which they thrive. Unlike scallops from other waters, they are as tasty raw as they are seared in a skillet or baked in a sea pie.

Moreover, because this is entirely a dayboat catch, the scallops arrive in port within hours of harvest and are usually shipped out within a short time frame, as fresh as a Maine morning. Deep-sea scallop fishermen, on the other hand, pack their catch in ice and frequently also in a solution of sodium tripolyphosphate (STPP), an additive that is "generally recognized as safe," according to the United States Food and Drug Administration.

Scallops are like little sponges, absorbing moisture and of course increasing in weight. These deep-sea scallops are sold—or they should be sold—as "wet" scallops and they are to be avoided. If you try to sear off "wet" scallops, they exude a milky liquid into the frying pan and will never brown properly. Consumer alert: even if you can't find Maine sea scallops, you should only buy "dry" scallops, which have not had anything added to them.

Once you have the best-quality scallops in your kitchen, you should use them quickly, within a day or two. In Maine we often freeze scallops in order to prolong the season; scallops freeze better than almost any other kind of seafood. But otherwise, we eat them raw (a squeeze of lime juice, a pinch of chopped green jalapeño, a little fresh cilantro will give them a delightful Mexican touch), or we cook them up in a variety of simple ways. I love to serve them to guests crowded around my kitchen table on a chilly night in January. With a brisk fire in the woodstove, a couple of rum toddies to start with, and a properly chilled Muscadet or Chablis to go with, scallops warm up even the coldest Maine winter. You don't need much more—a salad of bitter winter greens and a Maine apple pie for dessert. It's how we like to eat in Maine—simple, straightforward, and delicious.

But first, a couple of tips in the kitchen: (1) Be sure you get dry scallops. (2) Remove and discard the thick, opaque bit attached like a strap to the side of the muscle—it's tough. (3) Dry the scallops thoroughly with paper towels just before you start to cook. (4) Don't crowd the scallops when you sear them—they need plenty of room to brown perfectly.

SEARED MAINE SEA SCALLOPS
IN A TOMATO-PEPPER GRATIN

For a pound and a half of "dry" Maine scallops, take about a cup of chopped yellow onion and two finely chopped garlic cloves and sauté very gently in a couple tablespoons of extra-virgin olive oil over medium-low heat until they soften. Then add a sweet red pepper, cored and slivered, and cook some more, until the pepper slivers start to soften. Now stir in four to six canned plum tomatoes, breaking them up with the side of a spoon as they cook down. Add a spoonful of mild Spanish or Hungarian paprika, a sprinkle of salt, and several grinds of black pepper. Cook another five minutes or so, until you have a nice thick sauce, then set it aside while you brown the scallops.

Add about three tablespoons of olive oil to another skillet set over medium heat. Dust each scallop lightly in instant flour and drop it in the hot oil, searing each side until golden, about two minutes to a side. Remove the scallops to a lightly oiled gratin or oven dish.

When all the scallops are done, turn on your oven broiler. While it's heating, add about a half cup of dry white wine to the skillet in which the scallops cooked; bring the wine to a boil and scrape up any brown bits left in the bottom of the pan. Turn the tomato and pepper mixture into the same pan and cook it down to a dense sauce. Spoon the sauce over the scallops and transfer the gratin dish to the hot oven, broiling until the top is lightly browned and sizzling, about five to seven minutes. Serve immediately.

FOR THE LOVE OF GRITS

Alice Bingham Gorman

T HEY SAY YOU can take the girl out of the South, but you can't take the South out of the girl. Is that true? Take me, for example. I was born and raised in Memphis, Tennessee, but I was taken out of the South at age seven. During World War II, when my father was a Naval officer stationed at the Presidio, my whole family moved to San Francisco for a year. From our house, I could walk to the Pacific Ocean, a far cry from the Mississippi River. I discovered the sights and foods of Chinatown, the pagoda roofs, the hanging lanterns and dragons, the noodles and rice, so different from the cobblestones, the colorful bars, the live blues music, and the fried bologna sandwiches offered on Beale Street. Listening to the grown-ups talking at our house during cocktail parties that year, I overheard constant references to "The War." "What was happening?" "When would it end?" In Memphis, throughout my early childhood, any conversation about "The War" meant "The Civil War" and I knew that was over.

At age fourteen, I went away to school in the Green Spring Valley of Maryland. My French teacher loved to listen to me read an Alphonse Daudet story in front of the class. She actually laughed out loud at my "Southern accent." My roommate from New York was horrified that I brought a 45-rpm record player so I could play "Dixie" when I felt homesick. After three years, some of my Memphis friends teased me when I came home and occasionally referred to them as "you guys" instead of "y'all." They said I had become a Yankee. The word appalled me. Never, I thought, never would I become a Yankee.

At age twenty-one, before succumbing to the status of "old maid," I married a Connecticut Yankee, a Marine lieutenant who had moved to Memphis for three months of Advanced Flight Training at Millington

Naval Air Station. I would have moved anywhere, even Yankee-land, with him, but he decided to move to Memphis. After raising our three children and going through a divorce, I remarried in 1992. When my new husband and I decided that we wanted to live someplace that neither of us had ever lived, we both made a list of preferences. His list began with the Shenandoah Valley. I only listed Maine. From my summers in Maine with my first husband, I had fallen in love with the state. My new husband eventually agreed with me, and we made the move. Today I am a widowed snowbird who commutes between Maine and Florida (definitely not the real South!) every six months.

If the saying about the South never leaving the girl is accurate, what is it about the South that, after all these years, I still carry within me?

For starters, there are so many character traits, both negative and positive, attributed to Southerners that make me smile. Are any of those traits mine? I have met people who have never been south of New Jersey or East of Texas who once read *Gone with the Wind* and are quite certain that all Southern men are courtly gentlemen like Ashley Wilkes, and many women are conniving charmers like Scarlett O'Hara or soft-hearted, sweet-voiced ladies like Melanie. Others I know have formed opinions of the Southern life and the Southern people from movies like *Steel Magnolias*, *Forrest Gump*, and *The Help*. Certainly, novels and films offer some viable examples, but, often in the name of drama, they portray the extremes of Southern culture: the language, the accents, the manners, the work ethic (or lack thereof), the rural culture with its hunting guns, Bibles, and bourbon.

What the books and movies don't emphasize are many of the things I miss most about the South: the lacy pattern of dogwood and wild azaleas blooming in the spring woods, the smell of white magnolia blossoms in June, the jasmine and gardenias, the sound of a paddlewheel calliope on the Mississippi River, the guitars and banjos, the family gatherings on green lawns that go on forever, the tradition of hospitality and graciousness that many of us were taught by our mothers and grandmothers—and the food. Oh Lord, how I do miss the food!

I love grits. Grits for breakfast, grits for lunch, and even grits for dinner. No amount of bagels and smoked salmon or waffles with maple syrup can hit the spot with me like a breakfast plate of country ham and scrambled eggs with plain old grits. And come to think of it, I have often served a casserole of cheese grits at a dinner party in Maine that seemed to charm and delight even the most skeptical Yankee guest.

"This stuff is really 'grits'?" a person once asked, as if I had tried to put one over on him. "I must have the recipe."

And fried chicken, the kind soaked in buttermilk and breaded and bubbling away in a black iron skillet with hot bacon grease and Crisco. I recently stood in line for over half an hour at Popeyes chicken in Kennebunk, Maine, for two drumsticks (even though I knew they were not cooked in a black iron skillet). I just had to have fried chicken, and Popeyes is closer to the real Southern way than Kentucky Fried.

And how I miss all the Southern summer vegetables: fried green tomatoes and lady peas and okra and white corn. Most of my Maine friends have never even heard of lady peas, much less ever tasted one—a sort of cross between black-eyed peas and baby lima beans, but smaller and more delicate than either. I can still taste the white corn cut off the cob, mixed with melted butter and bits of green pepper at my grandmother's dinner table in Nashville, served along with Mary's biscuits, heavenly biscuits started from scratch with buttermilk and flour. I cannot remember a cocktail party at my grandmother's without the crunchy taste of country ham and beaten biscuits (and always a bit of Durkee's dressing). The best treat at her house, of course, was always the dessert, pecan pie (pronounced *puh-cahn*, accent on the second syllable, not *pee-can*, accent on the first). Just thinking about these delectables as I write them down makes me salivate.

Oh, yes, and then there's Memphis barbecue. These days practically every town in America has a sign out for some form of barbecue. Even in Maine there are roadside stands that advertise it, sometimes spelled BBQ. None of them tastes like Memphis barbecue. Western "joints" and restaurants in Texas and Montana—the now defunct Road Kill Café in McLeod, Montana, for instance—mostly use beef for their barbecue. Beef? Real barbecue to my Southern taste buds has to be pork. Pulled pork from the pork shoulder or pork ribs slow cooked in some form of a pit. Period.

In Memphis, the successful commercial barbecue tradition was started over sixty years ago by Charlie Vergos at the Rendezvous, a basement restaurant in a back alley downtown. The Rendezvous ribs are known as "dry ribs," as opposed to Corky's, purveyor of one of the newer favorites, which are referred to as "wet." In both cases, the meat begins to fall off the bone before you can sink your teeth into it. A barbecue sandwich from any of the local restaurants consists of pulled pork on a fat, squishy, toasted bun, coleslaw, and a spicy red, catsup-based barbecue sauce. I've dreamt about a barbecue sandwich and more than once been disappointed by optimistically ordering one from a menu in some other city, only to wonder what in the world I was eating. There's just something different, something special, about Memphis barbecue.

And one more haunting memory that reminds me of my roots every Thanksgiving: cornbread. No self-respecting Southern cook would ever, I mean ever, put sugar in cornbread. It is hard to imagine why some Yankee, many years ago, decided that cornbread needed sugar. Not only in regular baked cornbread, cut in squares, served with turnip greens (or anything else), but also in the left-over cornbread that is a requirement for the best Thanksgiving turkey stuffing. Whatever made Pepperidge Farm think turkey stuffing needed to be sweet? Through the years, I *have* succumbed to using a bag or two of Pepperidge Farm cornbread stuffing, but I always added salt.

So what it all boils down to is this: food matters. Taste develops early from regional and cultural traditions. Of all the delights I have discovered through the years—escargot in Paris, baby artichokes in Venice, Dover sole in London, tandoori chicken in Mumbai, or even lobster in Maine—my memory of grits has prevailed.

PANCAKE MORNINGS
Peggy Grodinsky

A RECENT MESSAGE FROM my iCloud account that I was out of storage led me to spend a dull afternoon deleting hundreds of photographs from my iPhone. There, among the many pictures of Trixie (The Most Beautiful Cat in Maine) and the obligatory beach walk pictures of my partner, Joe, and me, I discovered pancakes. Stacks and stacks of pancakes. Many shots—weekly shots, or actually weekend-ly shots.

Pancakes on red plates and on green ones. Pancakes shot from overhead and half-eaten ones shot from the side, drenched in syrup. Blueberry pancakes, banana-walnut pancakes, cranberry-pecan pancakes. Summer pancakes with peach-and-strawberry syrup (the strawberries from my own garden) and winter stacks with pretty pink grapefruit halves on the side. Fluffy pancakes from those days when I took the time to stiffly whip and fold in the egg whites and flatter ones from those days when I was lazy, or hurried, and didn't. Oven pancakes and griddle pancakes, though many more of the latter.

Round, golden, picture-perfect pancakes, and the occasional burnt or unattractively pale blobby stack. Not too many of the poorly constructed ones, though. I like to think that's because I am a practiced pancake maker. But let's be honest, like most people, I prefer not to broadcast my mistakes.

I grew up in the 1960s and '70s eating homemade pancakes with maple syrup every weekend. I have a fuzzy memory of our mixing imitation maple extract with sugar and heating it on the stove to make some kind of syrup when I was very small, but by the time I was old enough for distinct memories, we were buying the real stuff and it was a point of pride. This was not the era of real maple syrup, or real much of anything foodwise, but my mother grew up in Montreal, and we spent our summers with our cousins in Vermont, and we knew from syrup. We poured it into a jug and heated it gently on the stove in a pot of warm water. No cold syrup on hot pancakes for us.

Occasionally, I would form the pancakes into faces with chocolate chips for eyes, nose, and mouth, also shape them into mice or dogs by pouring the batter to form ears. When I was eight or so, I went to a sugar on snow celebration in Quebec—the syrup still collected in buckets then. Weird! But . . . a revelation! And that sweet-sour counterpoint still resonates in my food likes today.

When my grandmother died, we gave away her mink coats, but I inherited her griddle, a round, worn, cast-iron one some twelve inches in diameter. I was about twenty-four, just starting out in a household of my own, plus I lived in Vermont then, the maple syrup (and thus presumably pancake) capital of America. I have no memories of Nana ever making pancakes, none, so why she had the griddle in the first place is a puzzle. Actually, I have no memories of Nana ever cooking anything. She loved to entertain, but the cooking was usually outsourced. Still, I kept that griddle for some thirty years, until its black, comfortable handle deteriorated into loose flakes, and the entire mechanism swirled around whenever I tried to grip it, turning pancake mornings into anxious affairs.

I acquired the griddle toward the end of my know-it-all-days when my parents knew nothing and I knew all, especially about food and cooking. I was, after all, a new reader of *Gourmet* and an avid follower of the country's then-nascent food revolution, which was growing up alongside me. This was the era of Chez Panisse, nouvelle cuisine, and kiwis. One thing I knew for certain? Never, ever press on a pancake with the spatula after you flip it. All that height and fluff you've worked to create? Smashed. I smugly corrected my mother one pancake morning as she worked the griddle. She had a temper, and I have blocked out memories of her response.

So, real maple syrup, my supply usually sourced in Maine, but what about the pancakes themselves? Every few months, I make up a batch of my whole-grain mix. A friend bestowed the recipe on my sister Carolyn, who bestowed it on the rest of the family to help my beleaguered mother handle the several dozen guests who descended on our lakefront Vermont home each weekend. We made it every summer weekend for going-on thirty years, sometimes holding the pancakes in the oven until we had a sizeable stack for the crowded table, sometimes letting visiting cousins, siblings, aunts, uncles, and friends grab them as they came off the griddle—which strategy is better remains a cause for debate. As the host-esses, my sisters and I took turns manning the griddle.

This was years before my father died; the uncles died; my wise and beloved aunt vanished into Parkinson's and died; Mishka the lake-loving dog was struck and killed by a car that didn't even stop; and my sisters and I began to have aches and pains and wrinkles of our own. Summers, our big, boisterous, argumentative crowd gathered in Vergennes by beautiful Lake Champlain, canoeing every day, biking every day, kayaking every day, swimming every day, bickering every day, watching sunsets and storms over the lake every day, reuniting over dinner or over pancake breakfasts. It was our golden time.

One of the first times Joe and I ever spent the night together, I had The Great Pancake Meltdown. It is an event we still talk about, though I can't say we reminisce fondly. Why he didn't ditch me that day I'll never know. I made pancakes for him for the first time, supposing he would immediately appreciate what a talented cook I was and how many contented, leisurely, perfect Peggy weekends lay ahead if he played his cards right. The pancakes stuck, the pancakes burned, the batter ran off the griddle and pooled at the edge, inedible. My temper was as hot as that July morning, and I fell apart, pouting, whining, dissolving into tears.

Yet, Joe stuck with me then, and to this day.

I have so few rituals in my life. I've moved from state to state, with a few countries thrown in for good measure. I've held a lot of jobs. I've made dear, wonderful friends and then moved away and lost them without meaning to, without wanting to. I learned to speak Japanese and German, not fluently, but not badly, and then most of the hard-won words and sentences dissolved from lack of use. (I still remember "Pfannkuchen," though, the German word for "guess what?") But making pancakes on the weekend in every season—the dance between Joe and me as we set the table, make the coffee, heat the syrup, prep the fruit, whip the eggs, pour the batter, and flip—steadies me.

Wherever I am, pancakes connect me: to my childhood, to old friends, to places I love. To my extended family, living and dead, and to my nearer, if geographically distant, three sisters who just maybe are making their own pancakes for their own families at the very same moment I am cooking mine.

TOMATO SANDWICHES
Jonathan and Desmond Lethem

MY EXTENDED CLAN of family and friends spend our summers in East Blue Hill, in a farmhouse built in 1865. We spend a lot of time eating, and a lot of time thinking about food, and a lot of time on the porch. In the archaeology of East Blue Hill Porch Food, Desmond, my ten-year-old son, and I want to begin with tomato sandwiches. Not just any tomato sandwiches, but the tomato sandwiches that define the form, the archetypal tomato sandwiches that occupy the center of his consciousness of Porch Food to begin with. As Desmond says, "My earliest memory was of biting down on a tomato sandwich and having it falling apart in my hands."

The sandwiches in question are made with a combination of Tinder Hearth Bread and tomatoes from C&G, a local tomato grower with a farm stand. At the height of their ripeness, there is something eternal about them, and there is also something a little bit tragic about them that you'll discover by the end of our account.

Can Desmond describe the flavor? He can: "A low tone with a bit of a tomato taste, in this low undertone carried by the mayonnaise." How did the bread interact? "With the nice fresh bread as a foundation to anchor the flavor down. Crusty on the outside and soft on the inside, that helped to carry the sauce." I laugh at this word "sauce," but recognize its rightness at the same time. I tell Desmond his use of it has made me see that the combination of ripe tomato and mayonnaise did form a kind of sauce inside the sandwich. Those, incidentally, are the entire ingredients: bread, tomato, and plentiful mayonnaise. Nothing else but salt, pepper, and a few leaves of soft lettuce, though as Desmond points out, "The leaves don't matter, really."

So let's talk about the two ingredients that are specific—since no mayonnaise could fail to bind the two together. And salt and pepper are just salt and pepper. Tinder Hearth sourdough is baked at a beloved nearby bakery and pizza maker, on a communal farm in Brooksville that doubles as an outdoor dining area several nights a week through the summer, a site of delirious grown-up dining and drinking, and childhood dining and play. There's too much to say about Tinder Hearth the institution to go into here. We'll stick to the bread, which is enough. The loaves are prized, and in midsummer, they disappear within hours of their twice-weekly delivery to various outlets. Ours is called the Blue Hill Wine Shop. Desmond says, "We still have fond memories of waiting around in the Blue Hill Wine Shop (not actually waiting there to buy wine), but instead to buy the soonest, freshest shipment of Tinder Hearth bread. It was always a rush because of how quickly it sold out—if you weren't there when the truck arrived it was going to be sold out."

The sandwiches were best the day the bread was picked up. We often made them the minute we got home with the loaves. I'd cut it thick and use a couple of loaves to make a platter full of sandwiches when guests were coming. The result was, in Desmond's words, "comically large sandwiches, as big as your face." Then we'd eat them, either in the dining room or on the porch. Here's Desmond again: "We'd sit down on the dining table, which was a bit large—we either all sat together, and there were empty seats, or we sat far apart and it was weird—that table only felt full when there were guests over. I always felt excited seeing the mountain of half-sandwiches on the platter. I'd anticipate eating four to five halves, and then I'd be wrong, I'd only eat two to three halves. That ties in to how it was as large as your face."

Other times, weather permitting, or if Desmond and his older brother, Everett, were running around, and it didn't seem reasonable to try to pull everyone inside to the dining room, we'd eat on the porch. Desmond says, "A game we used to play on the porch while eating the sandwiches was guess what the color of the next car would be and from which direction it would come. Ninety-eight percent of the time you'd be wrong, but it still felt great when you were right. If someone was on a winning streak, you'd just copy them."

The difficult part of the story is the C&G tomatoes. These were by far the best tomatoes on the peninsula, and we'd buy them and ripen them on the windowsill. They had a special ability to catalyze with the bread and mayonnaise to make the "sauce." We weren't the only ones we knew who loved them—everybody who knew about the C&G stand preferred them. It was worth the drive. We thought of C&G as an institution. I'll let Desmond take over. "The place where we got the C&G tomatoes for the sandwiches always seemed so eerie and unreal. You just put money in the box and took the amount of tomatoes you wanted. Sometimes we'd just get a couple of tomatoes when we were in the area. It was a sudden shock when we went to get tomatoes from the stand and saw that it was closed permanently. The people we talked to at the gas station nearby just seemed confused, like it was incidental, as if they'd already almost forgotten about its existence. They said that C&G continued to grow tomatoes, but they shipped them out to different places. The stand wasn't important to them the way it was to us."

Once we couldn't get the C&G tomatoes, we could still make the sandwiches. "It was a hard change to go through," Desmond tells me. "But as long as we can find juicy tomatoes, we could still have the classic tomato porch sandwiches. And, if you think about it, the Tinder Hearth bread was the vital component, but we could still make tomato sandwiches without it. It was more like those ingredients were just perfect for the application we were using them for."

So it comes down to a last question. Was the tradition alive? We felt a bit disappointed. Could we still have the classic tomato sandwiches, or was it over? Then we realized that if we ripened good large tomatoes from the Blue Hill Food Co-op, we stood a fighting chance. In Desmond's estimation, "I'd say that two out of three tomato sandwiches we make are the original porch tomato sandwiches."

And as I told Desmond, "Two out of three ain't bad."

ON NOT BEING FRESH
Susan Minot

WHEN I THINK back to the food that I was raised on, I am not nostalgic; I am appalled. In my family we didn't eat real food; we ate mostly brand names.

In the '50s and '60s, when I was growing up, the word *fresh* described what you were not supposed to be as far as your parents were concerned. *Don't be fresh.* Fresh meant you were *talking back*, something you were not supposed to do. It turned out that fresh was also something they did not want for their food either.

I may have heard the word *fresh* in tandem with fish. Sometimes. But for the cuisine of my childhood, the *less* fresh a food, the more desirable. That there were seven children in my family may have made efficiency a priority, but it was also part of the times and considered an advancement to have food already prepared. Better than fresh was packaged, processed, frozen.

It's amazing we received any nutrition at all. No wonder our generation is full of addicts and people battling anxiety and depression. We were fed crap.

YES, WE ATE MEAT, one of the three food types that like a color chart made the tri-fector shape on each of our plates at dinner. Meat, starch, vegetable. With a hamburger, we'd have Minute Rice and peas (frozen). All vegetables were frozen: lima beans, "French cut" string beans, corn. Carrot sticks were a rare fresh food, though they were always peeled and cut into spears, lest they resemble the actual vegetable. The meats were hot dogs, frozen fish sticks, and the odd cube steak, which had the consistency

53

of corduroy, as if it had been woven. Spaghetti and meatballs slid out of a Chef Boyardee can.

With seven children, special choices could not be indulged. At dinner, we all had the same thing. We children ate at 5:30 in the kitchen and our parents ate "alone" at 7:30 in the dining room, the one time in the day I suppose they tried to be with one another, though we often hovered at their elbows, begging for bites of the lamb chops or scalloped potatoes, adult food, which glistened so appealingly in the candlelight.

Breakfast was the one meal where we were given a choice—of cereal. There may have been a hint of a grain in there, but I think the boxes—fun to read, often with plastic "treats" inside—were filled pretty much with processed starch, sugar, and God knows how many food dyes and chemicals. The names sing of the tastes of my youth: Frosted Flakes, Sugar Smacks (not to be confused with the yellow Sugar *Pops*, not to be confused with the similar-looking Cap'n Crunch), Rice Krispies, which really did snap, crackle, and pop, Cocoa Puffs, Fruit Loops, and Lucky Charms with their rainbow colors, and the "healthy" Corn Flakes, Cheerios, Shredded Wheat, and Grape Nuts.

It's a wonder our bones actually developed.

But we did drink milk, at every meal. Maybe milk was more natural then. And we did have ice cream. Hoodsies were round wax-paper cups with the three flavors of chocolate, vanilla, and strawberry, eaten with a flat wooden spoon. It was a golden era for popsicles: the heel-shaped fruit ices, Creamsicles, a (to my ten-year-old mind) sophisticated blend of cream and orange sherbet, and Fudgsicles, our mother's favorite popsicle bar. More exotic popsicles one would find away from home: the red, white, and blue rocket-shaped ice pop, the Toasted Almond bar—my favorite—with a center of "almond flavor," the cardboard cylinders that pushed a circular base up around a stick—maybe those were called rockets too?—and the nut-topped vanilla ice cream cone, wrapped in paper, stocked in the freezer at the sub shop.

Welch's Grape Jelly came in small glass jars decorated with *The Flintstones* cartoon line drawings etched in pastel colors onto the glass, which we saved and used as juice glasses. Two brands in one!

Lunch was often eaten from a tin lunch box, invariably a sandwich on white Wonder Bread. My favorite was baloney, no mayo, with a thin leaf of iceberg lettuce, the only lettuce I knew ever existed. Other sandwich fillings came from jars—peanut butter and Fluff, a white pure sugar marshmallow spread, which made the Fluffernutter; from cans: tuna; from plastic wrap: slices of American cheese.

WE DID EAT FRUIT. Green grapes. Bananas. The oranges we got were the ones made for orange juice, so we sliced them in half and ate them direct from their rind bowls. But most of our snacks had newfangled, brand names.

A Triscuit was a basket-woven cracker. Fritos were corn chips, made by Frito-Lay. We had Ring Dings, chocolate patties with a vanilla cream center, and Yodels, small bûches de Noël with a curl of white filling, each individually wrapped in thin foil. And can anyone who knew them ever forget the allure of Hostess Cupcakes with their loop-de-loop frosting design, Sno Balls made out of pink . . . what? Well, something springy with coconut sprinkled on top, and the famed Twinkies, fingers of soaked yellow cake with an extra sweet white filling, which were somehow singled out as being "bad for us" and off-limits. We also infiltrated the grown-up cocktail snacks, stuffed in the same corner shelf of the kitchen, above the counter so you had to knee up and balance while you rooted around past the eternal potato chips and Saltines to potato sticks in a cardboard cylinder, glazed party mixes of peanuts, tiny Wheaties and puffed corn, and dry roasted peanuts in a glass jar shaped like a peanut. Later came Cheetos, Pringles, and the short-lived, trumpet-shaped Bugle.

Our father liked fried pork rinds. Spam. Mum liked Pop-Tarts and Sanka.

I CAN REMEMBER some real food: roast beef and potatoes for big meals, my mother's oatmeal lace cookies, somehow both brittle and chewy, and her Irish stew (made with Campbell's tomato soup).

If I do have any wistful memories, they would land on ginger-ale floats, which in our family were called Treats, with the icy glaze that formed on vanilla ice cream. But I'm not sure anything outdoes in wonder the miracle of the growing silver dome—as it sat on the burner—of Jiffy Pop.

Now most of the food I eat is real and fresh and good for you. Kale. Avocado. Chard. Arugula. They are foods, not to mention words, that in my youth I did not even know existed.

BLACKBERRY LANDS
Myronn Hardy

During my childhood summers in Arkansas, my parents, sister, cousins, uncles, aunts, and I picked blackberries on my grandparents' farmland. They had a berry patch, a few long rows of bushes but the yield was bountiful. The rest of the land was reserved for soybeans and rice.

We'd fill five-gallon plastic buckets and place them on the picnic table near the paint-chipped barn. It was a contest to see who was the swiftest at filling the buckets, who could stack the most buckets on the table, and whose hands would become the most purple and sticky. I was never the winner. But I loved being there. I loved gathering the warm berries in my hands, and I liked how the white plastic buckets became ornate with our purple fingerprints. Once we'd filled the top of the weathered picnic table and the long benches, and before washing our hands, turning on that seemingly random barn faucet that spewed the coldest water in the world, we'd stand looking at what we had gathered, astounded by what that land had produced with my grandparents' careful tending.

Above us, above the table, willow branches swayed and curled in the humid air. The sweet, earthy blackberry smell was all around us, in us, on our washed hands. We ate handfuls, the berries breaking, releasing juice, the chewy bitter pulp and seeds opening and spilling into our mouths.

Many of the blackberries would end up in Ziploc bags for us to take back to Michigan where I grew up and lived at the time. Some went to Maryland with my uncle's family. My grandmother would spend days making preserves out of them. But usually, on the evening of our first big harvest, she'd make blackberry cobbler and serve it with a dinner of fried perch, potato salad, and tomato onion salad.

For that meal, we covered the picnic table with a plastic tablecloth and white dishes and silverware, making it feel like a celebration of how long my family had survived in this country. Dressed in short-sleeve shirts and khakis with our straw sun hats removed, we'd eat until the mosquitoes attacked our bare arms, legs, and necks.

I THINK OF HOW old those blackberry bushes are. Perhaps over seventy years, or even more. My great-grandparents were sharecroppers all of their lives. My grandparents were sharecroppers much of their lives but saved, borrowed, and eventually bought that land, their land. Some of those blackberry bushes were there when the land became theirs. They planted others later, and the summer blackberry gathering and harvesting became a tradition long before I was born, long before I was a possibility.

Blackberries grow in dark southern Arkansas soil, soil filled with the dark slain, slain family members, some I've met and known, many I've never met. I can't help but wonder what bodies feed those blackberry bushes.

On our flight back to Michigan, I would eat blackberries from a Ziploc bag. It was my way of reliving the harvest and holding onto the people and place that I was leaving.

IN MICHIGAN, IN elementary school, as I explored the woods with friends, we once came upon a blackberry bush. I was startled as I'd only seen them growing in Arkansas. The berries we gathered that day were smaller and less sweet than the ones from Arkansas. But they were delicious. And part of that deliciousness was the discovery that they grew where I'd spent most of my life.

Years later, when I lived and taught creative writing and literature in Morocco, a student of mine took me to his family farm in Agadir, in the south where his family grew blackberries for export to Europe. He pulled some of those berries from the bush and placed them in my hands. I ate one, then another. They were almost identical to my Arkansas blackberries. "My grandparents used to grow these," I told him.

"You are lucky," he said.

"How am I lucky?" I asked.

"You know sweetness," he said.

"The struggle of it. The struggle for it," I said.

He shook his head. "You're making me think, Professor."

I smiled as we continued to walk in the field. I remembered reading that the ancient Greeks used blackberries to cure ailments.

I wonder what they are curing in me.

I'M SO NOT A FOOD PERSON
Richard Ford

M Y ATTITUDE TOWARD FOOD and general eating—let's call it *relaxed*—I owe to my mother. *And* to my father, since as long as I knew him, I never saw him do anything but obediently *eat* my mother's food, never help cook, or even be around when it was *being* cooked.

My mother was at best an apathetic cook. And her overall production can be described as adequate. She had "her dishes." Meatloaf (not turkey meatloaf). Too greasy pot roast. Spaghetti made with ground beef and too few tomatoes. Skinny, hard-fried pork chops. Mac 'n' cheese. Over-crusty, deep-fried chicken—the jewel in her crown. All these complemented by vegetables sourced from cans, the whole finished off with a limited variety of desserts—half a canned pear with grated cheese and Miracle Whip, or sometimes an intensely sweet lemon icebox pie made with treacly Eagle Brand milk, vanilla wafers, and whipped cream on top. These dishes were proffered mostly on Sundays, never during the week, since my father, a traveling salesman, was away working then, and if she didn't have to cook for him, she didn't cook. Weekdays at home were catch-as-catch-can. Mini-boxed cereals or lumpy Cream of Wheat to start, some brutalist school lunch, then packaged fare for the evening. Sometimes we ventured out to Morrison's cafeteria, or brought home steam-table meals from the grocery. But absent that, it was salami, bologna, pimento cheese on Wonder Bread, tuna salad, potted meat, Vienna sausages, possibly a dog or a burger or whatever'd survived the weekend or could be spelunked from kitchen cabinets and gotten into with a can opener. Pizzas had not been invented in Mississippi in my youth. (I saw my first one in Pensacola, in 1957.) TV dinners *did* arrive sometime during my teens, as did frozen food, both of which my mother looked upon with favor.

I'm not complaining here and didn't then. This was simply what food was—whatever my mother put on the table. I ate it. I liked it. I understood that when I went to my friends' houses—after school or on Saturdays—there would be different, often heady aromas in their kitchens. Savory, exotic, rich-smelling things were being prepared and eaten there every day. My friends' mothers took an alternate view of cooking from my mother—who'd grown up in less than ideal circumstances in the Ozark sticks, and later lived in hotels where her stepfather worked. Cooking was not culture. Not celebratory or an occasion, not a source of pride or exultation. It was barely even a subject. At the end of the day, cooking to my mother was the obligatory response to the intransigent, human need to eat. She owned but one cookbook, a wedding present I never saw her open. Her directive to me all through our life together—I hear her voice to this moment—was "If you don't like it, I'll throw it away." I don't remember that ever happening, because—again—whatever she put on the table, I ate. I also remember her saying she didn't really like to cook.

Such a low-bar initiation to *cuisine* wouldn't *necessarily* foreshadow later habits and pleasures. It could as well have produced a boy with cravings for only the finest—the Caspian Beluga, the Périgord black unearthed *that day*, cod cheeks, tiny swifts on toast. It just worked out *other* for me. Of course, I'd rather have the really good than the dreary today. Ruffed grouse, shot by me, served on an endive leaf with foie gras and a poached egg—preferable to a grilled-cheese sammy with non-dairy American *singles* and a dill pickle scavenged from the back of the fridge. I always prefer fresh over tinned, and steer clear of items full of fat and dye and sugar and pre-servatives and growth hormones and antibiotics and microplastics. I don't eat fast food. My mother would approve, though not be fundamentally changed in her approach.

TODAY, I STILL eat anything and everything with few second thoughts. I'll eat virtually any leftover—cold or warm. I'm happy with breakfast for dinner, and still go for the odd chili dog or frozen chalupa. Eating's not my subject either. It's just a potentially pleasant habit I try to make the most of—something I do so I can have the strength to do something more inter-esting. I *can* cook and sometimes do—though in truth, I *fix* food more than I prepare it. I'm one of those "three-dish specialty" cooks. One for whom people say, with amusement, "Ford makes a mean . . . egg salad." Or, "Ford's *specialty* is . . . breakfast." Having been around enough farmers in my life, I don't pay much attention to where things are sourced—the word itself is slightly repellent. One salt is as good as another to me. A regular avocado as good as organic. Restaurants that insist I *have* to hear about all these tedious matters before I can even order, I usually don't go back to. Over the long Maine winters, I don't dream of opening my own small, farm-to-table bistro in Skowhegan with only one seating a night. The whole foodie business puts me off—just like it would my mother—the stigmata of a declining culture, one in which household pets are worshipped as deities and people use *only* Kenya coffee for their cleanses.

All this being true, I'm happy to say I've lived with an inspired cook for fifty-three years, someone who reads recipes for their plots, owns shelves of cookbooks, and routinely goads herself into culinary feats she's never tried before. I have it both ways, in other words. Wouldn't we all like that? I'm not advancing an advocacy here. Just telling a little tale. Mine's no better than yours.

Though, it must be said, when Kristina and I have a meal at home, we don't talk much about the food—any more than we talk about our surgeries or the income tax. There are just the two of us. No kids to corral. We cook—sometimes together. We eat together. We're observant of each other. Then we get up and go do something else.

SWEET ON MAINE
Karen Watterson

I N JULY OF 1969, eighty little girls sat cross-legged on the lodge floor of a Maine sleepaway camp, transfixed by one small television. As we waited for the historic moon landing, we began to fidget a bit. Some of us were no more than eight years old, and this may have been a monumental moment, but it sure was moving slowly. Sensing discontent, the kitchen staff arrived bearing trays lined with thick camp mugs, each one holding a scoop of peppermint stick ice cream glazed with hot fudge.

And history was made.

Men walking on the moon couldn't compare to my first taste of that ethereal pairing. I'm forever grateful to the staff for introducing it to me. Whether it was something they enjoyed themselves, or simply what was in the freezer that day, the combination is still my favorite.

I grew up in an ice cream–obsessed family. There were always several supermarket half-gallons in the freezer, alongside hand-packed quarts from Brigham's or Baskin-Robbins. My father would ask the scooper to pack the container with two flavors, placing them in *sideways*, so that when you dished it out at home, you could easily get some of each kind. This was a pain in the neck for the ice cream parlor employee, but he'd do it anyway, and my father always felt like a prizewinner with that special quart. We had plenty of mint chocolate chip, but rarely, if ever, peppermint stick.

Ice cream field trips were a regular thing in our family, no drive too far for a visit to the newest Boston-area scoop shop creating handmade, artisan (before anyone used that word) ice cream. We went to Somerville and waited in a long line at Steve's for mix-ins. There was a memorable scoop from Belgian Fudge, in Harvard Square, studded with actual chunks of fudge; the seemingly endless sundae menu at Cabot's in Newtonville; the deep metal bowls and extra-long spoons at Bailey's, with hot fudge and marshmallow sauce dripping onto the saucer; and pointy-top scoops of pistachio at Howard Johnson's.

In the late '70s, I hit the ice cream jackpot when I arrived at the University of Vermont. The city of Burlington was abuzz about the new ice cream shop that had taken over an old gas station on the corner of St. Paul and College Streets. Two guys named Ben and Jerry were churning out previously unheard-of flavors from a rock-salt and ice freezer, and people were lining up for a taste. The place became a mainstay of my years in Burlington, but I don't recall them ever making peppermint stick, a shame because their hot fudge was second to none.

In the '90s, I again started to spend summers on a sparkling Western Maine lake, this time with a husband and three kids in tow. Much to our delight, an ice cream boat would appear on weekends, stopping at docks with a freezer full of treats. This was so much better than an ice cream truck! We'd run down to the dock, waving wildly to make sure the driver saw us. When we finished our Hoodsies and Popsicles, we cleaned our sticky hands in the fresh water. On days when the ice cream boat didn't show, we'd hop into our own vessel and cruise down the lake to the dairy bar for soft-serve cones. The day wasn't complete until there was ice cream somewhere along the way.

That early taste of the state whetted my appetite for more, and I've now lived in Maine full time for close to twenty years. Portland was at the beginning of its rebirth as a travel and food lovers' destination, when I first came. Food blogs were just beginning to catch on, and I started my own called *Mignardise*, a French word for a small treat with your after-dinner coffee. It was the perfect vehicle for combining my love of food and writing. The blog eventually led to what I have always considered my dream job (so far)—food editor at *Maine* magazine. It's still astonishing to me that there's a job that let me eat all over the state, sampling specialties both traditional and updated. Dessert is still my favorite part of any meal, so much so that, in 2020, I started a new blog called *Sweet on Maine*, highlighting it all, with a particular bias toward ice cream. Beal's Chocolate Peanut Butter, Mt. Desert Island Ice Cream's Girl Scouts, and Gelato Fiasco's Espresso Chip are all favorites, but discovering those one-person, handmade ice cream producers, like Parlor Ice Cream Co. in Biddeford, whose signature flavor is an addictive Salty Honey, gives me a thrill. Featuring them on the blog gives those new businesses exposure to more ice cream lovers, a win-win for all.

That hot July night, decades ago, often comes to mind. I doubt there are many people who associate the first moon walk with ice cream. Two summers ago, I celebrated a milestone birthday, during the pandemic. I thought very carefully about what dessert I'd most like for the scaled-down celebration. I considered a fancy dacquoise, maybe a German chocolate cake, but there really was only one answer—a fudgy brownie topped with peppermint stick and hot fudge, with a candle planted like a flag on top.

PART II

HUNGER AND PLENTY

MY MOTHER, THE LUNCH LADY
Ron Currie

SHORTLY BEFORE I entered sixth grade, my mother, Barbara, took a job working in the cafeteria at the junior high where I was about to make my debut. Being eleven, of course, I had no choice in the matter. First lunch period in September, there was my mom: white uniform, hairnet, beatific smile. The lunch lady. Welcome to my nightmare.

For three long years, I kept my distance. If she was running the hot lunch line, I was in the à la carte line, and vice versa. No exceptions. I gamed the system, peeking into the service area each day to see where she was, and only then getting into line at the other doorway to receive my meal.

My mother remembers this. I never acknowledged her, she says. Never said hello. Rarely, if ever, even glanced her way. I was horrified by her presence. Because what could broadcast the fact that you were poor more loudly and clearly than your mother being a school lunch lady?

THIS IS NOT something I'm proud of now. In fact, I'm not very forgiving, in general, toward my younger self. He was obsessed with class. There are things I want to tell him now. You've got food in your belly and clothes on your back, kid. Your parents bust their humps providing you with such, and they don't need you slinking around all day ashamed that they can't afford to buy you Air Jordans.

Short of inventing time travel, I'm unable to communicate those messages to the eleven-year-old me, and in any event, I'm not sure they would have had much effect. He remains, for eternity, what he was: shy, sensitive, and dedicated to the belief that there's something inherently shameful about who he is and where he's from.

I did all the things poor kids do to make money—shoveling snow, delivering newspapers, picking bottles—but whereas the other children in my neighborhood also did these things as a matter of course, and didn't seem to think much about it one way or the other, for me there was always a bass note of shame vibrating beneath all our little moneymaking ventures. Walking the neighborhood with a shovel, knocking doors and asking if people wanted their driveways cleared for five dollars a pop, felt akin to being a beggar. I liked the paper route because I could do it under cover of darkness, before anyone was up to see me pushing a grocery cart full of the Sunday edition around. And as for digging in convenience store trash cans for sticky returnables, well, let's just say I only resorted to that after all the less-degrading options had been exhausted.

To THIS DAY I don't understand why I cared so much about being poor. I have no idea why it was the transcendent preoccupation of my early years. There is this: many of my friends had parents who worked as lawyers and doctors and accountants, and they lived in nice, clean houses in better neighborhoods than mine. Was I hyper-aware of class differences because I had friends who were better-off, or did I choose friends who were better-off because I was hyper-aware of class differences? Either way, I rarely if ever invited those friends to come hang in my neighborhood, let alone my house. Even our municipal basketball court was an embarrassment, at least to me: crumbling pavement, busted rims.

Saying hello to my mother, acknowledging her in the cafeteria? That was not going to happen.

I SIT DOWN with my mother at a coffee shop in Waterville, the mid-Maine city where I grew up, and ask if it hurt her feelings, that I so studiously avoided her for so long. She tells me no. I'm surprised, but I believe her, because she sees it totally differently than I did: to her, I was just self-possessed.

"You always kept to yourself," she says, meaning, apparently, not just at school but at home as well. For a moment, I feel a blush of pride. She saw me as independent, not paralyzingly self-conscious. But the pride fades quickly, because I realize the implication of her misunderstanding: I did such a good job of hiding from everyone that not even my own mother really knew who I was.

Back then, she did her best to respect my evident desire for privacy. She didn't follow me around the school, didn't inquire with my teachers as to how things were going, in part because she wanted to avoid hovering, and in part because she was just too busy. She had work to do, and that work did not include keeping tabs on her son.

There was another guy at the junior high, Scott, whose mother also worked in the junior high cafeteria. Unlike me, he would go up to her most every day. Sometimes, he needed extra money for lunch, because he'd somehow squandered what he'd been given that morning. Sometimes, he just chatted her up, because he was that kind of kid. Scott seemed to have no misgivings about his mom being a lunch lady, no misgivings period, in fact. He was always confident and good-looking and gregarious. The opposite of me, in short.

I barely remember that Scott's mother worked in the cafeteria, let alone that Scott was always talking to her. My mother reminds me of this. We have a laugh about it, the contrast between me and Scott.

I hadn't thought about him in a long time. I remember how he had such a big personality and was a good athlete and popular with girls. But after my mother reminds me of Scott and how he would chat up his mother in the cafeteria, I remember that when we were in our thirties, Scott committed suicide. There seems something significant embedded in these facts: Scott, self-assured, friendly, and dead by his own hand. Me, reserved, self-conscious, and still drawing breath. I'm just not sure what the significance is. Maybe it's something about the way shame moves and takes new shapes over the course of a life. Or maybe it means nothing at all.

AT THE COFFEE SHOP, I tell my mother that the worst thing, for me, was feeling that to a certain extent she was doing the bidding of my peers (and never mind that she did mine regularly; that was different!). If they said pizza, she provided pizza. If they wanted a chicken sandwich, she gave them a chicken sandwich. When they were done making a mess of the tables, she cleaned up after them. Of course, as the adult, she ultimately held the power in these interactions, but still: they were issuing orders, and she was taking them, a fact I didn't like then, and don't especially care for now. Call me old-fashioned, but I'm of the opinion that children should never be allowed to mistake themselves for the people in charge. And yet, at least in my eleven-year-old eyes, that was the case: my classmates were telling my mother what to do, and she was doing it.

However overblown my own preoccupation with the class aspects of Mom being a school lunch lady, class did figure into it for everyone. She tells me this herself. The sons of lawyers and doctors—always the sons, mind you—were sometimes arrogant and haughty with her. They demanded more than they were allotted, grabbed food instead of asking, ignored and laughed off her admonitions to behave. She was just a lunch lady, after all. They didn't have to listen to her.

For her part, though, and to her credit, she simply called for the principal and didn't let any of it get to her. Of course, she didn't! Because as cynical and misanthropic as her son can be, she did then, and does now, seek and see the best in people, particularly children. She did not confuse providing meals to kids with being their servant—even if sometimes they did. And though some kids could be a pain in the ass, as kids sometimes are, she still enjoyed the work.

"Really?" I ask. I'm not sure why I find it so hard to believe, but here we are.

"Really," she says. "Besides, whether I liked it or not was beside the point—I just needed the work."

When I think of the bill of goods called trickle-down economics, of people who work too hard for too little money, of jobs that seem almost designed to break your body and give you little in return, I think of my mom. It's not overstating it to say that watching her work had as great an effect on my political and moral convictions as anything (and when I say "work," I mean the labor she did in addition to parenting, which she covered about 80 percent of). She's the reason I understand and appreciate how hard most women work just as a matter of course. She's the reason I believe labor unions are the only entity that have done a damn thing for blue-collar people (and, more specifically, blue-collar women) in this country. She's the reason that, even though I make my living sitting at a desk, I still endeavor to have calluses on my hands, as ongoing proof that I know what it is to labor, and that I understand its value and its cost.

My mother has a more substantial and permanent reminder of the cost of labor than mere calluses. Her right thumb is fixed and rigid, more like the bony appendage pandas have on their forepaws than an actual human thumb. This is attributable to decades of hard work with her hands—carrying sheet pans, lifting stockpots, emptying garbage cans. Over the last couple of years, she's had surgery on the thumb so many times that I've lost count. Each procedure has taken place in Portland, where I now live, and afterwards I've picked her up at the surgical office, listened to and signed off on the post-op orders, gotten her situated in her hotel room, brought her to dinner, and checked to make sure she's taking the right meds at the right times. She's got other problems too, which constitute the legacy of her working life—a bad hip and feet, the result of years standing on the tiled floors (and underlying concrete) of service kitchens. Her back is a little wonky as well, which, ditto.

But it's the thumb I come back to as emblematic of a life spent making and serving food to others. Hand and wrist issues are epidemic among food service workers, particularly waitresses. In her case, the lower joint of her thumb had been worn down until it was bone-on-bone, and it got worse from there, the damage cumulative and implacable. The only silver lining is she's a lefty, just like her son.

Because watching her work through my childhood turned me into a class warrior, my first inclination is to view the state of her hand through that lens—like so many others, she worked too hard and too long for too little, and the inevitable physical cost of that labor is now hers to bear alone. It's unfair, even immoral, the way our economy commodifies and exploits the bodies of the poor.

But there's another, more generous way to look at it, and that's the way I'm choosing now, in part because I'm no longer the cowed, self-conscious boy mortified by the fact that his mother works in the school cafeteria. Blue-collar men often go on and on about how this or that on their body hurts, lest anyone should fail to notice how hard they work. Blue-collar women, on the other hand, sacrifice their bodies, bit by bit, year by year, with more smiles and fewer complaints than their male counterparts. And "sacrifice" is the operative word here. My mother did work for which she was paid a wage, that much is true. But the state of her thumb is evidence not just of the jobs she had but also of the fact that she was happy to provide for both others and her own. She liked making food for kids, plain and simple. That it happened to be something for which she got paid was almost beside the point. She wouldn't change it, even with the panda-thumb.

By contrast, there are a few things I *would* change—starting with choosing to get into her line at lunch on the first day of sixth grade.

GLASS BOTTLES OF LOCAL MILK
Arielle Greenberg

I GREW UP IN something of a bleak place at something of a bleak time. Though people not from New York rarely understand this, *upstate* New York—specifically in this case, the "Capital District" of deeply rural towns and small cities ringing Albany—has much more in common with rust-belt, lake-effect places like Cleveland and Erie than they do with cosmopolitan Manhattan. *Smallbany*, we called our capital city: it's the seat of a sleepy, provincial region. Other than a briefly glorious autumn, it is also a gray region, even when it's not snowing and raw, which it usually is. (The sparkling coastal winters in Maine are nothing like the slog of dismal winter months spent in the wake of the Great Lakes.) When it's not cold, it's humid. And in the 1970s and '80s, it was a place than had been hit hard by the recession, the closing of factories, and the state government's ties to New York City's economic ruin. I remember long lines at gas stations during the 1979 oil crisis and being late for school when our bus was locked in traffic caused by striking workers at General Electric.

In our own household, my mother cut coupons and saved dollar bills in hand-sewn fabric envelopes she kept in a drawer, which was the budgeting system. She was someone who cared about food and was a good cook, who painstakingly copied out recipes while waiting in doctor's offices or at the library. But we ate a lot of frozen pizzas and fish sticks and hot dogs and spaghetti and American cheese, inexpensive things. Sometimes when we went to the supermarket, she'd have each of us stand on separate check-out lines, so we could get away with extras on deals for tuna fish or canned soup that were supposed to be only one per customer. Each week, she bought a two-liter bottle of generic brand soda, which we opened on Friday nights. It went flat in minutes. Once it was gone, it was gone.

For a while, my mother had a part-time job as a "merchandiser" for the Mars chocolate corporation. This meant that she drove to rural convenience stores and gas stations and swapped the expired candy on the metal shelves for the new shipment, making sure it all looked nice and neat. As a result, our basement had bags full of past-date Snickers, Skittles, and Twix bars, which we'd haul up to stock in our kitchen pantry for us kids. It didn't matter whether or not this was candy we liked: this was the candy we had, for free, and so it was the candy we were going to eat.

I'VE SPENT A LOT of time in adulthood thinking about the concepts of abundance and scarcity. I consider these two poles the spectrum between which most of my anxieties and desires lie. I grew up with a deep sense of scarcity: scarcity of food, attention, time, love, money, praise. Upstate New York itself felt like a place of scarcity, even when we were picking Cortland apples off trees in endless orchards. Over the past decades, I have worked on deprogramming myself from that mentality and toward a life of abundance—an *attitude* of abundance, of believing in the *possibility* of abundance, of *trusting* that there is enough to go around and acting as if this is so even when sometimes it's technically not. And I can trace that desire for abundance back to the glass bottles of local milk at the Cowan & Lobel gourmet market in Stuyvesant Plaza in Albany, New York, in 1988.

Stuyvesant Plaza: The name conjures up the long-past glory days of Albany, when it was a city of railroad barons, émigrés from Holland. In fact, it's an outdoor mini-mall, a small cluster of thirty-five shops in a U-shape on an ugly stretch of highway in the unremarkable township of Guilderland. When it opened in 1959, Stuyvesant Plaza was a novelty: malls hadn't really taken off yet. Like many other things in the Albany area, it fell on hard times in the '70s and seemed like it might close, or become a low-end discount center. But in the mid-'80s, someone took a risk and decided to spruce it up and focus on filling it with independent retail. The strategy succeeded. Even though it seemed destined to be overshadowed by the big indoor mall just up the road, Stuyvesant Plaza was something special, something different: a carefully curated selection of shops that connoted quality, tastefulness, and, yes, abundance.

Accustomed as I was to penny-pinching and making do, I loved the whole vibe of refinement, the whole genteel gestalt, of Stuyvesant Plaza. I remember that there was a jeweler who made custom pieces, and a brunch place that offered fancy pancakes on flowery dishes, and a furrier (still there!), and a quaint old-fashioned toy store (still there!), and a lovely book-store (still there!), and a gift shop that sold pewter candlesticks and delicate baby gifts (still there!), and a home stereo store that smelled like static elec-tricity (still there!). I haven't been back in ages, and to me Stuyvesant Plaza is a tangled teenaged memory of aspirational delight, set to a soundtrack of piano concertos. But the place is still going, independent retailers mixed in with chains like Talbots and West Elm.

Another memory: a Crabtree and Evelyn shop, which smelled like lav-ender soap and sold gauzy nightgowns and quilted tea cozies and tins of lemon shortbread cookies. A houseguest once brought us those cookies as a gift, and I savored each crumbly bite and then saved the tin, which had a gorgeous illustration of a lemon tree and a traditional English folk poem on it. I put my pencils in it and kept it on my desk for *decades.* That tin symbolized everything I knew I wanted one day: things that were delicious, unusual, exquisite.

But even more than the tin of British lemon shortbread cookies, I re-member the glass bottle of milk I saw at Cowan & Lobel.

COWAN & LOBEL had started as a cheese shop and reopened as an upscale market in Stuyvesant Plaza in the '80s. When I first went there as a teen-ager, I had never been to a gourmet food market. We shopped mostly at the big local chain supermarkets, Grand Union and Price Chopper, and some-times at the tiny kosher butcher and the family-run bagel shop. My mother had a brief "health nut" phase, which meant I got to help her fill paper bags from the dusty bulk bins in a one-room co-op, but that was short-lived. My parents were concerned mostly with getting as much food as we could to feed our family of five on as little money as possible. If there was a deal to be had, or the miraculous occurrence of "double coupons," we stocked up and kept the extras in the basement, where they usually expired before we consumed them. And our food had to be kosher, by the particular rules we followed. This combination of shopping via religious restrictions and tight budgets and hoarding deals was scarcity mentality in action.

Cowan & Lobel, on the other hand, was a place that *oozed* abundance. (In the '90s, Rachael Ray worked as a counter girl at the deli there, work-ing her way up to buyer, the foundation of her rise to culinary-comfort superstardom.) The merchandise, a mix of exotic packaged products from around the world and locally produced goods, was displayed for optimal enticement, piled high and spilling out of artfully arranged wooden crates.

The cranberry cream scones were baked fresh each morning. There was an extensive meat and exotic cheese selection. It was much smaller than a typical supermarket, and so the carts were daintier and rolled more smoothly than typical carts, to make them easier to maneuver around the aisles. No matter that I was a fussy eater with an unsophisticated palate and no spending money: from the moment I walked in, I wanted absolutely everything in the store.

We didn't go to Stuyvesant Plaza often. My mother, who did not shop for pleasure and prided herself on being *hamish* (Yiddish for unpretentious), no doubt thought it was snobby, as well as a waste of time and money. But I found any reason I could to get dropped off there, and later, when I had a boyfriend with a car, I had us stop there on our way to punk shows and art house movies.

I can't remember if I was with my family or my boyfriend the day I was at Cowan & Lobel and paused in front of the display of local milks beautifully bottled in thick, traditional glass bottles. I grew up on plastic gallon jugs and cardboard containers of skim milk: I had only seen heavy glass bottles of farm-fresh creamery milk, the company names painted on in thick raised lettering, in old movies. The milk bottles stopped me in my tracks.

I don't think I was even a big milk-drinker by then. But the traditional quality of the packaging and the simple, pure product inside were beautiful to me. This milk cost more than the kind of milk my family bought, and the very fact that one could choose to spend a little more to pour their morning milk, milked from happy local cows from a glass bottle rather than milk that came from a miserable dairy factory and out of waxy paper or plastic, was a revelation. In hushed tones, I said aloud, to no one, "All I want is to one day have enough money to buy the milk in glass bottles and not feel worried about it."

SLOWLY, OVER THE COURSE of my adulthood, I started to shed the habits that came from the scarcity I'd learned at home toward something more abundant. I spent my twenties working in New York City, where my winsome, sophisticated boss taught me to go to the tiny independent Old World bra shops on the Upper East Side to get a proper fitting, and to spend $60 for one good French bra that would last for years instead of $20 for a cheap one from the mall that fell apart within weeks. I gave up drugstore lipstick for the kind that came from the counter at a posh department store. I walked seven blocks out of my way to get one perfect marzipan tart instead of a whole box of Oreo cookies from the bodega for the same price. At the flea market, I learned to spot antique clothes in real silk velvet (a bargain then!) and mixed these rare pieces in with contemporary discount fashion. I started eating really good Malaysian and Thai and Cajun food. I could tell an excellent (or mediocre) chocolate chip cookie just by looking at it. You could say I was developing taste, but I think I possessed taste for quality and thoughtfully made goods all along: I just didn't feel able to choose it over cheap, convenient quantity.

LATER, WHEN WE STARTED coming to Maine, one of the things I loved most about it were all the old-fashioned markets full of traditional goods. As we drove up the coast, I would make our family stop at every little food co-op, locally owned bakery, and artisanal food shop. One Maine summer vacation when my daughter was a toddler, I bought her every flavor of Westbrook's Smiling Hill Farms milk, each gorgeous color shining through the glass: the muted lavender of the blueberry milk, the buoyant pink of the strawberry, the melty sunset shade of the orange crème. I had made it: I had become a person who could—who chooses to—buy local milk from a glass bottle.

I am by no means rich, but these days, I make all my food choices around quality, an investment in my local farmers and a commitment to locally grown and ethically raised food, and an attention to packaging for the sake of the planet. I spend more money on food for my family than is probably typical; I probably spend less than average on kids' clothes (which I buy secondhand) or gadgets and toys (which I rarely buy at all). Our refrigerator overflows with organic produce from our year-round CSAs, tubes of Asian and European condiments and glass bottles and mason jars full of nuts and kimchi. Our pantry is stocked with carefully chosen goods, each treasured like the gift they are. My cookie jar is full of homemade treats studded with chocolate chunks I chop off thick, pricey bars, rather than chips from a bag. And mostly, I don't fret about these choices afterward.

I've gotten so used to shopping and eating like this that I want to stop and remind myself that I once did not know if I'd land here. The trick to abundance is noticing it, being grateful for it. I don't want to forget those glass bottles of milk from Cowan & Lobel.

NOURISHMENT
Stephanie Cotsirilos

O NE MORNING IN roughly 1957, my mother's hand curved around a white-and-red can of Red Heart dog food. Her spoon was poised to scoop out half the contents into our female boxer's bowl. Mom had probably extracted the coveted baseball cards from Red Heart's packaging and set them aside for my brothers. Today, Amazon sells a 1954 Complete Set—its cards including Mickey Mantle with a bat resting on his shoulder and Stan Musial smiling under his cap—for a discounted $8,750.

"You give that to your dog?" Eleni asked in Greek. A family friend from the Old Country, she was well into her fifties and had crossed the Mediterranean and Atlantic to come live with us, to help while Mom fought the aggressively metastatic breast cancer that had surfaced a few years earlier, when Mom was twenty-nine.

Mom hesitated over the dog's bowl that she'd washed and was about to lay on the floor of our suburban Chicago kitchen. Her hair was brown and wavy, her eyes hazel, her lipstick a bit orange, her cheekbones broad and slightly Slavic in the manner of her parents' Ionian island. She looked alive and well to me, never mind that after the birth of my youngest brother, her gynecologist prematurely dismissed the mass in her left breast as a "milk lump."

At an aunt's suggestion, Mom had traveled to Mayo Clinic in Minnesota to check out the "milk lump." Her radical mastectomy was scheduled for the next day. Dad resisted instructions to start saying goodbye. Mom kept on going, left breast or not. She and Dad agreed they'd live as though she had forever in front of her. No sappy photos in the house, please, nothing to suggest a memorial. Their pact worked, apparently. She lived another twenty-five years. On the day she opened the can of Red Heart, she was probably at the front end of that survival journey and was perhaps unsure—no, certainly unsure—how long it would last.

Puzzled by the question, "You give that to your dog?" Mom looked up at Eleni. Eleni was blue-eyed, her thin dark hair pulled back into a bun, her low-hanging breasts in a dark cotton dress enveloped by a sweater. She said, "We ate that during the war."

She didn't say which war—World War II or Greek Civil—though it didn't matter much as both were among the most brutal of twentieth-century Europe. Mom explained to me later what Eleni told her: cans of Red Heart had washed up from some freighter onto Greek beaches or were smuggled into villages, with Red Heart becoming the primary protein source for Eleni and her loved ones and neighbors. Without saying so, Mom and Eleni agreed that Red Heart would never again appear in our home.

Their pact forced me to consider that nourishment held meanings I'd never thought of. I became alert to lessons that followed. My Greek grandmother's insistence that we stop the car during summer vacation in Michigan meant she'd spotted roadside vine leaves suitable for dolmades. Yet plucking the leaves and placing them in her handbag to later wash, blanch, and wrap around ground lamb and onions humiliated my mother and father. Waiting inside our idling sedan, they tried to assimilate themselves away from her peasant roots.

Was I ten years old during the Red Heart episode? My precise age doesn't matter as much as my growing awareness that the incident and many after weren't entirely about food. They had something to do with another reality—that amid the flat January cold icing our northern Illinois home's casement windows, we lived well. We wore sweaters indoors during off-cycles of forced hot air and slathered on hand cream to fend off dryness. We had matching print-upholstered armchairs. We had more than enough food and could choose what we ate. We were finally where we belonged. Immigration stopped with us. No one thought I'd end up anywhere else, and certainly not in Maine half a lifetime later.

IN EASTERN MAINE'S WOODLANDS, where I moved in 1995 with my four-year-old son after my husband's death, I learned about unexpected sources of protein. Other than Red Heart, that is. And other than the foods I'd embraced during my decades in New York City, far away from the Chicago of my vine-leaf-plucking grandmother. In Manhattan, I became accustomed to proteins pan-seared, crisp on the outside, pink on the inside, drizzled with reduction sauces. On a bed of something or other.

One autumn, north of Bangor, I ran into Maine's secretary of state while we were both shopping at Hannaford's. At the time, I lived in the largely rural Second Congressional District, where it was common to run into government officials purchasing groceries. Wearing camouflage pants, the secretary explained he'd been deer hunting. This was a practice that sent shivers through animal rights activists and many of my progressive friends, yet, as I chatted with the secretary, I began to understand: a freezer full of venison could see neighboring families through a hard winter of rising heating oil prices or cratering income from seasonal work. There was no shame in sharing the venison or asking for it or bartering for it. To the contrary, doing so reflected a sense of community and mutual support. I grasped this as I stood beside a refrigerator full of artisanal yogurt, whose prices would have appalled my other immigrant grandmother. She cultured her own tangy yogurt—the Greek kind, which has become popular as of this writing—in Pyrex containers placed along a sunlit kitchen windowsill. My cousins and I didn't like that yogurt. It made our mouths pucker. It goes without saying that no one in our families considered desecrating yogurt with syrupy preserved fruit.

I came to yet a different understanding of venison's role a few years later, after the November night I survived a car crash on I-95 northbound from Augusta. A buck appeared out of nowhere onto the highway lane in front of me. There was no time to avoid slamming into the animal with the front end of my vehicle, or to avoid living through endless seconds of awful crunching sounds over my darkened windshield. The buck's body must have lain across it as I tried to keep my vehicle straight toward where I imagined the road headed and prepared myself for the pain of dying.

I didn't die. My windshield cleared. My car came to a stop, straddling empty interstate lanes. No buck. I got out and tried the passenger-side door to retrieve my cell phone, then stepped back fast when, at my touch, the car's blasted computer sent the vehicle into reverse. Accelerating slightly, it backed itself toward the highway's shoulder and slid down the embankment to come to rest at the bottom, headlights blinking on and off like a Pixar creation.

I hustled to the roadside. Shawl around my neck, earrings intact, purse at my elbow, I almost raised my hand to hail a passing taxi as I might have in Manhattan. Instead, a truck pulled over thirty yards from me. The driver leaped out of his cab and ran in my direction to see if I was okay while he punched numbers on his phone to call the state troopers. He said he'd seen it all. Moments later, a young woman pulled over in her white pickup. She suggested we sit in her truck while the other driver went back to his rig. Since we didn't know who he was, she was offering safety. Of course, she and I didn't know one another, either. A few moments passed before she asked me where the buck was and whether it was dead. If it was not, she could put it out of its misery. She was returning from a hunting trip of her own and had firearms on her vehicle's rack. She chose one and we walked toward the median with the truck driver, who was also interested. The buck was dead. The truck driver whistled his admiration at the antlers. This animal was big.

Later that week when, courtesy of my insurance coverage, I showed up at the Toyota dealership to replace my totaled vehicle, the salesman asked whether I'd claimed the buck's meat. He wanted details. Since I should not have survived the wreck, he also asked if I prayed a lot. When I said no, he offered to pray for me. Skepticism be damned, I was grateful for prayers, though I'd been too clueless to even consider claiming the venison. Doubtless someone else did. Maybe the truck driver. Maybe one of the troopers. Not the woman in the pickup, since she drove me home. I struggled with the idea of consuming the buck's flesh, which I could only envision as belonging to the animal, whoever he was. I was not hungry enough to consider his muscle and sinew nourishment for me.

So why did Mom and Eleni feel shame about the Red Heart dog food? Its moist meat may have come from cows, pigs, sheep, goats—or horses, I suppose, before using horse meat in pet food was outlawed in the United States. People in my childhood home ate the flesh of cows, pigs, sheep, and even goats, grilled, roasted, broiled, and in stews.

Decades later, in fact—after I'd become a mother myself—I discovered that it was normal for guinea pig, or *cuy*, to appear grilled, baked, and stewed on restaurant menus everywhere in my son's native Peru. Indigenous Andean families, like his forebears, raised small muddles of *cuy* in their stone homes and harvested as needed for afternoon soup, the little claws facing upward from a bowl in which the skinned creature lay, more honestly butchered than supermarket shrink-wrapped chicken thighs.

What was so terrible about Red Heart? It was this: the product's graphic designers had deployed images of dogs all over its label. In Eleni's mind, the branding established an hierarchy that, for an instant in our suburban kitchen that winter, placed her on the same level as our boxer.

There was another layer to the shame. It had to do with plenty versus bare sustenance. Granted, Mom was working hard against the odds of a lethal disease that struck strangely early in her life. Yet she was the beneficiary of daily comforts derived from the American dream that her parents and Dad's parents had bet on when they immigrated. She and Dad made good on that gamble. Eleni's people, on the other hand, may not even have made their way to the betting table. They had stayed behind and lived through everything my grandparents escaped. When she pulled out the can opener for the Red Heart, my mother probably had no idea how bitter it would be for Eleni to consider the calculus behind the different wagers her people and mine had made.

What sustained Eleni? In part, the detritus of a cargo ship bearing manufactured products for increasingly prosperous Americans, while Greece scrambled to recover from civil strife and flattening earthquakes, to construct primitive toilet facilities on once-fragrant hillsides. Yes, Eleni had survived on dog food, but she'd sustained herself more deeply on the dignity of her hands' work and the strength she'd had, at the age of nearly sixty, to pull herself across continents and join our family in a cold, flat place. She was soft and hard, her sharp eyes those of a mountain villager, her affectionate fingers gnarled and stronger, probably, than my father's. She found the wherewithal to send monthly checks back to her daughters in Greece so they could overcome catastrophe or open their cupboards to hints of abundance.

WHEN I MOVED to Maine in 1995, I didn't meet many Greeks and when I did, I didn't identify with them. The few I came to know specialized in cooking with beef, lamb, chicken, and fish—if they were not vegetarian. Forget venison. It wasn't on life's menu. Forget wearing blaze orange to hunt for winter protein.

I didn't yet understand that Eleni's hands might also have curled around a rifle had she lived among Eastern white pine and needed to feed her family through till spring. That perhaps on this score she and the secretary of state had more in common than I did with either of them.

So I ask myself: would I open a can of Red Heart and eat it? If it were necessary, of course I would. Then I'd wash and stack the remaining cans near the woodpile and bring in logs and kindling for the woodstove I first learned to use in Maine. I'd coax the fire with small, dry twigs from the yard, blow gently, add larger pieces of scrap wood, and exhibit the patience necessary to nourish flames. I'd figured out that if I fed the stove in the ways it needed, it would warm me when I most needed warmth.

AFTER THE FALL
Elizabeth Peavey

I WASN'T GOING TO go back out.
 I was on a deadline, trying to finish some website copy for the organization where I had just started volunteering. I told myself, "You've already done your good deed for the day."

The organization, Cooking for Community, is a Portland-based grassroots group that formed in April 2020 as a crisis response to the pandemic. We raise funds to hire struggling restaurants to make nourishing meals to feed our most vulnerable neighbors. I was brought on board to be a "Story Guide."

My "good deed"? Earlier, I had heard a rattle out on the street. It was recycling day, and any urban dweller recognizes the sound of a shopping cart filled with bottles and cans. I had a contribution to the cause. I was living in an apartment in the back of a Victorian home on Portland's Eastern Prom, and I had not taken my returnables back since I moved in several months prior. Instead, I stored them in a kitchen closet that stretched under the stairs, where they magically disappeared. But the time for spring-cleaning had arrived, and there was a solution just outside my door.

I scooted down and gathered a handful of bags from the closet. I didn't want to lug out too many in case my neighbors were watching and would peg me as the "Lady in the Carriage House Who Tipples." I perched on my doorstep and gingerly tossed the bags to the curb. I was wearing my *indoor* sneakers, and I didn't want to step out onto a sidewalk that might be coated with COVID cooties. I had a pair of clogs parked on the stoop for outdoor tasks, but I didn't feel this moment merited a shoe change.

A man was working the recycling bin across the street. His cart was festooned with bulging black garbage bags that dangled over the sides like fenders on a tugboat. I called out: "Sir! Sir!" He turned and gave me a smile as bright as the sun coming from behind the clouds. I gestured to the bags before me. "Oh, miss," he said, "thank you so much." His Jamaican accent made his words sound regal and gracious, as though I had just knighted him Sir Bottleman of the Eastern Prom. I insisted he was doing *me* a favor, and I thanked him, and then he thanked me again, and we both laughed and waved, and I was back up at my desk before he had probably even crossed the street.

Pleased, and a bit puffed by my own beneficence, I returned to the sentence I had been working on: "Because in this beautiful, bountiful state of Maine we call home, everyone deserves a seat at the table." My words hung in the air. I heard the cart rattle again, and I said to myself, "Elizabeth Peavey, you can do better."

And ordinarily, I would. I'm a problem solver. I was a lecturer of public speaking at the university level for over twenty years. I've taught writing equally as long. And I now guide institutions and organizations to more effectively craft and share their stories. I help people find solutions. But my world had been tipped off its axis by the pandemic. In a matter of two days in March 2020, all my work—speaking at conferences, lecturing in crowded auditoriums, bringing people together in boardrooms—vaporized overnight. And while I can do my speaking and training online, my clients were all in triage mode, just trying to figure out how to navigate this new landscape. Additional programming was out of the question. People weren't even answering my emails.

Add to that, at sixty, I was marginally considered in an "at-risk" group for COVID. For me, it was less my age than my tenuous living situation. I had left my marriage and home the year prior and had been condo surfing ever since, while I tried to sort out next steps. My carriage house was intended to be a winter rental, extended only because of the pandemic. Who knew how long I could stay? Further, what would happen if I got sick? I had no one to take care of me. I couldn't bring the virus into either of my brothers' or any of my friends' homes. Which meant I had to be cautious and careful about everything—money, contact, contagion. I felt useless. Working with Cooking for Community had been one way to help. But writing blog posts and web copy wasn't the same as connecting with people. And that's when I realized my human connection was rolling a shopping cart up the street.

I stuffed a bit of cash in an envelope, grabbed a few more bags from the closet, and put on my mask and gloves. I then removed my indoor sneakers and changed into my outdoor clogs before clomping up the side-walk, looking for my friend.

When I caught up with him, he beamed as he greeted me. I put down the bags between us and handed him the envelope. He saw the cash through the cellophane window. "Oh, miss, thank you," he said. "It's hard out here." He continued to look down. "I've lost all my work. I tried asking people for a quarter, but no one wants to give. I get some food here and there, but sometimes it's a peanut butter sandwich, and I can't eat the peanuts." He then squared his shoulders. "So I had to have a talk with myself. I said, 'Be a man. Find a way to get some money.'" He gestured at his cart. "This was the only thing I could think to do. I take these bottles down to East End Redemption, then I go to the grocery store to buy tuna fish and bread."

As I listened, something clicked in my brain. I thought of Amistad, one of Cooking for Community's partner organizations that serves people who, for myriad reasons, can't or don't access conventional social services. I asked the man if he had ever heard of them. I explained they deliver prepared meals to people on the street. "They find you," I said.

The man's eyes lit up. "Miss, I have not had a warm meal in three months."

I repeated the name of the organization. "Amistad. Can you remember that?"

He looked at me. "You have a number?"

Well, of course, I had a number. Suddenly I was filled with an urgency I had not felt in weeks. Here was a chance to act, to do something. I asked him to wait for me, and I took off down the hill, clogs clacking on the undulating brick sidewalk, on my way to save the day.

I DO NOT RECALL going down. I only recall the sound of plastic shattering: my glasses flying off my face and exploding on the bricks. I didn't move for several minutes. I just lay there, sprawled facedown on the sidewalk that only moments ago I didn't want my precious, safe-to-run-in indoor sneakers to come in contact with. Slowly, I took potential-injury inventory. *Did I hit my head? Did I pass out? I don't think so. Elbows? Knees? No, they feel—but ouch. My hands.* I turned my right hand over. Road rash. Speckles of blood beaded in my palm. And the left? I couldn't turn that one over at all.

At that moment, I did not know that it would take me two days to muster the courage to have them examined. Or that when I did, I would find myself with one broken and one sprained wrist. I couldn't foresee the challenges I would face managing on my own with a busted wrist for the next six weeks, or the nearly three months of physical therapy that would follow when the cast came off. Or that I would still be wrangling with the insurance company deep into December. No, at that moment all I knew was I had to get that man Amistad's number before he disappeared.

Somehow, I dragged myself up to my desk, Googled the number, and even though I could barely hold a pencil, managed to scrawl it on a slip of paper. I hobbled my way back outside, retrieved my clogs, which had also flown off, and went to deliver the number. I found my friend bent deep into one of the big blue recycling bins. He lifted his head and smiled when he heard me call to him. He hadn't seen a thing.

I HAVE NEVER been on the street, but I've been down and out. Somewhere in my misguided youth, I bought into the romantic notion of the starving artist. I thought occasionally sleeping on trains or in my car was necessary to my education as a writer. An easy notion to entertain when each time I dragged myself back to Maine, broke and homeless, my friends and family patiently bailed me out.

But even playing at poverty takes a toll on the soul. You learn the fine line between fragility and stability, and how quickly your world can come crashing down around you. You never forget the ache of want or the comfort of being offered a meal when you're feeling forsaken and forgotten. In that way, food nourishes beyond what's on the plate or in the box or in the bag; it feeds the spirit. We all stumble. It's a gift to be able to both extend and receive a hand, even a banged-up one.

EATING THE EXCESS
Kate Russo

W ORKING IN RESTAURANTS means never eating when you're hungry. Between ages eighteen and thirty, I worked as a busser/ hostess/server/bartender in half a dozen different restaurants in Maine, Martha's Vineyard, Boston, London, and Maine again. All those years, I ate when I wasn't hungry, and I worked when I *was*. My stomach rumbled when I set down an imposing heap of fried calamari in front of a young family at a seafood restaurant. The parents would "ooh" and "ah" at the mountain of squid, while I stared spitefully at their children who regarded the fried fishy rings as punishment. At a Boston restaurant, my mouth wa- tered when I jealously handed over the ricotta cavatelli—drizzled with just a little bit of truffle oil—to a couple on date night. The man claimed it was delicious, but the portion too small. His date looked up at me and complained the opposite, saying, "Too rich for me." *I could eat a bucket of that, lady. A bucket,* I wanted to tell her, but I had my tip to consider. At a high-end French restaurant, I raged as I returned half-eaten plates to the kitchen—abandoned frites, the unconsumed scallop, the untouched side orders of beautiful buttery mashed potato, the little glass pot of foie gras mousse with only one scoop taken out, the crisp bread lying beside it cold and brittle. On such occasions, I did what any starving employee would do: I stole a surplus frite while no one was looking. Same with the leftover bread roll. I even stuck my finger in the little pot of foie gras. I don't even eat meat, but I couldn't help myself; I was furious that they left it.

They meaning the kind of customer who ordered and wasted foie gras. *They* ate out most nights. *They* were on a first-name basis with all the chefs and front-of-house managers in town. *Was it all right?* I asked. *(It's foie gras mousse. Of course it's all right!) They* said they wanted to save room for their onglet steaks. *They* also left half of those very steaks to make room for chocolate ganache torte and another bottle of Krug. *They* didn't want to go home stuffed, just pleasantly full. Looking at me like I was nuts, *they* explained all this. Diners' eyes are bigger than their stomachs (and their bank accounts are even bigger than their eyes). There's always excess. If the plate is clean, it signals stinginess, and these diners don't want to appear cheap.

After all, they're usually there to impress with the food, not to *eat* it.

The night I stuck my finger in the pot of foie gras because I wanted to know what the fuss was about, because that *poor fucking duck*, right? Well, he was delicious, obviously. It tasted decadent, like a rich and fatty meat milkshake; I wanted to spread it on McDonald's French fries. I mean, it *was* 9:00 p.m. and all I'd had to eat that day was a bowl of overcooked penne pasta smothered with Bolognese that had been pushed through a sieve to remove the beef, because, *Oops!*, the line cook forgot I was vegetarian. Again. "Shouldn't be any bits in it," he said, pushing the bowl across the pass to me. By "bits" he meant ground beef. "It's fine," I said, because he wasn't going to make me my own special sauce, was he? (And, for the record, there were "bits" in it.)

There's a frequent misconception among customers that restaurant staff must eat like royalty. "How wonderful to have this chef cooking for you every day," they say. But working for a talented chef is, I suspect, a bit like living with a talented comedian; everyone thinks your life must be a laugh a minute, but the truth is, being a chef and being a comedian are both performances. If you haven't paid for a ticket and it isn't showtime, you're shit out of luck. No food, no jokes.

Most restaurants do something called "family meal," which is usually prepared by a cook low down in the pecking order. It's often an "everything but the kitchen sink" kind of dish—a casserole pot full of things one day from going off, ingredients the cooks had too much of, all of it bound together with white rice or a penne pasta. The sauce is usually red. It might contain a strange collection of vegetables: canned tomatoes, endless zucchini, mushrooms, and something weird that didn't sell well. Beets, maybe. Beans are usually involved, often ground beef.

Family meal serves two purposes. The obvious is to feed the staff, to make sure everyone is carbo-loaded for what will inevitably be a long shift, but this is not its *main* purpose. I promise you: no chef I worked for ever gave a shit whether or not I actually ate the slop he put in front of me. The main purpose of the staff meal is to get on the same page. It's a business meeting in disguise. It's about starting the night with the pretense that we are all one big happy family. An opportunity to talk about specials and discuss what to push that night—*Sell the sea bass! We have loads.* At the best of times, family meal is a deep breath at the beginning of a shift. A chance to joke about last night's customer—the one who thought gnocchi was pronounced "ganotchi." *What a moron*, we laugh, united. As a staff, we need to start off laughing because in forty-five minutes we'll all hate each other and be calling one another assholes and threatening to slit each other's throat if the other person doesn't get out of the fucking way. Family meal is a lie restaurant folk tell themselves.

Ironically, working in restaurants makes real family life difficult. Our *actual* families are at home or at work. *They* aren't eating, yet. They'll be eating later, at a normal time, *without us*. Their dinners probably won't involve a combination of ground beef and beets. But for many restaurant lifers, *this* is their family, so we loved and hated each other in equal measure, because that's what families do.

When I worked at a French bistro in Rockland, Maine, dinner service started at five. This meant we had family meal around 4:30. I'd rarely worked up an appetite, but I did my best to consume what was on offer. *(Hello kidney beans, my old friends!)* I'd push the food around and listen to the chef talk about the specials and laugh at the recounting of last night's parade of idiotic diners. I'd psych myself up for the night ahead. When the customers arrived thirty minutes later, I waxed lyrical about the delights of dishes I'd never eaten. "The steak frites is delicious." (So I'm told.) "You have to try the duck breast; it's our signature dish." (It's not. We just need to get rid of it before it goes off.) "The mussels cooked in white wine are the best I've ever had." (Mussels cooked in *anything* were the emperor's new clothes of any restaurant I ever worked in. So long as there was ample garlic in the sauce, the customer always agreed with me.)

By 8:00, I'd been selling and smelling braised duck, pan-fried scallops, roast chicken, triple-cooked frites, and bubbling French onion soup for hours. It didn't matter how much penne pasta with canned tomatoes, kidney beans, kale, and grated cheddar I'd eaten at 4:00; I was starving. I wanted what *she* was having, and *he* was having, and *they* were having.

I SPENT A SUMMER in college working in a hotel restaurant on Martha's Vineyard. Most of the time, despite the sweeping sea and lighthouse views, the restaurant was snoozy, virtually empty at lunch time because guests were at the beach. Dinner was a civilized, if stuffy, affair that involved crisp white tablecloths that were loathed equally by the restaurant staff and hotel laundry staff who had to steam the steak blood out of them every night.

The meal everyone came from miles around for was the weekend brunch. The buffet was insane—it snaked around the restaurant's long wooden bar and across to several tables lined up in the back of the restaurant. It started with a raw bar—a guy standing right at the entrance shucking oysters. Next to him were bowls of accompaniments: horseradish, mignonette, cocktail sauce. Cooked and peeled shrimp on a bed of ice came next, just in case raw oysters weren't your thing. If you weren't a seafood-in-the-morning person, don't worry, lining the bar were dozens of silver chafing dishes containing blueberry pancakes, French toast, and waffles. No need to choose. *Have one of each.* After that, how about sausage? Patties or links? You *still* didn't have to choose. Bacon? *Of course!* Eggs: scrambled, scrambled with smoked salmon, scrambled with chorizo, scrambled with parmesan cheese and truffle oil. *Don't like scrambled eggs?* Lucky for you there's a guy frying and poaching eggs at the end of the bar. And, yes, an omelet guy too. On the low tables were salads: lobster salad, steamed mussel salad, orzo salad, a couple of potato salads, asparagus salad, simple green salad, panzanella salad, crunchy vegetable salad. I could go on. Done yet? Not a chance. I haven't mentioned the bagel station: raisin, onion, everything, and plain. Also, cream cheese—low fat, full fat, chive, and dill. Smoked salmon, too, obviously. Platters and platters of smoked salmon. Hard-boiled eggs, because maybe you didn't like any of the other types of eggs, and lastly, a toaster oven for your bagel. Yes, you had to do this yourself. *I know . . . sorry.* Oh, and fruit, of course! Which fruit? All the fruits.

This epic brunch ran from 9:00 to 2:00. There was no staff breakfast beforehand. Half a dozen of us servers were expected to be there at 7:30 to set up. Smarter people woke up really early and ate something before arriving, but I've never been able to eat first thing in the morning, so I always arrived on an empty stomach. We laid out this grand buffet, polished baskets filled with forks, spoons, and knives. We folded stacks of napkins and draped white cloths on the tables. We sliced butter into rectangles exactly an eighth of an inch thick onto small round white plates and topped the slices with crushed sea salt, before placing a plate at the center of each clothed table. We arranged the salads artfully with explanatory labels in front of each.

THEN WE STOOD back and waited for the diners to arrive. As the diners took their seats, the chafing dishes started to come out, carried by cooks in white chefs' jackets with sleeves rolled up to the elbow, arms covered in burns. The omelet and egg cooks took their positions. The oyster shucker was already shucking madly away—some guests took the opportunity to down an oyster on their way to the table. Once the customers had taken their seats, we took orders for mimosas and asked who wanted toast for the table. *White? Wheat? Multigrain? Rye?* When a chafing dish was half empty, we took it back into the kitchen to be replaced. The cooks spooned the remains on top of the next full and ready-to-go chafing dish, which we carried back to the dining room. From the large restaurant windows, we glimpsed the beautiful sunny day outside—tourists on bikes, guests lounging on the wide wraparound porch, the sea lapping gently in the distance. But we had to move quickly. The dishes were piping hot, smelling of butter, fat, and dough, and customers were waiting. When someone spooned a portion of salad, a server would take the large silver spoon and rearrange the salad, so the divot was covered over. The salad looked brand new for the next guest to scoop. All this accomplished, we just stood there and watched while the guests piled their plates high—with even more food. We waited until they needed something from us. And they *would* need something from us: more mimosas, more toast, grated parmesan, olive oil, truffle oil. They saw tuna tartare on our dinner menu, could they also have that? *No, they could not.* Standing behind the salad tables, we waited, a chorus of rumbling tummies. We smiled. We answered questions. *Yes, the orzo salad has pine nuts. No, the pancakes aren't gluten free.*

Eventually, the customers were full. They rose from their tables, leaving behind half-eaten eggs, smoked salmon, bagels with bites taken out, cold bacon, and soggy pancakes. I remember feeling as if I might faint, staring at the remains. After stacking the abandoned plates onto a large oval tray, we balanced the towering remains on our shoulders and teetered back to the kitchen, where we used the customers' forks to scrape the excess into the large kitchen bin.

As brunch went on, we stared at the clock: 10, 10:30, 11:30 (halfway!), and so on until 2:00, when the last of the guests were just finishing up. Actually, they were done hours ago. At 2:00, they were just drinking mimosas and Bloody Marys. As they drank, we watched the food in the buffet change temperature—warm things going cold, cold things going warm. Each of us holding a cardboard take-out container, we servers hovered in the restaurant's corners waiting for the last of the guests to finally rise and stagger out, because that's when we were allowed to attack the buffet.

And attack it, we did. There were mountains of leftovers: pancakes, waffles, all those scrambled eggs. All the oysters shucked, but uneaten. The lobster salad. *Lobster!* The bagels—*eat them or they'll go hard.* Fruit—*so many enormous strawberries.* We filled our boxes. (We weren't allowed plates.) It didn't matter that the eggs were cold, the oysters were warm, the pancakes rubbery. Because we weren't allowed to eat in the dining room, lest the guests see us eating their excess, we took our feasts downstairs into the staff room, where communal tables had been set up. There were no windows down there; the sea view wasn't ours to enjoy. My box usually contained a mixture of salads, a bagel with cream cheese, and oysters, which I slurped first with cocktail sauce to mask their temperature. No mimosas or Bloody Marys for us, just tap water. It didn't matter. We didn't need booze. We were a family having a meal, finally off our feet and brimming with stories of ridiculous customer behavior. We sat around plastic tables on metal chairs and howled, recalling the customer who asked for poached egg whites and complained bitterly when he cut through and found no yolk. We ate out of our cardboard containers with unpolished cutlery and stuffed our faces with sweaty salads, room-temperature waffles, and limp sausage. Yes, we were in the basement, but it felt like heaven.

STONE SOUP
Anne Elliott

I N THE SPRING and summer of 2002, my colleague Marina and I sat at our desks on the edge of a hedge-fund trading floor in Midtown Manhattan, observing like anthropologists. What fascinated us most were the frequent deliveries of food. Lunch was a given, as on many trading floors employers feed their people to keep them in chairs. But these men—mostly men—rarely sat still in these chairs. The older ones stood with heavy phones tucked between cheek and shoulder; the younger ones had wireless headsets and roamed the floor talking to invisible people, tossing their stress balls into the air. Every so often, a sudden whoop would emerge from the floor, then boxes of pizza or milkshakes or cupcakes arrived, and the whole assembly would swarm. Had a stock or bond gone up? Had someone lost a bet? What were they celebrating—or what sorrow were they drowning—with all of this food?

Some days saw several sudden deliveries. Marina and I began to chart them: *Deliveries vs. Dow.* Was there a correlation between the number of pizza boxes and the S&P 500? I plotted the food flow against several market indices: NASDAQ, ten-year Treasuries, junk bonds. We hoped that if we found a reliable pattern, it could be a leading indicator, perhaps one we could harness into a predictive model, like skirt hemlines or unemployment numbers. Were we witnessing correlation or causation, and if the latter, what was causing what—did gluttony cause markets to rise and fall, or the other way around?

This hedge fund was big enough to move markets. Any theory was on the table.

We kept our theories to ourselves, for the most part, as we watched the CEO walk around the trading desk like a slender king, watched the traders scramble to straighten their ties as he shook his head at the excess food, then at the excess bellies of some of his young employees.

Neither Marina nor I had grown up with a safety net. I came from a family of clergy, educators, and artists, meaning our choices—I suppose we did have choices—were those non-lucrative passions that leave one barely making New York rent. In the early 1990s, after a family illness put me behind financially, I had done the unthinkable: applied for a temp job on Wall Street. There, I found mentors and discovered a knack for database design, and my day job became a kind of game. Putting on my cheap suit was theater, speaking their lingo was persona, and besides, it couldn't last forever—someday I would see my escape hatch and dive through it into the full-time artist's life. But someday didn't quite happen. After the events of 9/11 traumatized my Wall Street firm, culminating in layoffs, I moved with a handful of associates uptown to the buy side, from a place that crafted bonds to a place that consumed them.

Marina had grown up in Soviet Russia, where scant resources had little to do with one's vocation. More to the point, she grew up in the Ural Mountains, a part of the country so frigid that even growing one's own food was difficult. She came to the States via a refugee program for Russian Jews that offered job training in computer programming. Her first days in the city were spent—like mine—in a cold apartment in an outer borough, making do.

There we were, improbably together, improbably friends, writing code to help asset managers hedge their convertible bonds. What joined us was our shared love of simple, elegant solutions to complex problems. And we shared a fascination with this curious tribe in front of us.

Each morning, she and I logged on to a website to order the free lunch—a perk for us too—from a handful of local restaurants. She looked forward to Italian day; I looked forward to Japanese day. We ordered extra to take home, maxing out our daily budget. We grew used to summoning food at the click of a mouse. Her calamari must not have lemon, and nothing green must come in her takeout box. My salad must not have dressing, and my sushi must be rolled with brown rice. For people with memory of recent poverty, we had certainly become picky, sending back dishes that did not match the tick boxes we had clicked on the screen. We didn't have allergies. We just had preferences.

To amuse, Marina regaled me with stories of the old country, particularly about food. She knew I loved to hear about cleverness, and food in her Soviet city was a matter of problem-solving. Your connections would tell you what was available and where: bread on this line, butter on that. If the store did not have cheese, you made cheese, for which she gave me the translated recipe; it instructed crafty cooks to use the milk carton as the mold. If the store did not have cognac, you made your own cognac, for which she gave me the recipe too: some cocoa, some honey and spices, and a whole lot of vodka. Damp summer days were for foraging mushrooms, then jarring them in brine, she told me, nostalgic for the birch forests of her youth. She gave me that recipe, too, and brought some pickled mushrooms in to share. Old, stale bread could be made into a fermented drink, and this recipe I actually tried at home. Kvass: it was a little like beer.

Her favorite Russian snack was raw yellow turnip, for which she gave me seeds, smuggled into the States by her husband. The seed package, under bold Cyrillic lettering, sported a cartoon of an outsized turnip next to a gnome. I planted a seed in the window near our bank of desks, and we babied it, watched it leaf out, then develop a bulb at the surface of the dirt. Perhaps our turnip could become a gnome house after hours, when the trading floor was dormant. The turnip, the mushrooms, the homemade cheese, all of it had a fairy-tale feel for me, like that old yarn about stone soup, a favorite childhood fable. The fable appealed to my inner communist and my outer problem solver: A crafty traveler shows up to a town carrying nothing but an empty cooking pot. No one will share food with him, but he builds a fire and boils water in the pot, tossing in a stone from the river. Curious folks wander by and ask what he is making. He talks up his stone soup, how delicious it is, but suggests it would be even better with *a garnish*. Townspeople, one by one, bring garnishes: a carrot, a potato, an oxtail, some oatmeal. At the end of the story, all sit down for a tasty stew. Plenty for everyone.

Meanwhile, on the hedge-fund trading desk, we witnessed daily birthday cake, unlimited lattes. Holiday baskets from brokers full of wrapped pears, waxed cheese, summer sausage, seedy mustard. Other brokers sent lunch—on top of the lunch we had already eaten: thick steaks and creamed spinach and onion blossoms with horseradish; fancy boats of sushi for Pearl Harbor Day, which many on the desk found funny. The traders and portfolio managers would lay out the food and circle it. Much went uneaten and sat on top of a file cabinet, until someone volunteered to throw it away in the pantry.

A rumor went around about a woman who picked and ate uneaten food from the pantry garbage can. Another rumor: the same woman had been spied vomiting in the lavatory, then guiltily avoiding eye contact in the mirror as she brushed her teeth. People giggled at this rumor: male people, that is. The women eyed each other sadly, but we did not dare chide the laughter for fear of becoming its next target. Two guys from the desk staged an experiment: they ordered extra seasoned fries with their lunch, ate three bites, threw it in the garbage can with the lid open, then lurked outside the pantry door, peeking through the window, to see if she sampled it. They burst back onto the desk, laughing—not even hiding it; their experiment had worked. The woman had stood over the bin and eaten several fries, before skulking off to the bathroom.

Marina and I confessed to each other, when out of earshot of the desk, that we had seen her in the bathroom, too, doing what she did. She was an attractive, professional-looking woman, neat clothes, coiffed, manicured. Lucky for her, she did not work on the trading desk. I feared I would see her in the bathroom again. I would not be able to hide the heartbreak on my face.

Maybe this tribe we were studying was a little bit evil. So, what did that make us, watching from the sidelines, charting, judging, but not intervening?

We stopped charting the food indicator. It wasn't funny anymore. We finally pulled the turnip from the dirt and cut into it. It was not sweet, as we had expected. The place where it had grown was far too warm. It was bitter. I wondered if this place, if I were not careful, might turn me bitter too.

I was only beginning to understand something. Under the cruel laughter and stress-ball squeezing and bulimia-baiting, these people had a hunger, and the flow of food could do nothing for it. Hunger for success, for importance, for a bigger bonus than the guy sitting across the desk got. Those who had this hunger might not see how it was killing them. One's own plenty was impossible to see when the next person had more of it. Gratitude, when the air was full of competition, was near impossible.

Gratitude. Marina and I had survived September 11th. We had made do in unsafe apartments. We had plenty of gratitude, and it filled our conversation. We talked about the stone soups of our lives, the ways we made something from nothing. Resourcefulness could be celebrated. Stone soup, the soup made of nothing, how beautiful! If people won't share, you can trick them into it! What I didn't think of, not until recently: this beautiful soup was based on a lie. The traveler was a con artist. The townspeople guarded their resources for good reason. They had families to feed.

Before long, the firm got wind that Marina and I were building something from nothing: trading applications that could not be bought. Bernie Madoff had startled the world to attention at how much freedom was to be had on a hedge-fund trading floor. Our whole industry had become rife with suspicion of trickery—cooked books, faked trades—and homegrown software was harder to audit. Clients would not tolerate it. Management split the two of us up, away from the trading desk—put me with the risk department, put Marina with a team onboarding third-party software to replace the software she had lovingly coded. Our new offices did not have many walls, but we could see the handwriting on them. We had been through layoffs before.

One morning, the chief operating officer came to my desk with a frown. "I just want you to know—"

"Someone I love is no longer here?" I said. He nodded, pity in his eyes.

Marina's whole department was pushed out, to be replaced by consulting firms with liability policies and configurable personnel. Time for me to start looking for that escape hatch I had planned for. I had been working in the industry for over twenty years. I had never intended to work beyond one year.

My husband and I made a plan to move to Maine, where we had many friends, the kind who socialized with potlucks, making a better kind of stone soup, the kind where nobody has to trick anybody into it. In Maine, I would be able to forage and farm and pickle all I wanted. DIY would be de rigueur, along with the gruff friendliness of sharing surplus zucchini or hand-dug clams. Livelihoods could be cobbled together from seasonal gigs and side businesses. Making do was a way of life. We made all the arrangements to move, and I gave my notice.

On my last day at the hedge fund, someone ordered me a cannoli cake. I brought two cases of Moxie to share, to give them a taste of Maine. I actually hate Moxie. It tastes like poison to me. But suddenly—without prompting, without trickery—from hidden compartments in desk drawers, emerged garnishes: whisky, rum, vodka.

Turns out Moxie tastes pretty good with a garnish.

After the closing bell, I sat in a conference room drinking rum and Moxie, pigging out on cake I didn't need, laughing with my colleagues, several of whom looked at me with jealousy. They surprised me by understanding: I was relinquishing my future in data design to turn my mind to the present. They were looking around for an escape hatch, too, weary from the vigilance required to stay alive in this place. Half of us were on medication for blood pressure.

Marina and I stayed friends, of course. She came to Maine for a visit, bringing a very full cooler. Inside it were the Russian treats she had introduced me to, ones I now craved: grated-cheese salad on thin rye toast, blinis and blintzes, sour cherry sauce. She knew I couldn't find them here. But we couldn't eat everything, so I put some of it in the freezer before I sent her off with her cooler refilled with seafood from the Gulf of Maine.

Coronavirus came along, and my husband and I found ourselves avoiding shopping, eating our way slowly through the freezer, finding mystery foods like gifts from the past, making do. I discovered a curious triangular package, a Georgian cheese flatbread Marina had brought, and warmed it up. So comforted was I by the bread that I texted Marina to see how she was holding up. We laughed about how her Soviet skills had led her to the only toilet paper in New Jersey. We shared news of our old colleagues. We talked about who was still working, who wasn't. Who was sick, who wasn't. Too many heartbreaks to count, so we didn't count them.

The CEO of the hedge fund died young a few years ago, just after I moved here. All the money in the world could not keep illness away. I sympathized with his family. I dreamed, during the pandemic, that I ran into him, on the snowy street, here in Maine. "Anne, you're still here?" he said, as he had said to me once on the trading desk, thinking he had laid me off.

"For the moment, yes," I said, as I had said back then.

ZAKIA'S DOLMA
Kifah Abdulla

I CARRY A METAL bowl as I wait for lunch in a long queue of starving prisoners of war. The bowl has become my most important possession. I have nothing besides it, a broken spoon, shoes, and a prisoner's uniform. I use my bowl for bathing, a pillow when I have a chance to sleep, and also as an instrument—I play on it and sing, though only in a low voice. I shovel snow in the winter with it, by order of the prison officer, and in the summer, my bowl serves as a hat, protecting me from the desert sun.

I was called to compulsory military duty in service of Saddam Hussein, whose party I disagreed with, just days after graduating from college. I left my home in Baghdad for the battlefields of the longest war of the twentieth century. The war was between two neighbors in the Middle East—Iraq and Iran—and in the sepia dust and heat of the desert combat zone, my world as a peace-loving university student was transformed.

For years, I fought without allegiance to either side. My unit was decimated, though I escaped the wreckage. I trekked for many days across the desert without food or water, traveling only at night. At last, I was captured by Iranian forces who first mistook me for one of their own, treated me well, and fed me, but then learned the unthinkable—that an Iraqi could look like an Iranian—and I was sent to a war prison in Tehran.

THE PRISON IS low and windowless, so my eyes hurt when they let us outside to bathe in the midday heat. We receive our meals inside, though, and in the dim light, I am given just enough to keep me alive, and no more. For breakfast, it's a thin piece of bread the size of my hand and a small piece of feta cheese; for lunch, a simple cup of rice; and for dinner, a gray-green

98

soup, which tastes abysmal because meat is first boiled into it. I am so opposed to the meat soup that I prefer to be hungry. For over eight years, I
have eaten only cheese, bread, and rice.

HUNGER SETTLES INTO a prisoner's guts, wilts the body, and leaves one
hollow-eyed and dry-lipped. Some prisoners turn violent, stealing other
prisoners' food, but others experience peaceful hallucinations when starving. When strange visions find me, I let them come. Other times I focus on
all the foods I loved before the endless war.

In the lunch line, my prison friend tells me about the delicious food
he ate in his civilian life. We share an exhausted laugh. Then, as we shuffle
forward, it is my turn to wet his mouth, and I tell him about my grandmother's dolma.

WHEN I WAS A CHILD, I lived with my grandmother and she cooked for
me because my mother was often away at work as a nurse. I was too embarrassed to tell my mother the truth when she asked me whose cooking
I liked better. My mother always laughed and kissed me, saying, "I know
what you mean. I love my mother's food too."

My grandmother's name, Zakia, means "perfume," and my grandmother
infused my childhood with the smells of her cooking. Rays of deep sun-
light filtered through an opening in the ceiling, and the aroma of black
tea with cardamom filled the air. Zakia made hundreds of different dishes
without using a cookbook. She never forgot a recipe or mixed up her
spices. She was an excellent chef and baker, and although she made almost
limitless pastries, bread, pickles, jams, and desserts, dolma was her specialty.

FOR DOLMA, ZAKIA went to the market (with me by her side) for fresh
tomatoes, eggplant, zucchini, onions, green peppers, red cabbage, grape
leaves, garlic, green fava beans, and chard. Then she would buy freshly
ground meat before we returned home to find my grandfather lying on a
couch under the shadow of an abundant vine in the front garden. His head
was usually near his old radio, listening to the news of the world, before the
war, while sparrows chirped on the branches of fig, berry, and eucalyptus
trees. We had food growing everywhere then, all around us! He would clap
his hands once we showed up, saying, "Great, you arrived safely! I hope
your shopping was easy?"

"Yes, it was, but we walked a lot," my grandmother would say, then rest a little by sitting on the clean, cool cement floor, while I brought water for tea. Then it was time to make the dolma.

In a large bowl, Zakia would mix rice, ground meat, salt, garlic, lemon juice, sunflower oil, tamarind molasses, and a blend of black pepper, cardamom, coriander, nutmeg, and cloves. She took the skin off the onions, made a slit halfway down each one, removed each layer gently, stuffed the shells with the ingredients of the mixture, and hollowed and stuffed peppers, eggplants, zucchini, tomatoes, and potatoes. She then wrapped vine leaves and cabbage leaves around the mixture, added green fava beans to the bottom, and neatly layered all the stuffed and rolled vegetables in the saucepan. She laid the stems of chard on top, and finally, added tomato sauce, covered the saucepan, and brought everything to a boil for ten minutes.

Once the dolma was ready, Zakia slipped the dolma onto an enormous tray, and my grandfather would pick up her scented hand and kiss it gallantly. "Thank you, you are wonderful," he would say. The rest of the family would join us to sit on the floor and eat.

IN THE PRISON LUNCH LINE, I close my eyes and speak: "Each vegetable has its own amazing taste, despite the same ingredients being mixed and cooked together. I always savored the smells and the textures of each vegetable, eating them slowly, one at a time."

"Stop, stop, that's enough!" my friend in line says as our turn to receive food approaches. "I am almost full of remembering the good food, and I don't want to lose my appetite for today's special meal!" He asks me to promise that after the war, we will meet again, and he will get to try my grandmother's cooking.

That never happens. Years will go by, and my friend and I will part when we are transferred to two different prisons. I never found out what happened to him, though I did at last return to Baghdad, and get to spend time with my grandmother and again enjoy her dolma before she died. Now, in my new home in Portland, Maine, I often think of my grandmother. I will never forget what it feels like to starve, sustained only by dreams.

CONNECTIONS
Michele Levesque

I AM LUCKY. I've never gone hungry because of a lack of food. I was raised in a middle-class family with a mostly stay-at-home mom and a working dad. They watched their pennies and bought stuff on sale, but my mom had the luxury of calling the local butcher for an order that we would pick up on the way home from school. I went to a private school that didn't have a food program. My mom packed my lunch every day until she realized I was coming home hungry because I was throwing away a perfectly good ham sandwich, just because I didn't like it. To me, that is the definition of privilege: to have food and waste it. From then on, my mom put me in charge of packing lunches for the whole family. This meant three different types of sandwiches, as I wanted tuna or egg salad, my brother wanted a plain, dry ham and cheese, and my dad liked things I didn't consider food, like Spam, pickle mustard, and cold meatloaf. In my house, dinner hit the table at 6:00 p.m. and wasn't over until dessert was served. Then we started again the next morning with choices like cereal and milk, fruit, English muffins, and sometimes even donuts or cinnamon rolls. Food was plentiful and it showed.

I have, however, gone hungry because of my relationship with food. I have deprived myself, and at times I've excluded entire food groups from my diet, hoping to change my physical being, my mental state, or, let's be honest, my jeans size. At age twelve, I gave up soda, and in high school I learned the stomach-filling benefits of coffee. Then I gave up snacks. Deprivation seemed to be the answer to a smaller me. Save calories for the good bits, I thought, as I consumed my go-to high school lunch of a chocolate bar and a strong cup of coffee. At one point, I purposefully ate cabbage soup for three months straight! Now what teenage girl would intentionally do that to her intestinal system if she wasn't desperate for something? Following the cabbage experience came calorie counting, Weight Watchers–style, fad diets that involved scrupulous almond counting, and days of fasting that inevitably ended in binge eating, because I didn't seem to have the willpower to stick with the diet that I was somehow convinced would change my life.

Despite these struggles, I am now a firm believer that chicken soup does cure the common cold, and some of the best conversations I've had happened while breaking bread with friends and family. Food starts and prolongs conversations, evokes memories, and unites us. To this day, the smell of roasting chestnuts transports me to my first holiday season in the Big Apple, where I experienced that nutty aroma for the first time.

We all have some special food tradition. Some people have a special cake for their birthday. Others get together to bake cookies or make tamales. In my family, Christmas means tourtière, a Québécois meat pie, and Aunt Blanche's fudge cooked on the stove, then tucked tightly into cans for distribution to friends, teachers, and family. At Thanksgiving time, a mash of turnips and carrots sits beside the turkey. My husband's aunt makes tomato aspic for Thanksgiving. Since most of us don't eat it, it's become a bit of a family joke. Yet the day wouldn't be the same without it.

Family tradition can include heated arguments about cooking or preparation methods. Whose process is correct or superior? Which sister got it right? Once, I came across a poignant collection of recipes titled *In Memory's Kitchen: A Legacy from the Women of Terezin* that celebrates the beloved dishes and rich traditions from the women of the Czechoslovakian concentration camp. Even in times of hunger, personal heritage prevails through stories of food.

At fifteen, my first job was at Hall's Seafood, a fish market in my native Rhode Island. I had no idea how that job would change my life, leading me eventually to my current restaurant El El Frijoles, in an old barn behind my house in Sargentville, Maine. At Hall's Seafood, Emily ran the market side of things. Her husband, Tom, spent his days as a lobsterman. In my early days, I was nervous, well aware that I barely knew what filet of sole looked like, let alone how to cook it. One day, Emily asked me if I liked linguini and clams. I didn't know. Clams were a bit exotic for my meat and potatoes family, but I said yes. What a lunch!

Whenever I could, I asked Emily how to cook this fish or that shellfish, and I would repeat her directions, word for word, to anybody who needed cooking advice. Because of Emily, whenever people complain that they don't like bluefish because it's too oily, I respond, "Just brush it with some tasty mustard, salt, and pepper, and sprinkle it with some bread crumbs and then broil it for ten minutes per inch."

My curiosity didn't stop with the fish! I soon became interested in the origin of different foods. I wanted to know how Hall's Seafood worked and how all the products arrived in our display case. The scallops, for example, were delivered by a local guy who scalloped to cover the extra supplies he needed for his swordfishing boat. The first time I popped a fresh scallop into my mouth, my relationship with food changed forever. How could something actually taste like the sea? How could a food taste like where it came from?

After high school, I left Hall's Seafood for New York City to pursue a career in the visual arts. But my food adventures continued. I sampled New York–style pizza, had meals at "hot" new restaurants, and rewarded myself with expensive treats from Balducci's. I loved walking into Chelsea Hot Bagels. The windows were so steamed up, and rivulets of water pooled on the floor, and all of us, packed in there together, were sweating just like the fogged-up windows. I always ordered a (sublime) everything bagel with vegetable cream cheese and smoked salmon. The bagel place closed long ago, but I still search out similar experiences, for the quality of the bagel or the nostalgia. Or both.

Throughout my life, I have always returned to some form of food service to pay the bills. I moved to the California Bay Area to go to graduate school. At the time, I didn't realize I was entering the mecca of modern food. I found a job at a small Italian deli working the counter and helping the eighty-five-year-old owner make ravioli. He taught me to make *arancini di riso* and the perfect aioli for artichokes. Before meeting him, I'd never eaten an entire artichoke and had no idea how to approach the strange vegetable, but now my eyes were open, and I just wanted more.

From the Italian deli, I moved back to a fish market, but one housed in a European-style marketplace. The marketplace had a coffee roaster, a produce market, a wine merchant, a butcher shop, places for amazing bread and pasta, and an anchor restaurant with a young up-and-coming chef. I learned all about West Coast fish, from Dungeness crab to Hawaiian ono and yellowfin tuna. I was surrounded by many young people, including chefs, finding their way in the increasingly competitive food world. My fish-market position gave me constant access to fresh, healthy food and the people who were interested in consuming, preparing, and talking about it. I made lifelong friends with customers and coworkers. Food became central to my social life, and though I was still pursuing a career in the visual arts, I soon came to understand that gallery openings were often as much about food as art.

Over time, my Friday evenings shifted from overindulgence to more intimate gatherings of friends, celebrating Shabbat and sharing an amazing meal. And even those Shabbat dinners have evolved, too, into family gatherings and potlucks, where I am more aware of the challenges of raising a child in a climate of chemicals and fast food.

AT THIS POINT IN MY LIFE, food is how I make my living. I set out with the intention of recreating a typical San Francisco Bay Area taqueria. Over the years we have morphed into something more. We sourced local produce, talked a farmer into growing black beans for us, and combined traditional Maine ingredients with Mexican-inspired flavors. I feed lots of people, too many to count in the summer, and a small group of regulars in the winter months. I feed people on vacation, carpenters grabbing lunch, my hungry family after a long day, the random visitor to the peninsula in the winter. I love each experience for a different reason. I aim to make people feel welcome. Whenever I feel the urge to encourage a regular customer who always orders the same carnitas burrito to try something new, I pause and remember my experiences at Chelsea Hot Bagels, where I always ordered that same amazingly delicious everything bagel with vegetable cream cheese and smoked salmon. Something else on the menu might be just as good or even "better" than that carnitas burrito, but food is about more than taste. Don't get me wrong: delicious food, made with fresh, quality ingredients, is necessary for excellent eating, but in each bite we often feel a sense of nostalgia and memory that has the power to transport us to a different time and place. The quality of a meal can change a person's entire day, and being a part of that has become a central theme in my life.

So, as I clean up Monday's breakfast, I ponder Friday's dinner and how I can make something from what others consider nothing. I'm always planning, creating, and trying something new, and each day I work hard to push the boundaries of what eleven-year-olds, some of the most discriminating critics around, might be willing to try. My goal is to make people feel welcome and satisfied, no matter their age, background, or food traditions. Good food can do that.

FORAGED, STOLEN, BEGGED!
Bill Roorbach

A T POPHAM BEACH, with my family and some friends and their kids during home-school days some years ago, I brought along a cookie sheet to make salt, as it was a science day. Later, we looked into tide pools to inspect hermit crabs and bivalves, sea urchins and stars, the various shells left behind, also the tides themselves, the angle of the sun, the nature of bodies in surf, the quality of Dad's nap in such active conditions.

But the salt is germane.

All day we kept the cookie sheet going—a bucket of sea water to evaporate, then the next, faster than you'd think in the hot sun and wind, the salt rime slowly thickening till by day's end we had enough to brush into a half-cup jelly jar and label REAL POPHAM SALT. It tasted more metallic than the mined salt back home in Farmington, and saltier in some ineffable way, with the tiniest hint of ocean to it.

Over the following months, we didn't much use it—too precious!— and slowly it pushed its way to the back of the spice shelf while our home-school novels and plays and poems and essays and book reports got written, and the language and math and history programs were absorbed, a couple of morning hours sufficient. Afternoons were for whatever, including our gardens, lots of vegetables, a modest array of herbs. Food is science, of course, and also art, and philosophy. That is, it was *all* school, whatever food thing we did, from canning to cooking to digesting, converting, eliminating, composting, everything a cycle.

Come spring, I got the wild thought to make a meal only from things foraged. What if we were hermits? How would we eat? On a downed popple log (*popple*, we'd learned, being the New England term for eastern aspen, also called white poplar), my daughter, Elysia, and I spotted spring oyster mushrooms, smooth white and growing in stacks like pancakes. We gathered as much as we could carry in a wind-tossed Walmart bag we'd pulled down earlier from high branches using a makeshift pole. Bright blue, it got a second use. We'd been heading to find ramps, sometimes called wild leeks, something in smell and taste between onion and garlic, but the greens more delicate. They grow in the rich streamside soil in rare patches. I'd brought a trowel with a long handle, a cherished gift of my newly departed mother, I'm remembering now—that she was newly departed, I mean, which makes this 2006, likely May—and with the trowel and its very British long handle, we dug ramps. The bulbs are thin as your pinkie finger, the leaves broad as your wrist, stems a purply red and white, all edible. Except for the icky cowl enveloping the bulb, which we washed off in the cold stream that bloomingly warm day. Back home, we read up: the bulbs are modified leaves, the plants themselves spring ephemerals. That is, their leaves emerge quickly and photosynthesize madly while the hardwood canopy is still bare, sending energy to the roots. When the trees above leaf out, ephemeral leaves die back. The plants then use the summer for bulb and root building, spreading into greater patches. Ramps don't flower till early August, throwing up a white spray that fades quickly, leaving black seeds similar to other onion types. We will collect these when the time comes and Johnny Appleseed them over likely looking spots (and in fact have successfully created new ramp patches all through the home forest in Farmington, which in spring is among the first green, if you want a clue).

The stream washes away the dirt, the cowls get stripped off the bulb by eager hands, the leaves shed the water leaving iridescent drops, and we make bundles, not more than we think we'll eat in a day or two. They go on top of the bag of mushrooms, and we feel lucky once again that the wind brought us a vessel when Dad forgot his bucket, even the trash at our service.

The crawfish trap has but one creature in it. Little monster pulls back defensively. We count the legs, same as the crabs of the ocean; we marvel at the claws. I let it pinch my thumb and it's not kidding around—no bruise or cut will ensue but give it credit. I'm thousands of times its size. We won't eat this one; there's too much wisdom in its bite. Off it scuttles backwards.

"You should never kill anyone," Elysia says, soon to go vegetarian. We watch the stream for a half hour, long enough, we've learned, for the sun to travel 7.5 degrees across the sky. In olden times you might have built a weir to catch a fish or two. We can hear a pair of black ducks quacking. How might we have approached them as a meal—*I mean back in the day, sweetie, when you had to eat whatever you could eat, one death preventing another.* She thinks maybe a spear, and so we carve spears from very straight, very light-weight viburnum sticks. I always had a knife at my belt then, a Leatherman, with all the tools you needed. We could have used a sharp rock to shape the spears, though, we really could have. And we laughed a lot practicing with them—likely all ducks were safe from us. She'd used a bow and ar-row at camp, and we discussed how that invention likely sprang from the effort to get a spear to fly straighter and further. A great conversation as we collected fiddleheads, the first growth of ostrich ferns (and other ferns, okay, but those fiddleheads are so oxalic that they taste bitter, and some are plain poison). The serendipitous Walmart bag was serendipitously full, so we stuffed my pockets, and I had plenty of pockets. We wanted enough largesse for three meals, we figured. Three meals for three of us, Mom—a painter and textile artist—back up at the house making her work.

We had it on good authority that the Gunthers were away. And if we wa-tered their chickens, they might not begrudge a couple of foragers enough eggs for two of those meals. We crept like old-time brigands through the wood behind their farmhouse, up along the barn's side, sticks between our teeth like knives. The chickens contentedly clucked, only made a fuss and outcry when we opened their door. But they knew us, settled down. The hose was right there, and we rinsed and filled their self-waterer. They didn't even need food—there was plenty for them to forage in the yard, and plenty in their self-feeder. And eggs galore. The long days had all eight of them laying daily, and with the Gunthers away, there were seventeen eggs. Elysia made a pouch of her smock, and you never saw someone so careful, all the way home over rock and stump and brook and wall.

You can do with ramps whatever you might do with a leek. Braised is particularly good. They're a little strong for soups at *your* house, maybe, but not at ours. The greens wilt in a pan the way spinach wilts, the bulbs grow clear, caramelize like onions. You can bake the bulbs like garlic too. But we were making omelets.

We washed the oyster mushrooms carefully, all the tiny, shiny-black beetles from the gills (my mother called them pleasing beetles, because they don't hurt the mushroom much).

Slicing the mushrooms, I realized our foraged and commandeered meal needed some fat. Some butter, to be exact.

Needing wise counsel, I asked Elysia: *What should we do?* Obviously we could not just use the butter in the butter dish. But there was butter in our freezer, and our freezer was in the barn. And I tried to spin a justification.

"No, *Dad*." We'd just seen *Oliver* at one of the local schools. "But we could *beg*," she said. And dressed for the role, hiking boots and big socks, her smock all dirty from our earlier adventures, cheeks freshly smeared with garden dirt, we hiked to the house of our new neighbors, because it couldn't be someone we knew *at all*. And it should be she alone, like the guttersnipes of *Oliver*. We didn't have very near neighbors. We approached the chosen house from the woods, pickup trucks and Confederate flag in the drive. From behind a large white pine, I watched the poor little beggar girl go to their forbidding front door. She knocked not at all timidly. I could hear her piteous tone, the delight and joy of the neighbor woman, whose name I still don't know. I had told Elysia not to go inside and she did not, though invited, and very shortly the lady of the house, plump and serene, was back with a whole pound block of Land O'Lakes.

Beggars can't be choosers!

And back through the woods we cavorted, the neighbor left with charity in her heart and questions about the professor just through the woods and down the road. I hoped a thank-you note on a nice card would suffice to quell rumors and perhaps it did, dropped that night under cover of darkness in her mailbox with a basket of Easter goodies, never another encounter or word.

Home we giggled a lot and cleaned fiddleheads of their husks (a kind of papery afterbirth only present in the proper kind), boiled a huge pot of water, the French method, a rapid boil so it doesn't slow at all when the green vegetables go in—fiddleheads same as any other, the high heat keeping them brightest green. And the salt.

Wait.

"Sweetie, salt," I said consternated.

"Popham!" she cried.

That had been all the way back in summer, but sure enough our science-day salt was back in the shelf with the mace and the alum and the great unknown soldiers of baking past.

"Real Popham Salt!" we cheered. And didn't we salt that water!

The butter was salty too. I tasted quite a bit, as it melted in the pan. The mushrooms shrank a great deal as they sautéed, turned a nut light-brown. I chopped the ramps while Elysia, standing on her favored cooking chair, dropped the fiddleheads into the rolling, salted water. (Of course, she was being careful, *Dad.*)

In with the mushrooms went the ramps, which cook quickly like so many wild things. We put them on a plate, wiped out the pan, put it back to heat. The girl beat the eggs with great whisking focus, added salt, a little more. Pepper was forewent. Butter was generous.

And thus were the ramp-mushroom omelets with fiddleheads prepared, and shortly consumed.

Foraged, stolen, begged!

TURTLE
Justin Tussing

T WO MEN KNOCKED on our front door. It was a late morning in the spring and the men were giggly. They had a present for my father. One of them lowered the liftgate of their pickup, revealing a green-black boulder the size of a compact spare tire. No creature is as fluent in stillness as a turtle, but this wasn't the stillness of a turtle but of its corpse.

The men had come across the animal while carrying guns, which might suggest they were hunters, but hunters have rules and seasons. These men, drinking buddies of my father, liked to shoot animals in the woods. Sometimes they shot deer during deer season, but they also shot deer during duck season. They shot pheasant out of principle: the birds flew too slowly not to shoot.

They'd been out on a ramble when they'd stumbled upon the turtle in a bog. Camouflaged by the algae that grows on their shells, snapping turtles spend most of their lives waiting for fate to deposit some morsel of protein within reach of their beaky mouths; they are opportunistic, like my father's friends.

I recognized both men. Brownie moved slow and talked slow, a sentient flannel shirt. The other man's name was Billy Fairchild. Billy had quick eyes and resembled an Irish setter—he had a reputation as the most prolific poacher of winged game in the state of Connecticut.

When the men stumbled upon the creature, they had time to consider the effects of their actions. If they shot it, they'd have to hump it out of the woods. And neither of them knew how to clean a turtle. They were at an impasse. Then Brownie thought of my father. He figured, even if he was stranded in Connecticut, an Ohio farm boy might know what to do with a turtle; this suspicion was sufficient cause for him to set the barrel of his shotgun against the diamond-shaped head of a living dinosaur.

Bang.

My FATHER DRAGGED the turtle out of the truck bed by its meaty tail and walked its ungainly pendulum to the back of the house. After setting the turtle upside down on our flagstone patio, he sent me to get his folding knife, a cleaver, and a pair of pliers.

I watched my father walk the knife blade between the carapace and the cross-shaped plastron covering its abdomen. Next, he traced each of the turtle's appendages, the four stubby legs and its long tail. When he wrenched off the plaston, it was like lifting the hood of a car—order lurked inside, but it was a confusing sort of order. While the outside of the animal was a somber brown, the inside was gaudy with jewel-toned organs, sheets of bright red muscle, and immaculate white tendons. Black blood pooled in the shell. Perhaps one can't make a silk purse out of a sow's ear, but after he'd pulled the skin off the legs, the inside-out tubes resembled pearlescent opera gloves.

Limbs were disjointed, as was the tail. The shell was carried to the side of the yard, so its contents could be decanted into the weeds. With the organs removed, the shell contained one last secret; rows of ribs, acting like flying buttresses, suspended the turtle's spine. It was elegant and sturdy. And it was also the reason my father had sent me for his cleaver. Tucked inside that sanctum, between the backbone and the shell, lay the tenderloin.

The four of us—Brownie, Billy, my father, and I—headed to the Giant's View Inn, on Whitney Avenue in Hamden. The name referenced the Sleeping Giant, a series of small hills which, when viewed from the proper vantage, were said to resemble a sleeping colossus. The "Inn" was purely aspirational. There were no rooms for rent, and the only foods available were cellophane bags of peanuts. The GVI was a bar. I would have been eleven or twelve that spring, but I was already something of a regular. My father would set me up at a café table with a Coke and some quarters, for pool or Asteroids, while he played cards. Though they didn't serve food at the GVI, there was a kitchen with a hulking cast-iron stove.

After consulting with the bartender, my father was granted access to the kitchen. While Billy got the stove ready, my father made aluminum foil packets stuffed with turtle meat and Lipton's French Onion Soup mix.

While the men played cards, I sipped my Coke longing to be old enough to sit at that bar.

THE GVI CLOSED its doors thirty years ago. A life insurance franchise occupies the space. Whenever I drive by, I have the impulse to stop and ask the people working there how it feels to calculate risks and consult actuarial tables in what once was a glorious den of poachers and gamblers.

When the meat came out of the oven that day and all the regulars gathered at the bar, my father pushed a particular pouch to me, saying, "Eat this one," because the packet contained the tenderloin, which was the choicest cut, and I was his son. Everyone said it was the best thing they'd ever eaten. I ate the turtle. I loved it. I didn't even mind the pieces of shattered bone.

RED HOT HEAVEN
Donna Loring

I AM A PENOBSCOT tribal elder.

I grew up on Indian Island, the home of the Penobscot Indian Nation, a mere one mile wide and seven miles around, located in the Penobscot River, thirteen miles north of Bangor. If you look at a map, this is central Maine, though anyone living in Portland would consider it "wicked" far north.

Seventy years ago, when I was growing up, Indian Island consisted of about forty or fifty houses and approximately three hundred people and felt even more remote. My brother and I lived with our paternal grandparents. My grandfather was away most of the time, hunting or fishing. My grandmother was from a very strict conservative Baptist family who had disowned her because she had married an Indian. Still, she insisted that my brother and I go to the Baptist church three or four times a week, though almost everyone else on Indian Island was Catholic. Heaven, we were taught, was a wonderful place with many mansions and streets of gold. Until we got there, we had to live on Indian Island and deal with the state-appointed Indian agent. The Indian agent approved all requests and issued invoices for food, clothing, fuel, or any other needs a family might have.

Life was not easy for any of us. The island had no running water, so we got our water from a well, which was on our property but about a football field away from our house, down a steep grassy hill over a mud path. We'd place a galvanized five-gallon bucket at the end of a long wooden pole that my grandfather had shaped into a hook. We'd lower the pole into the well about ten to fifteen feet down and pull it up slowly, so we didn't lose a lot of water, and then take the bucket off carefully so as not to drop it down into the well. Once that was done, we lugged the water all the way back home.

There was only one thing I hated more and that was when it was my turn to dump the honey bucket. It was bad enough to have to do it in the first place. The idea of having to dump someone else's! That was the epitome of disgusting. My brother and I took turns doing the duty. We would fight every morning about whose turn it was. One day, I decided I wasn't going to fight about it. Not really thinking the scenario through, I picked up the honey bucket and dumped it over his head. What a mess! I immediately suffered the consequence of my actions. Cleaning everything was no fun, to put it mildly, especially given all the water it took and trips to the well! I envied the town of Old Town, just across the river with its running water. They got a water district in 1925. We lived without running water until the late 1960s.

I didn't realize it then, but water wasn't our only problem. The Indian agent was in charge of the allocation of funding and resources for all the Maine tribes. Tribal members suffered if this agent did not like them, and some paid the price of his dislike or disapproval with their lives, freezing to death upon his refusal to issue a voucher for heating fuel or starving when he refused them grocery money. We were always struggling to keep food on the table and to afford wood and oil to keep our house warm. The system purposefully kept the community in poverty, aiming to force the able-bodied and the young off the reservations and into the larger society, so there would be no more tribal governments or communities. No more "Nations within a Nation."

MY GRANDMOTHER WAS a product of the Depression. She kept the old stamps the government issued for rations during WWII. She was always focused on the next meal, often planning for weeks, or even months, ahead. Her pantry was stocked to the hilt with canned goods and government commodity foods. These were delivered on an irregular basis, arriving at the agent's office in big brown cardboard boxes, with goods like rice, flour, peanut butter, cheese, sugar, powdered milk, and canned meat. Most of this food was fatty and full of sodium, contributing to a high rate of diabetes and cancer in our communities. Still, as kids, we were always excited to get the boxes. My favorite item in the box was what we called "That Meat," which lead to my taste for my favorite food: hot dogs.

Back then, another favorite was breakfast. My grandmother made something she called "Cockrobin." I didn't realize until years later that "Cockrobin" was a mixture of flour, salt, and water. My grandmother made it when we had nothing else. Still, I loved it. My aunt Ernestine says that one morning, when I was four or five, she was taking care of me and asked what I wanted on my oatmeal. I said pepper. She made me repeat my answer and asked me why. I said I just liked the taste. She laughed and put pepper in my oatmeal. After I recovered from my choking fit, I realized I had equated pepper with sugar. I never asked for pepper on my oatmeal again.

My brother and I were oblivious about our grandmother's worries. We lived a carefree life as far as food went. We would go outside to play and mostly had a great time. We would come home to eat lunch and go out again.

In summers, we spent many hours exploring the woods, picking blueberries, strawberries, and blackberries. We'd pick the berries just to eat them; they somehow tasted better that way. Sometimes, we managed to bring some home for Gram to make blueberry cake, muffins, or whatever she wanted. She was a really great cook. We were always eager to eat whatever she baked. Her yeast bread was the best, and she would make a dozen loaves and freeze them. No matter what she made, though, my favorite food remained hot dogs. Munching down Grammy's baked beans and hot dogs while listening to the Lone Ranger or one of our other favorite radio shows was my idea of heaven.

I was never what you might call a food connoisseur. I would refuse to eat anything that looked, smelled, or tasted funny or slimy. That left out foods like eel, clams, lobster, deer meat, muskrat, rabbit, and fish. But I did eat all the staples: oatmeal, eggs, bacon, yeast bread, beans, corn, squash, potatoes, and macaroni and cheese. I had a fascination with color in food, and if hot dogs were my favorite food, Red Hots, a red spicy hot dog, were my favorite of the favorites. When given a choice, I always ask for Red Hots, even over filet mignon, lobster, chicken, or seafood. Red Hots were fairly common in Maine until the company moved out of state. They are sold now by a different company. They are not the same. Less tasty and snappy. (Hot dog casings are made from animal intestines and that's what causes the snap.) I prefer my food to not talk back to me. My idea of heaven wouldn't be mansions with streets of gold but a Red-Hot place. No, not that place! A miraculous place with the original Red Hots. I guess it would be Red-Hot Heaven.

FOR THE WINTER
Tanya Whiton

I'VE ALWAYS BEEN hesitant to write about food, because in my family, food was about class. It was aspirational—a signifier. As the only daughter of a career Naval officer, it was considered important for me to know how to assess the quality of things. How else would I grow up to be what I was expected to be: a discerning, gracious hostess? From the age of six, I carted trays of hors d'oeuvres around at cocktail parties, wearing a velvet dress, white tights, and Mary Janes.

"Would you like to try a grapefruit ice?"

Even then, I chafed at the performance.

But food was also—although I didn't understand this until much later—about diplomacy.

A favorite story of my father's was about Queen Victoria's modeling of etiquette: when a visiting dignitary from another country mistook a fingerbowl full of warm water (for cleaning one's fingertips) as a beverage, the queen picked hers up and drank it too.

The upshot of this lesson for me?

I had to eat whatever was put in front of me. No questions, no complaints. Because at some point, I might be having dinner with someone whose customs and cuisine were very different from my own.

Yes. As you might suspect, food, despite—or perhaps because of—the amount of attention it was given in our family, was ultimately about control. To be overweight was not simply a health issue: it meant that you (the officer in charge) did not run a tight ship. From the age of twelve onward, my weight and appearance were the subject of constant, brutal scrutiny.

What food was decidedly not about, for my ambitious baby boomer parents, was necessity.

That was something I had to learn on my own.

AT FIFTEEN, WE moved to a tiny base at the end of a Down East peninsula, thirteen miles from the nearest town. I attended a high school that served five communities, the economies of which depended almost entirely on a luxury food item—lobster. And as the cost per pound fluctuated, so did the fortunes of my classmates.

One year it was new trucks; the next, Tyvek covering gaps in the siding. At school, there was a social hierarchy based on who could afford to bring their own lunch. Nothing in my experience had prepared me for the poverty that I would encounter in the homes of my classmates.

But I still didn't *get* what that poverty meant, in the most elemental terms.

Two encounters changed that.

The first was at the local IGA, where the management allowed customers to run tabs if they were unable to pay. I was standing in line behind an older lady, a pink puffer coat over her winter clothes, when the clerk, a girl only a few years older than me, cut off the woman's tab.

She didn't bother to lower her voice.

"Sorry, you can't have those. You haven't paid up in three months."

And with that, she swept the woman's items off the conveyor into the returns basket. The older lady opened her mouth to speak, closed it, and walked slowly out of the store without saying a word.

The second happened when I picked up a friend on the way to school. I hadn't been to her house before, and when I pulled into the dooryard, I was confronted with an old glass-fronted restaurant cooler filled with moose meat.

It was a horror show: red, gory, dripping blood down the white walls of the interior. More meat than I'd ever seen. I was still gaping when my friend got in the car.

"What in the hell is that?" I asked.

"It's a moose," my friend said.

I forgot, in that moment, the only essential part of my education about food: diplomacy. I continued to stare, appalled.

"You're going to eat that?"

"It's for the winter," my friend said.

For the winter.

The anger and shame I felt—and still feel as I write about those moments—are in part about the privilege in which I was raised. Even having
these emotions seems like a luxury. Food is not an abstraction. It ultimately
isn't *about* anything. It's not about control, or social class, or even love. It's
the most basic necessity next to water, and yet we live in a country, one
of the richest in the world, where 13.7 million people don't have enough
to eat.

I NO LONGER live Down East. I live in Portland, which, when I moved
here, was a funky little backwater, a town with only a few high-end restaurants and a *lot* of bars. Watching the transformation of my beloved city
into a "foodie destination" has been painful. It's not because I don't like
restaurants. I do. I worked in the service industry for twenty years, starting
with a summer job at a fish-fry joint in the town where I went to high
school. That restaurant opened in May and closed in October, because the
people who lived in the community year-round largely could not afford to
go out to eat. It was for summer people, people from away.

What I see in the way people often talk, write, and behave in relation to
food and "foodie" culture reinforces the idea that food, and access to it, is
about class. This behavior also, in a more insidious way, reflects a desire *not*
to see that even here, in Maine's largest and most prosperous city, people
are hungry.

The reason I've never written about food was because my efforts to do
so always seemed, in one way or another, to separate food from what it is:
how we live. That, in her kind, down-to-earth way, is what my high school
friend was trying to tell me.

A BEAR IN A DUMPSTER
Jason Grundstrom-Whitney

I REMEMBER COMING OFF an acid trip and being ravenous. A month earlier, I had tripped and seen the Cosmic Christ in San Mateo through three lit crosses against the night sky.

Back then, I lived with friends, but they pulled out of Frisco for work in Phoenix. I stayed on, intoxicated by the rich tapestry of street musicians, the sound of the Bay Area Rapid Transit as it pulled in to stops, and the various cultures and languages of the city. I listened while on LSD; the drug felt like a wormhole taking my consciousness beyond the confines of metal, steel, broken asphalt, and cardboard dreams.

I soon lost the apartment and was homeless. Some nights, I slept in abandoned buildings, either under construction or about to be torn down. I had nothing to eat and no money. Just the backpack I had used for the last two years of hitchhiking around the United States. I adamantly wanted to be on my own and away from Maine. I was not ready to stop the drugs, despite what they had already cost me. I had been barred from Division I sports, lost a football career because of a broken back, and a girlfriend had passed away.

All this happened during the recession of the early 1980s. No work anywhere. I walked for miles and used false addresses on job applications. And I wasn't the only one. I had never seen so many families with children homeless on the streets.

ON THAT MORNING when I was coming off a trip and feeling so ravenous, I walked into a McDonald's to wash up. My hair was wild. My eyes feral. People watched me as if I had escaped a zoo and animal control had yet to be called. I will never forget those eyes, so damning.

When I left the McDonald's, I was still hungry. Then I smelled fresh bread from a nearby deli. Next to the deli was a dumpster. Having dined several times from the confines of similar metal walls, I climbed in and found day-old bread, softened by the dew from the morning's fog.

I tore into the bread and then found and ate a bruised apple. People walked by as if they did not see me. My long wild hair blew westward as I faced the prayerful sun of the east.

Was I invisible? Had I ever been here, and where was *here*? I couldn't tell if I even existed anymore. The passersby and their non-seeing eyes seemed to confirm my fears.

I let out a bear growl, and a man holding onto a cup of coffee jumped and spilled the liquid over his immaculate black coat.

"What the hell!" he yelled menacingly. His eyes were frightened, but he acted brazen, knowing that steel separated us.

I growled again. Louder this time, and then I snarled. My hair whipped my face as the wind now blew from the northeast. He jumped again and took off, his coffee cup landing on the street.

After another couple of bites, a woman in a fur coat walked by. A tiny dog peeked up from under her collar. The dog started to yip. The woman looked at me and made some derogatory comment about the homeless, addressed to her dog, Pierre.

I growled loudly and she ran away, the dog yipping.

I HAD SEEN people attack those who wore fur coats in the city. They threw red paint. One time, I saw paint land on a little girl who was with her mother trying to find a shelter for the night. The paint fell on the child's head. She looked like a young Carrie. The paint thrower was oblivious and unapologetic. He walked away satisfied, having nearly hit his target.

Before I climbed out of the dumpster, I put some day-old bread into my backpack like the mendicant in *The Way of the Pilgrim*. I had no Jesus Prayer. I only had my prayerful wonder at being alive another day in a world that made no sense.

I EXPERIENCED MANY other nights and lived in many other places where I had nothing to eat. Once, as I hiked alone in the backwoods of Glacier National Park, I survived on a bag of granola for a week. Other times, in inner cities, I had to take a bus several stops to get to a proper market with affordable food. The corner stores were often overpriced and focused their sales on alcohol, tobacco, and sugar, making money off diabetes and addiction.

I HAVE BEEN in recovery for many years now. I am grateful and amazed at the plenitude of food options I have. When I returned to rural Maine, in the mid-1990s, to explore my Passamaquoddy roots, I learned how to garden and offer the excess to the homeless through a local rural community action ministry. I learned to garden with the Three Sisters, as corn, beans, and squash are mutually supportive. However, I never forgot those condemning looks when I ate in dumpsters, so I have chosen to work as both a licensed alcohol drug counselor and an activist on issues like homelessness, sexual and physical abuse, substance use disorders, end-of-life care, mental illness, and Native rights.

Gardening in recovery helped me to feel intimately connected with the Earth again. I would hoe while barefoot, hair tied back in one or two braids as I deftly plucked weeds and watched for infestation in both the garden and my mind. I nurtured, cared for, and caressed the soil, and, in doing so, helped my body expunge toxins and grow in strength. At times, my addiction made "one day at a time" seem interminable, and I had to take it one second at a time. Everything was organic. For many years, I did not use a rototiller, as I wanted nothing gas-operated to touch the sacred soil. Just a strong pitchfork and muscle.

Gardening grew me and helped me to pass a skill on to my children and the brothers and sisters with whom I currently work as a co-occurring specialist at Riverview Psychiatric Center in Augusta. As I grew, I began to see the Cosmic everywhere, in all eyes and all beings. I became clearer about what I needed to work on. As with the changing seasons of the garden, I knew when to prepare, to fortify, to harvest, and then to lay to rest.

No longer a bear in a dumpster.

OPENINGS
Gabriela Acero

GROWING UP I never ate Lunchables or fast food but rather fruit leather and homemade mac & cheese started with a roux. After my parents moved to Maine from New York City, we picked apples in the fall, received an annual drop of fresh blueberries from the barrens in August, made a summer pilgrimage to the coast for lobster, and tapped maple sap on Maine Maple Sunday in March. This was life.

My father came from a restaurant family in Cucuta, Colombia, and he and my mother found a mutual love for cooking and hosting that wove its way into our day-to-day family rhythm. My mother threw Solstice parties on top of the usual holiday events simply because she wanted more excuses to get people together. They were my first mentors in the art of hospitality, and without realizing it, they set me up for a lifetime in the restaurant industry. I still get swept away by the magic of a perfectly executed night of service, a feeling that I remember well from their long-ago dinner parties.

WHEN I GRADUATED FROM COLLEGE, I felt (and still feel) very committed to helping people and working in a field that improves the lives of others. After two years at a national nonprofit, however, sitting at a desk was killing me. I was uninspired and getting bitter. Then I heard about a former classmate who had left her job in health insurance to work as a floor manager at a large restaurant near Washington Square. I was fascinated partly because she did not strike me as someone who would do something so off the beaten path, and partly because I couldn't believe that I hadn't thought of it first. I contacted her, and, within a week, she hired me as a part-time host. A few short months later, I left my nine-to-five job to work full-time as a maître d' at the restaurant, a casual, fast-paced pizza/pasta joint.

The staff was one of the most involved and invested of any restaurant I've ever worked at. Our pre-shift meetings were full of conversations ranging from how to solve a service problem to recent meals at other establishments to strategizing about how to connect our guests with a new wine on our list. The restaurant was a corporate giant, part of a large hospitality group, the leader of whom was later ousted as part of the #MeToo movement. (Italian restaurants, NYC, corporate giant. I'll let you figure it out.) There were many structural problems in the company with regard to equity and worker protection, and one could easily assume it was the type of place where the "customer is always right" mentality prevailed over respect for the staff. However, somewhat magically, this specific restaurant, at least for the time I was there, was a surprisingly progressive, safe, and supportive environment.

I recall a busy evening when our barista, an elderly Bengali gentleman, was delivering coffee to a large table and accidently spilled one of the beverages on a guest. He immediately apologized and notified a manager of the situation, while promptly returning to his station to remake the order as quickly as possible. He did everything as perfectly as he could in light of a mistake that does, unfortunately, sometimes happen. The manager, a Black woman, immediately went to the table to offer a follow-up apology, as well as a card with information to cover any dry-cleaning expenses. The guest replied with something like "Well, that's what you get for hiring people like him." Naturally she was shocked but didn't miss a beat. She quietly told him that that sort of language and opinion was not welcome in our establishment, and, while she was sorry there had been a spill, it did not excuse his comment. Then she presented the check and asked him to leave.

Her decision to ask the guest to leave was not questioned, and there was no disciplinary action or retaliation against her. The general manager had intentionally built a diverse team and, more importantly, created a work culture where members of that team were trusted and encouraged to make decisions they believed were right and good. And then those decisions were supported. It seems like a small thing, but in an industry where one bad Yelp review can ruin a business, it was something special.

Eventually, I wanted to move on to a slower-paced, more hospitality-oriented restaurant and accepted a management position at a small, chef-owned restaurant in Williamsburg. On paper, it was a perfect fit for me. The reality was quite different. There was almost no communication or oversight, until a problem arose, which usually prompted some sort of emotional outburst. I was fired after about six months after our bouncer hit a belligerent customer in self-defense. The bar manager smoothed it over but did not want to tell the owner. I was not on duty that night, but I knew about the incident and agreed to keep it quiet, which, in retrospect, was not the right choice. Unfortunately, when it all came to light, I was the one to take the fall. The bartender had helped open the place and was good friends with the owner. This was the first time I saw how easily favoritism could hold sway in a restaurant setting.

I SPENT THE next several years learning my trade. I worked in fine dining and was part of a seven-person (total!) team that earned a Michelin star within a year of opening. I worked at a raucous wine bar that had one of the best lists in the city, maybe the country. I helped open several projects, some of which were amazing experiences, and some of which I wish I had not been a part of. I learned about pop-ups and event production. I held probably twenty different roles over the next five years. I even cooked a bit! This faux graduate school allowed me to stretch myself and scratch every inquisitive itch I had. But it also opened my eyes to systemic problems within the hospitality industry: psychological abuse, physical violence, sexism, racism, etc. All of these things are inextricably tied to the structural realities of the industry. The restaurant business model lends itself to the perpetuation of these problems. Restaurants are businesses that are only able to function because a third-party (guests/customers) tip makes an evaluation of quality that makes up the income for half the staff. Front-of-house employees (the people who are typically interacting with consumers) don't make minimum wage; the majority of their income does not come from their employer. Meanwhile, back-of-house employees work grueling hours for minimum wage. No one gets healthcare, time off, or benefits. Race, gender, legal status, appearance, and physical ableness all influence hiring and whether employees are able to grow or are kept at the bottom of the barrel slogging in grunt jobs. The longer I worked in the industry, the more I wanted to reimagine the model.

The pandemic made problems in our industry clearer. In early December 2020, I saw an uncomfortably long list on Facebook of all the businesses in New York City that had closed due to the pandemic, a majority of them restaurants and bars. Several were places that I frequented and loved. I had moved to Maine the year before COVID broke out and was selfishly relieved that I was riding out the pandemic in a rural and relatively safe environment. Midway through summer 2020, I got notice that my unemployment was going to run out, and so I panicked and got a job as a server in Portland. Immediately, I was thrown back into the reality of a restaurant just trying to survive. There was no luxury of reimagining the model. It was just nose to the grindstone, pushing the square peg of take-out and "distance dining" into the round hole of a restaurant that was used to having a booked-out dining room every night. It was awful. I tried to present ideas for how to rearrange space to make the flow to the outdoor dining area easier. But suggestions were often met with "Well, we've always done it this way" or "The owner will hate that." Everyone was just exhausted and stressed and didn't have the bandwidth to even attempt to think of different ways of doing things. Of course, when you are just trying to make the machine run, you don't want every little cog to have its own ideas and try to make changes. You just want it to run. But some of the most creative and thoughtful people I know are those cogs.

I left the restaurant after someone tested positive for COVID and then doubled down on my explorations of how to run a restaurant differently. By that time, my partner, a chef, had also left his job. We started seriously discussing how to open our own business, which, shockingly, felt like the best course of action, despite the global pandemic.

I LIKE TO SAY that I've always wanted to own my own restaurant. That goal is sort of what's expected, especially when talking to non-restaurant folk. When I first started working in restaurants, many people were bewildered. They thought it was cool and fun and exciting, saying perhaps I could write a book about the experience or that they were jealous because I got to eat so much free food. Invariably, they eventually asked, "But what are you going to do next?"

Imagine if every doctor was met with "OK, that's great, but when are you going to be director of the hospital?" or every lawyer with "Congratulations, but when are you going to start your own firm?"

And the truth is, I don't know that I ever sincerely wanted to own a restaurant. On a personal level, I have always been uncomfortable with the idea of being tied down or locked in to one thing and one place for the rest of my life. I have also seen so many owners who despite being good people were struggling to make ends meet and thus made choices that hurt their employees. My ego made me think that I could run a business successfully, but I never wanted to be put in that position.

But in a surprising confluence of events, my partner and I were able to buy a building in Camden and begin making plans to open our own restaurant, wolfpeach, a Maine twist on a classic chophouse. As of this writing, I am still shocked it's happening and extremely uncertain how I feel about it. I have no idea if we will be able to pull it off, but we are trying to build a business that aims, in part, to address the myriad of problems we have both witnessed over the years, while simultaneously honoring the deep love we feel for sharing food and drink, for true hospitality. We don't have major financial backers or investors, and we are not expecting huge monetary success. Our goal is to run a stable business that does not have tipping, that pays everyone equally (back and front of house) and provides healthcare, bonuses, and time off. Despite everything negative I have witnessed in the business, I don't know what else I would do. I love turning down the lights, unlocking the door, and diving into a swirling night of service. I don't want to give that up.

I FELL IN LOVE with this industry before I even knew it existed, as a twelve-year-old sitting with my parents and their friends at dinner party after dinner party. That love only deepened over the years as I witnessed how much more restaurants are than simply a place to go eat good food. I have shared intimate moments with complete strangers, making their birthdays and anniversaries special. I've pulled out all the stops for major mergers. And I've even held someone as they cried after their father's funeral, and the place they felt most safe was the restaurant they used to eat together, the restaurant where I worked. This is the magic of restaurants, and it must be protected because it is the most human aspect of the industry. And the only way I see to do that is to change the way the system runs. Perhaps it is idealistic, but if we have learned anything from the last year, it's that broken things must be changed and small joys are what keep us going. So we are diving in full force and cannot wait to welcome you and see if this little experiment works.

PART III

LOVE AND LOSS

PRIZE INSIDE
Debra Spark

T HE GOOD THING about Cracker Jack was the prize. The bad thing? It was the worst-tasting treat in the world: the disgusting oversweetness of the stale popcorn, the way the caramel coating jammed itself between your molars, and the vaguely industrial taste of the peanut. You could like sugar, popcorn, and nuts and still be disappointed. Though there was another virtue beyond the prize, and that was the saying printed on the prize wrapper.

Once, Susan, my best friend in junior high school, found a wrapper that said "Beware of red-headed twins."

I was a red-headed twin.

My twin sister, Laura, thumbtacked the wrapper to the bulletin board in our bedroom. It was funny for us, of course. But objectively, why issue this caution? What was going on with the 1970s-employee tasked with penning Cracker Jack bon mots?

Even if your parents wouldn't pony up for Cracker Jack, if you were a child in the 1960s and 1970s, you were all about sugary breakfast cereals and the box prize. Only here, too, the food was rather disgusting. Who, presented with real candy, would opt for the "marshmallow treat" of Lucky Charms?

Clearly, what the world needed was a genuinely tasty item in which a prize was contained. And that item, though it took till my own late-age motherhood to discover it, is the Kinder Egg.

A foil-wrapped, hollow chocolate, the Kinder Egg is thin-walled enough to hold an often-hard-to-open, yolk-yellow plastic capsule in which a tiny toy, sometimes needing assembly, sometimes not, is encased.

———

I FIRST ENCOUNTERED the Kinder Egg in London, in a down-at-its-heels mini-grocers in Swiss Cottage. I was in the country to do research for a novel, thanks to a two-week stay in an apartment that I had won in a raffle. I seem to have known what the treats were, even before I bought them for my son, Aidan. Perhaps Susan Kenney, the worldly professor-friend with whom I was sharing the apartment, filled me in. She had also advised me to load up. The eggs—their toys considered a choking hazard—were banned in the States.

From then on, the eggs accompanied my son through childhood. Not because I managed to get back to Europe, but because they suddenly became legal in the States. Intermittently, a fancy food store four miles from my home sold them. (Rosemont Market, nota bene, Portlanders.) Every time Aidan and I went in, he demanded one. To my parenting discredit, I always gave in. What would have been a special treat in another family became a routine pleasure. "He wants what he wants when he wants it," my husband and I joked about Aidan, both of us uneasy about discipline, unsure when to force things, and when to let things go, as he bumped into his teenage years.

Eventually, I figured out that the local supply line for Kinder Eggs was not Rosemont but an unusual place in Waldoboro, Maine, called Morse's Sauerkraut. The same professor-friend who'd roomed with me in London let me know about Morse's, surprised I didn't know of it, though how would I know? It's not on the road to anywhere. Instead, if you happen to be travelling along Route 1—the road that tourists take to the coast—you make a left at a bread bakery, then drive seven miles, each mile suggesting you are not headed where you intend, the road entirely rural and residential, mostly mobile homes, older cottages, and split-levels. Plenty of trees and shrubby greenery but none of the tailored flower beds you see in more affluent parts of the state. At just the point when you think, "No, this can't be right," an abandoned barn appears, its red paint peeling, with the word Morse's, white and also peeling, painted on. So, you've come to the right place, only decades too late. But if you look to your left, you see a windowless red-brown building, part wood, part concrete block with a sandy parking lot and a surprising number of cars. A small sign illustrated with dancing sausages announces that this is, indeed, Morse's, a "Euro deli."

The door opens onto two rooms packed with food stuffs, the epony-
mous sauerkraut is on a far wall in a refrigerator case next to a cheese
and sausage counter. Closer at hand: an array of Dutch, Viennese, Swiss,
and German cookies, candies, and other treats. In between are shelves and
refrigerator cases laden with pierogis, Knorr bouillon packets, elderflower
spritzers, exotic spices, fancy mustards, and more. The exterior of the store
is in Waldoboro, Maine; the interior appears to be in Europe. And maybe
not in the twenty-first century.

IF AIDAN AND I had been focused on Kinder Eggs for years, Morse's
proved that there were more things on heaven and earth than dreamt of in
our imaginings. "Oh, Mozartkugl!" I exclaimed on my first visit, immediately seeing a foil-wrapped bonbon with a picture of Mozart on the top.
Had my red-headed twin been visiting Morse's with me, she'd have understood both my fond feeling and desire to weep. The candy—a layer of
pistachio marzipan wrapped around a smooth chocolate paste, the whole
thing robed in chocolate—was first manufactured in Salzburg in 1890. The
sweet was a favorite of our younger sister, Cynthia, who'd discovered them
during a college semester studying abroad, happy months that ironically
exposed her to the winds from Chernobyl. The result? A cancer that ended
her life at twenty-six. Or at least this is my unproven hypothesis. No one
really knows how she ended up getting breast cancer at age twenty-one.

But candy is not supposed to make you cry, so on that first visit, I
pushed further into Morse's to wander past chocolate babkas and boxes
for making rösti. I leaned over to look at some bags piled in a basket and
saw Hopjes.

Hopjes! They were a coffee-flavored sucking candy that I didn't even
like but associated with my paternal grandmother, who doled them out of
her handbag, a purse that also always held half a banana. "For potassium,"
she'd say and offer it up if a child was feeling peaked during an endless
museum visit. Once, at the hostess stand at a fancy restaurant, I had seen
her open her pocketbook and dump the entire contents of a mint bowl
into the interior.

I didn't know that they (whoever "they" were) made Hopjes anymore. I
didn't know, in truth, that the candies were ever available *anywhere* save for
my grandmother's purse. It was as if she'd materialized right there in the
store to give me a nudge and her regular entreaty—how crazy it made me
during my teenage years of incessant dieting—to have something more to

eat. (Fun fact: In 1792, one Baron Hendrik Hop, having accidentally let his sugary, milky coffee evaporate on a heater, asked a confectioner to try to replicate the caramelized result. Hop's doctor had told him to stop drinking coffee, and now he had this alternative addiction.)

At Morse's, in pre-COVID days, small plastic containers with samples dotted the store, offering a tiny cube of cheese or a pretzel for dipping in hot sauce or an olive, sauerkraut being enough of a no-brainer that no forkfuls of the stuff were on offer. After all, the store has been selling it for long enough. Virgil Morse first offered the fermented bounty of his cabbage field to a Waldoboro store in 1910. He didn't have his own establishment—the Kraut Haus—till 1953, when Virgil Jr. built the curious building that still stands. He casted its concrete blocks out of the ground, quite literally, beneath his feet.

I GOT IN ON the "encourage someone else to eat" action one day, when I arranged to meet Rachel Isaacs, a rabbi I particularly admire, at Morse's. She'd been in Maine for several years but never heard of the place, and I liked the idea of indoctrinating her. She is charming, outspoken, and a lot of fun. Not to mention impressive. In 2014, at thirty-one, she was named one of the country's most inspiring rabbis by *The Forward*. Two years later, she went to the Obama White House to deliver the Chanukah invocation, her partner, Melanie, and their baby by her side. By the time we arranged a rendezvous, I'd come to understand Morse's as part of eighteenth-century immigration patterns. The Germans who brought sauerkraut to America also brought settlers to inland Maine, though, in truth, initially, I only knew this from careful study of Morse's website. I came to Maine in 1995 to take a teaching job, and in all the years since, the immigrants I'd most heard mentioned were French-Canadians and Somalis. Also, if you stretch the definition of immigrants: downsizers, retirees, and other adults whose happy memories of childhood summers brought them back to Maine for long-term residence. And no reason to slight *this* varied group's culinary contributions to Maine, which include ployes, tourtière pie, African vegetables, roasted Brussels sprouts, and kale salad.

WHEN I ARRIVE for my visit with Rachel, she's already been at Morse's for a few minutes and is as delighted as I by the plethora of goods on the shelves. I have the idea that I will tell her, at some point, that I once wrote a short story where a woman bites into a Kinder Egg and finds a little rabbi inside. My finest literary moment, as I see it, and I am not really joking. But maybe that would not be something an *actual* rabbi would find amusing.

Walking around the store, Rachel says, "I used to think all this stuff was Jewish, until I realized it was just European." We pass a shelf with boxes of Turkish delight. As a child, I had been fascinated by the treat, simply from reading *The Lion, the Witch and the Wardrobe*. C. S. Lewis made the stuff sound fantastically delicious, only I hated it when I finally tasted it. Rachel laughs, when I relate this, as she'd had the exact same experience with the book and the candy.

Morse's has a tiny restaurant, where various meat products are on offer, not so enticing since I am largely a vegetarian and Rachel is kosher, but we slip into a dark wood booth and make a meal of pierogis and sauerkraut. We talk about this and that: Colby College, where we have both worked; Trump; Israel; our families; her partner's pregnancy; what it was like to go to the White House. I share some worries about my son. Emotionally, I have had a crazy year, though what did I expect? I had a teenager, a (plastic) case I couldn't always pry open.

Was he OK? Or not?

I like the meal with Rachel but probably won't try the restaurant again. It's not the sauerkraut or beet relish that attracts me to Morse's but the candy and specialty foods, which were not part of the original vision for the store but added in 2003 by subsequent owners.

Before Rachel and I leave, I notice some chocolate eggs by the cash register. These are not *actual* Kinder Eggs (which were illegal again on the day of my visit with Rachel) but a rip-off version, produced by a New Jersey company. I feel haughtily dismissive. Profoundly uninterested. The very experience of visiting Morse's has taught me that I do not, in fact, want candy and a toy. I want something hard-to-find with Old World panache. The Kinder Egg and the store are one and the same as my imagination: unremarkable on the outside, magical within.

And then I *do* see a Kinder Egg. There are just two, perhaps leftover from when they were last legal, and I know I should encourage Rachel to take both, since she is the one with young children.

But that's not what I do. I make sure one of those eggs lands in my own basket. My greed does not go unpunished. At least in my imagination: I picture myself making a break for it, hopping into my car, and peeling out of the parking lot. Before long, I hear a siren, see a flashing light in the rearview mirror, and have to pull over.

"What have you got in there?" the policeman asks threateningly, hitting his billy club in his hand. *God, not another red-headed twin on this shift!*

"Nothing," I say, at first, of my contraband.

And then the truth: What do I have in my red Subaru Legacy? A Jewish immigrant to Maine from the wilds of Boston, a late-middle-age writer, a sister and mother, a college professor tilling not cabbages but minds, a purchaser of an illegal Kinder Egg.

The ticket he issues has one word: "Beware."

When I get home, my husband, Aidan, and his girlfriend are all in the kitchen, everyone in a light mood. School is almost out for the year, and, in general, we've all been on the upswing after a difficult winter. I start to unload items . . . an Appenzeller beer, because my husband and I went to Switzerland on our honeymoon; a dandelion and burdock soda, just because it sounds so weird; and amaretti cookies, to which my son is allergic but which I like because I know a trick where you form the wrapper into a column, light it on fire, and watch it rise into the air while still aflame.

And then I present Aidan with the Kinder Egg. It's been years since he's had one, given the ban. He makes a *whoo-hoo, whoo-hoo, whoo-hoo* war cry and takes a victory lap around the house, up the front staircase through the upstairs bedrooms, and down the back staircase, shouting all the while, a performance that is 98 percent camp and largely to show off for his girlfriend.

And here it is . . . the real virtue of the Kinder Egg: how giving it provides its recipient pleasure.

For a Jew, I have some surprisingly Calvinist tendencies. I've always been focused on good habits, responsibility, hard work, and delaying gratification. But against that, I have another inclination borne of seeing lives cut short: *Enjoy it now. Buy the egg. Go after the delicious prize of your child's happiness.*

7-ELEVEN CONVENIENCE
Susan Conley

A T FIRST TONY was a friend in a dive bar on Haight Street who taught me how to throw a dart. This was the winter of 1991, and for the first time in my life, I was going on actual dates with actual humans: a long-haired hippy gardener who left wildflowers on my car windshield, a nerdy bookseller who took me to see stand-up comedy, and a braggy football player who'd been a wide receiver at the University of Southern California and was now a personal trainer. Tony stood in the smoky bar, dart in hand, and told me that my love life was like something you could buy at 7-Eleven.

"Convenient," he smiled while his dart sailed toward the bullseye. "But not quality."

Who *was* this guy? And why did he think he knew anything about me? The little I knew about him was that he was saving money to go back to China, where he'd spent the last year hitchhiking through the northern provinces taking photographs, and that he painted houses in San Francisco for a living. I worked at a cutting-edge women's rights law firm, where I wanted to flip power structures, and where I took phone messages and filed reams of legal forms and felt as removed from the cutting-edge as humanly possible.

There was a 7-Eleven one block from the house that my friends and I rented on Fulton Street. My bedroom cost $300 a month, and my three roommates and I loved this 7-Eleven. One of us went there almost every day for sweet-n-sour shoelace-candy, or condoms, or dinner. The corner 7-Eleven was our supermarket. It sold milk and butter and eggs and packages of macaroni and cheese and Oscar Mayer salami and tubs of ice cream. We were twenty-two and far more interested in cigarettes and sex than in food.

When it was my turn to throw the darts, I missed the bullseye badly. Tony only gloated a little. I knew he was dating a woman who lived two doors down from him on Steiner Street, and this was my counter. "What could be more convenient," I said, "than next-door love?"

After he won, he bought us each a whiskey. "Let's make a bet," he said. "Which one of us can stop going to 7-Eleven first?"

I think I knew that he was flirting with me. Or that at least he was asking me to break up with the gardener, and the bookseller, and the physical trainer, and I didn't really want to do any of these things. I was from a speck of a town in Maine where it had been a thing to meet a new person every couple of years. It felt like my life was finally beginning in California.

"Deal?" Tony said.

"Deal," I said, giddy from the darts and whiskey and Tony.

Weeks went by. One night my three roommates and I ended up at Tony's apartment for dinner—we were waitresses, and assistant social workers, and wannabe paralegals, and we weren't there for the food. We were there for the beers and cigarettes and company. Tony had roommates who played guitar in rock bands and were line-chefs and rock climbers. My friends and I liked to play a game where we'd guess which one of us would sleep with which one of them.

Food mattered to us only fleetingly. Mostly as calories. Sometimes my gardener was at these pop-ups, and sometimes my physical trainer. Sometimes Tony's on-again off-again girlfriend. But on this night, none of them had made it, and the United States had just invaded Iraq. We crowded around Tony's little kitchen, all planning to skip work the next day and protest in the streets. He stood with his back to us at a four-burner gas stove, cooking noodles. He had a little pile of chopped onion on a cutting board, and a smaller pile of garlic, and he slid it all into this enormous, cast-iron wok where it sizzled. Then he took the cleaver and sliced some ginger fingers paper-thin and put them in, too, with chili paste and splashes of rice vinegar and soy.

No one ever cooked for me then. No one ever cooked back then, period. It was all about 7-Eleven. My friends smoked and drank, while I kept watching Tony at that grease-splattered stove. The noodles went in last—a long egg noodle that he got fresh from a Chinese market downtown. The heat looked too high to me. The wok crackled and hissed. But Tony calmly turned the noodles over and over with a giant wooden spoon, flat on top like a paddle. He wore a blue T-shirt with a picture of the solar system. A big arrow next to planet Earth read "YOU ARE HERE." I thought it was the greatest T-shirt ever.

I was falling in love, though I didn't see it yet. My roommates poured more wine and flirted, while I fixated on the noodles, which were really about Tony and how patient he was, cooking them; how he seemed to want to feed us, without us even asking him to. He doesn't remember any of this now, twenty-five years into our marriage—how I gushed about the lo mein when he doled it out on the paper plates. The noodles had a perfect chewiness, and you could taste the egg and flour if you thought about it. But you didn't, because the noodles were just the delivery system for the flavor punch of ginger and garlic in the paste of chili and soy. The food didn't transport me as much as ground me in that dirty, fabulous kitchen, which now smelled like some idea of home.

Later after dinner, he showed me a stack of black-and-white photos he'd taken in China that had just been accepted by a downtown gallery. He vaguely remembers this part. How my eyes kept going to the photo of two women selling Hami melons by the side of the road. And how, at the end of the night, Tony gave me the photo. I have no memory of why; I just know I wanted it, and that he somehow intuited this, and that it changed my life. I tacked the photo next to my mattress on the floor at our house on Fulton Street and stared at it before I went to sleep. It showed a vastly different world than the one where I pretended to understand how to write good deposition questions or fooled myself that I loved the gardener, or the bookseller, or the physical trainer, or that they loved me.

It's a long plane ride to China, and then a much, much longer truck ride to Yunnan, where Tony had hitchhiked to take the photo of the women selling the melons. It's easy now to see that he was not fazed by inconvenience. I will go further and say that Tony never liked 7-Eleven. At least not for dinner. And that he won the bet we'd waged at the dive bar.

Not long after he broke up with his girlfriend, my roommates and I had a dance party. When Tony got there, I took him upstairs to my bedroom to see where I'd put his photo. But when we got to my bedroom, it felt like a bad set-up—show the man who you think you love that you've hung his photo right next to your bed. But I had. And I did. I know now that

I was trying to prove to him that the photo really moved me. And that I was capable of being moved. That I was about more than 7-Eleven food or convenient love.

"We should get out of here," I told him and led him back downstairs. When we got to the front door, I asked if he was leaving, and before he could answer, I kissed him goodbye on his cheek.

"No," he said. "I'm not leaving." And kissed me back on the lips.

LEARNING TO EAT
Genevieve Morgan

FOOD HAS NEVER been my friend. To clarify, I like food, and there are certain items I love (tangerines, chocolate pots de crème, tomato and mozzarella salad, peanut butter on saltines), but I am notoriously nonchalant about the act of feeding myself. This may be my WASP heritage exerting its preference for martinis and cheese and crackers for dinner. Or it could be that when I was growing up in Manhattan in the late '80s—as the daughter of a skinny ex-model mother and as a "lifer" student at an all-girls' school—eating felt like a hostile act, something to gird oneself against and engage in only when desperate. No adult was doing any regular shopping or cooking in my house. Why would they when the goal was to stay effortlessly thin and attractive? The fridge stayed bare except for a tub of margarine (excellent on rice cakes), some milk, eggs, and butter, and a few bottles of wine. I drank a lot of Diet Coke, ate handfuls of No-Doz, licked the top (only) of yogurt containers, neurotically counted numbers in my head, and organized the clothes in my closet by color to keep my mind off being hungry.

My sparse diet was a choice, not fate, and looking back, this seems the height of privilege, but at the time it was my norm. I really didn't know anything else. Halfway through high school, most of my friends and I had succumbed to some combination of mild anorexia or bulimia. Later on, we found Marlboro Lights, the Scarsdale diet, and the Jane Fonda workout tape. Those were heady, low-blood-sugar days, and—surprisingly—most of us recovered by graduation thanks to discovering romance, sex, Danceteria, and Scorpion bowls at restaurants that didn't ask for IDs. On weekends, my friends and I would stay out until 2:00 a.m., then descend on an all-night diner to feast on pancakes and scrambled eggs with chopped ham to sop up the booze before crashing.

By college, I was eating more regularly. I had a full-meal plan, Domino's delivery, and a boyfriend who actually loved me (and my body), so I packed on the full freshman fifteen. (I assume. I had stopped weighing myself by then.) My new fleshiness became apparent to me only when I tried to put on my "city" Fiorucci jeans to travel back to New York for winter break. I pulled the waist up over my hips okay, but when I tried to button the top button, it popped off and flew around the room, ricocheting off of my roommate's Billy Idol poster. Strangely for me, given my prejudice against fat, I didn't care. I was happy. I was in love. And I liked hanging out at the cafeteria with my friends. I can't say I noticed the taste or freshness (or lack thereof) of the cafeteria food, but I do remember meals as happy experiences, finally—moments in the day to laugh and bond. Food was the portal to joy, a social lubricant, and I didn't really care what I put in my mouth as long as I was sharing it with my friends.

That all changed the summer I drove to California with my boyfriend. He grew up in Marin County, and until I crossed the Golden Gate, I had never seen produce like the fruits and vegetables they grew there. I went to one of the original Whole Foods in Noe Valley and was dazzled—as in, struck agog—by the pyramids and colors of huge lemons, mangoes, and melons. The rows of crisp misty greens and moons of rutabagas and turnips that seemed to be an altogether different species than the limp iceberg lettuce and anemic celery stalks we used to buy at Gristedes in New York. San Francisco in the early 1990s was a world where food and its presentation were works of art. We take it for granted now, because beautiful food and delicious restaurants are seemingly ubiquitous, but back then the Bay Area was a pioneer. And I hitched myself fully to that chuck wagon, embracing Californication.

I began to meditate and do yoga. I learned more about seasonal vegetables. I took a rigid moral stance against eating animals. In those days, it was called "eating macrobiotic." I can't say I was fully vegan, but I was vegetarian for several years, until I started dating the man who would become my husband. He came from cattle people and full-on carnivores. As our feelings for one another deepened, I had to make an uneasy truce between mating and morality. (Bacon helped.) Looking back, I see now that my strict vegetarian stance was another way to freakishly control my food intake—much healthier than my Manhattan days, but still, food had not yet become my friend. It had evolved into a taskmaster, requiring me to monitor its origin and purity before consuming it. I was way ahead of my time in this respect, demanding organic this and locally grown that.

By the time I had children, I was working in publishing and editing cookbooks. My years as a Californian had instructed me on the health properties of proper nutrition. I had morphed from vegetarianism to a whole food diet and viewed food largely as fuel. Again, I was impartial to flavor or feel—I just wanted it as clean and power-packed as possible. It had grown in importance and regularity in my life, but not in enjoyment. Instead, I made it a functional partner, helping my children grow healthy skin and bones, resist disease, and marshal brain power. I insisted on a lot of healthy fats (arguing with the pediatrician who, at the time, wanted me to serve my kids skim or 2 percent milk) and big protein-filled breakfasts. I was sure to make the kids eat a Brazil nut or two (surely the most repulsive nut to a kid that there can be) to add zinc to their diets. I packed balanced home lunches and restricted soda and junk food in a way that would have been completely alien to me as a kid but felt motherly and right. I monitored my nuttiness. I didn't want my kids to feel detached from eating in the way I did. I knew by then that food could be a source of real inspiration and joy to people, as well as fundamental nutrition.

I just didn't feel it myself.

About ten years ago, after a routine physical to obtain life insurance, I was given a surprise diagnosis of a genetic illness that eventually causes kidney failure, called PKD (polycystic kidney disease). One of the side effects of decreasing kidney function is nausea and GI distress due to increased toxins that build up in the blood stream. Kidneys remove impurities from the blood, so when your kidneys aren't working, your blood runs dirty, like gas in an engine with a bad carburetor. This makes food taste funny, and you just feel really, really sick. All the time. Moreover, PKD causes the kidneys to grow. Some can get bigger than a football. Over time, mine became large enough to push against my other organs, including my stomach. I found myself unable to eat more than a few bites at meals before feeling awful, like I had a vicious hangover. The irony of my situation was not lost on me. After a lifetime of trying to avoid eating, I was now in the position of being physically unable to do so. One of the symptoms of advanced kidney disease is—wait for it—anorexia. I had come full circle. By the time I was in end-stage kidney failure, even the smell of food sickened me, and

I was reduced to eating a tangerine section or two and ginger snaps or the occasional bowl of Thai coconut soup and rice. My body had finally given up on food, as I had wanted it to do for so many years—the only problem was, it was also giving up on life.

Then, God or fate or the universe or karma and the Western medical system intervened, and I received a kidney transplant that saved me. It may seem improbable, but I was actually in a restaurant when my phone began to ring off the hook. I silenced it. I was meeting an old college friend and our advisor, who lived in Maine. I watched them eat mussels and grilled swordfish at a restaurant called Scales, on the Portland waterfront, and we talked, but my phone would not stop buzzing. Finally, I picked up. It was, as they say in transplant world, "the call." A nineteen-year-old from Florida had died and he or she (I still don't know) was what they call the incredibly rare "no-fault" match; in other words: perfect for me. I had only been on the transplant list for a year—most folks have to wait many more before they find a match—and here, before me was, literally, the opportunity of a lifetime. A miracle.

It has been two years since that night, and since then I have been slowly coming back to life and learning to live with my new, turbo-charged young kidney. It took several months, but little by little, I began to feel hungry again. At first, I could only eat cold, dry, salty stuff. Crackers and celery with salt. Then I wanted fruit. And then cucumbers. And then, strangely, meat. A lot of meat. This craving corresponded with a month-long binge session of Scandinavian thrillers, Spanish melodramas, and French spy shows. Some say transplant recipients take on aspects of their donor, so I speculate that mine loved salty meat, mysteries, and spoke another language fluently. And, possibly, based on my newfound distraction by food, to cook. Within a year, I found myself thinking about my next meal with anticipation and—dare I say—gusto. I began to read cookbooks, to plan meals that I would gleefully shop for and cook. My closest people, long used to feeding me, were happily surprised to get dinner invitations. Because my new kidney was taking out the garbage, I felt clear and well after I ate, and my palate branched out. I craved chili sauce and lemon pickle relish. I wanted hot dogs with sauerkraut and fish chowder and red and yellow bell pepper slices. I stopped thinking about food as a "have to" and dove into it for its flavor, its texture, its seasoning, and the way it makes me feel—warm and energetic and content.

Admittedly, I'm sort of a hybrid person now, my DNA metaphorically mingled with my donor's, and something elemental has shifted with my resurrection. Today, along with my deep gratitude for the person who saved my life, I am grateful for the bounty of food available to me, lucky as I am. It took losing the ability to eat for me to recognize and rejoice in the availability of food: its power, its medicine, its joy, its sociability, its necessity, its blessing, and its vitality—indeed, its life-sustaining properties. I know what it feels like to be set *unwillingly* on the outside of food's conviviality and nourishment, and I have been given an opportunity to re-learn how to eat. This time, I am doing it fully and with the greatest of appreciation and some extra, happy pounds.

It took me decades to see the real face of the enemy, and it is not eating; it's starving.

LAST SUPPER
Maureen Stanton

M Y FATHER DIED not long after his eightieth birthday, after a rough
year of declining health from melanoma, which had spread from
a tiny spot on his knee—overlooked by the dermatologist he saw every
three months—to his lymph glands, and then over the next four years to
various parts of his body. He underwent several courses of radiation and
then infusions of an immunotherapy drug, ipilimumab, whose name seems
out of Lewis Carroll's "Jabberwocky," to no avail. On a Saturday in May,
from a hospital bed in his living room, which we'd positioned so he could
glimpse the ocean in the distance out his picture window, he exhaled his
final breath.

In the weeks following his death, which was over Memorial Day weekend, I found myself craving hot dogs. Whenever I was in town for errands,
I looked for hot-dog stands or food trucks, which seemed more promising
than Dairy Queen, which was where I ate the first hot dog in an attempt
to satisfy my craving. Steamed and then reheated in a microwave, the DQ
dog was far removed from the platonically perfect version in my imagination—grilled in bacon fat till the skin bubbled, nestled in a buttered and
toasted top-split roll, and slathered with mustard. Plain and simple: no chili,
no onions, no ketchup, no relish beyond my eating of it.

I'M NOT A regular eater of hot dogs, mainly for health reasons, though
I usually have one or two during the annual summer vacation with my
siblings and their kids. Then we grill out every night, and my meat intake
quadruples from normal life. I'm well below average on the bell curve
of hot-dog consumption by Americans, who eat some twenty billion an-
nually or fifty million daily (triple on July 4th), which is about seventy

frankfurters person per year: a wiener and a half for each of us every week. This calculation assumes that everyone is eating the same number of hot dogs, but I suspect the 80–20 rule applies, in which 20 percent of people eat 80 percent of the hot dogs, people like Joey "Jaws" Chestnut, the current record holder in Nathan's Famous annual hot-dog eating contest, who in 2020 downed seventy-five franks and buns in ten minutes. Joey is skewing the stats.

But there was a time when I ate a lot of hot dogs. At fourteen, I got my "working papers," a glorified permission slip from my mother, and was hired at Schaefer Stadium in Foxboro, Massachusetts, then home field of the New England Patriots. I worked in the concession stands, which I recall had an extremely limited menu: hot dogs, pretzels, bags of chips, and Schaefer beer. I was not old enough to pour beer, so my job was filling hot-dog orders. The concession traffic was steady pre-game, then a mad rush at half-time—lines twenty-people deep and eight across, orders of six or eight or ten dogs—and then stragglers until the game ended. I roasted the franks on a hot-dog roller, a grill with eight or so horizontal stainless-steel tubes that rotated. I'd line the valleys between the tubes with thirty to forty hot dogs, then watch them slowly brown. My pay was $2.10 an hour, noted in my diary of 1974, plus tips and all the hot dogs I could eat, which was usually six per game, about one hot dog an hour, a far slower intake than Joey Chestnut's but still an impressive gastronomic feat for a fourteen-year-old girl.

I developed a ritual for cooking my hot dogs during the lag times. I'd place a fresh hot dog on the grill, then watch it rotate, a calming almost hypnotic meditation, waiting for the first sizzle and spit of fat, for the skin to burst. When the hot dog split right down the middle, I'd fill the seam with mustard and nest it in the softest bun from the steam drawer.

MY FATHER, TOO, had a hot-dog-related job once, at the Boston Sausage Factory in the North End. He was nineteen but said he was twenty-one to get the job; he was working his way through college. My father was a great storyteller, a raconteur. When I drove him into Boston for medical appointments, he'd point to something in the landscape that triggered a memory. I learned more about my father's childhood during those drives than in the fifty-four years I'd known him. "What an interesting little world inside that building," he'd said of his job at Boston Sausage, though the factory was long gone, closed in the 1970s. "There was Old Harry," who made a trip to the blood bank weekly to sell a pint of blood, his money spent at the next lunch break on a different pint. Harry and a few others stuffed hot dogs and sausages in their socks or wound a string of them around their waists and walked out of the factory. "Willie James, the new England heavyweight boxing champion, was in charge of the ham kettle," my father said.

My father's job was most often on the cold-cut line. "Basically, I had to chop the end off a roll of bologna or other meat, and feed it through a slicing machine, which ejected eight piles onto a conveyor belt." The piles were then packaged by workers at the end of the line. The four belts were overseen by several women in their twenties—all of whom my father developed a crush on, he confessed. The women teased my nineteen-year-old father, embarrassing him with their risqué humor. "That entire operation—grabbing the butcher knife, slicing off the end of the bologna, peeling the skin off the roll of meat, and feeding the machines lead to a lot of double entendres," my father said. "'Oh Patrick, my machine is empty!'"

Sometimes his job was to watch a conveyor belt loaded with skinless frankfurters, plucking off any misfit dogs bearing remnants of skin. Hot dogs and rolls of cold cuts were cooked and poured into elastic stockings and hung to dry in a cold-storage room. On lunch breaks, my father and his coworkers played stickball in the cold-storage room, using a broom and a bologna end for the ball. "We had to scramble sometimes when the meat inspector showed up," he said. At the end of his shift, he rode the subway home, reeking of bologna and smoke. The scraps from the slicing machine were piled up and then shoveled into a furnace. "I couldn't eat bologna or hot dogs for years after that job."

The only upside of my father's illness was that I spent more time with him, on the drives to and from medical treatments in Boston, and at restaurants afterward. My father was hypoglycemic, so he had to eat every two hours to maintain his blood sugar. When I traveled with him in Ireland for a week in the mid-1980s, the final leg of my post-college backpacking trip, and the last time I'd spent significant time with him, also in a car, we'd had to stop frequently to find a snack, most often a toasted cheese sandwich at a pub somewhere along a winding country road. Once, we bought a rotisserie chicken at a grocery store and drove around looking for a scenic picnic spot. It's not difficult to find a lovely vista in Ireland, but somehow we failed, and since my father was growing weak and nauseated, I pulled over as soon as I found a safe place. Turns out, we picnicked on greasy chicken in the parking lot of a hospital.

At the post-appointment dinners, my father would order whatever he wanted—appetizer, entrée, a glass of wine, and then dessert and coffee—the tables turned now since I was paying. For much of my adult life, my father always treated when we dined out. I worked for nonprofits for a decade and a half and then spent another decade as a freelance writer. I never had much money. After my father's second divorce, in his seventies, which was contentious thus expensive, and the economic collapse in 2008, he was worried he'd outlive what was left of his retirement. In the last two years of his life, he lived on little more than his Social Security check, just enough to cover his bills. He'd forfeited his monthly luncheon with some old friends and had even canceled his beloved *Boston Globe* subscription. The elderly ladies in his condominium complex passed their newspapers to him when they were done. For my father, dining out was a treat, and it was a treat for me to watch him enjoying his meal.

The spring of 2014 was the culmination of eight stressful months of my father's declining health and increasing need for care. Since my father lived alone, twice a week I'd drive to his condominium in Gloucester to take care of him, cooking, cleaning, paying his bills, arranging appointments, driving him into Boston for radiation or check-ups, sleeping over at his place when it was clear he could not be on his own but never actually sleeping on his lumpy couch in the too-hot, too-bright living room. I'd wake from my tortured dozing at every rustling from his bedroom, worried he'd get up to use the bathroom and fall. One night, I found him entangled in the safety railing alongside his bed, one leg caught in the lower bar of the rail, the other leg in the top bar, his head hanging off the end of the mattress. It was one of those absurd moments when I wanted to laugh and cry at the same time.

In the final two weeks, the hospice nurse doubled my father's drug regimen; he'd become agitated, clawing at the air, semi-conscious and mumbling about a business meeting—he was back at his job as a systems analyst, work he'd loved. Once, after a doctor visit, stuck at red lights in downtown Boston, he enthusiastically explained "queueing theory" to me—the mathematical study of queues, or waiting in line.

We'd arranged for nurse's aides to cover Memorial Day weekend, so I drove home to Maine on Thursday night. But I had a nagging thought—*What if he died with only a home health aide by his side?* The next morning, Friday, I drove back to my father's place. He'd been asleep all day, but woke briefly at dinnertime, smiling when he saw me standing by his bed. "Mosey," he said, his nickname for me as a child.

The following morning, Saturday, he was due for a dose of painkillers at ten, but I held off. I wanted him to regain consciousness so that my brother Patrick and my sister Sally, both traveling from Maine, could say goodbye. Around noon, my father began to stir. I worried that I'd done the wrong thing in skipping the dose, that he'd become distressed or would try to climb out of bed, so I gave him the painkillers two hours late. My sister and brother showed up shortly after, and within minutes my father's breathing became erratic, the heaving, halting Cheyne-Stokes respiration pattern that signals impending death.

THE DAY AFTER my father died, my sister Sue and I were looking at burial plots in Gloucester. (Ever the procrastinator, my father hadn't finished his end-of-life plans; he didn't want his life to end, so he didn't plan.) Sue pulled into a Dunkin' Donuts to use the bathroom. In Massachusetts, there's a Dunkin' Donuts on every corner—351 in the state and six in Gloucester, where my father lived. As with hot dogs, I rarely eat donuts. They aren't worth the calories, but while my sister was in the Dunkin' Donuts' bathroom, I had a sudden yen for a glazed cruller, so I walked into the store and bought one. When Sue came out, she asked what I bought, and I said, "I had a strange urge for a cruller."

"Oh my God," she said. "Dad loved crullers." Before visiting my father, Sue would always stop at the Dunkin' Donuts on his block and buy him a cruller. After Sue told me about my father's love for crullers, we bought a few dozen to share with mourners at the cemetery. My little nephews, Sam and Ben, tossed bits of cruller into the grave, a snack for my father in heaven, they believed.

Back in Maine after the services, I launched into the complicated task of executing my father's meager but disorganized estate. I was exhausted from the months of caring for him, so I hadn't processed the loss. I didn't cry at his funeral, or the burial, or the luncheon afterward, or in the weeks following his death.

I didn't connect my desire for a hot dog with my father's death until I was eating my fifth frank at Schutty's, a food truck in Bath, where the setting—across from a gas station and adjacent to a used-car lot—belies the quality of the food. Usually, I went to Schutty's for fish tacos with Asian slaw or blackened-haddock burritos or fish and chips, but I'd never thought of ordering a hot dog there. At Schutty's, though, I found the hot dog that finally satisfied my yearning, the hot dog of my dreams: fried in grease, on a butter-toasted bun, with a generous squirt of bright yellow mustard.

As I was eating, it came to me why I'd been craving hot dogs. Two days before my father died, my brother Mike and his sons, Sam and Ben, who were six and four, had visited to say goodbye. The hospice aide kept shushing us, insisting that my father needed quiet, though I imagined that even in his deep opiated slumber, he would have enjoyed his grandsons' laughter and squeals. I took the boys into the hallway and gave them wheelchair rides, persnickety neighbors be damned. We decided to go to Tony's for lunch, to let my father rest, to let the nurse's aide wash him. Tony's, an Italian restaurant, was a block away, so my father was a regular there, so familiar to Tony that one day he noticed my father looking gravely ill, his skin ashen, and he suggested that my father go to the hospital. My father had been having a silent heart attack, and Tony's advice had saved him.

In his last week, my father hadn't eaten much, a bite of this or that. His mouth was so dry, probably from the cocktail of drugs. To hydrate him, we held a "lollipop" to his lips—a sponge on a stick, soaked in water. But that afternoon I'd asked my father anyway, "Do you want us to bring you something from Tony's?"

"A hot dog," he'd said.

Tony's menu had fifty or sixty choices. You could get just about any combination of anything—hot or cold subs, roast beef, turkey, pastrami, capicola, burgers, slabs of lasagna oozing cheese, homemade meatballs, eggplant parmigiana, pizza slices, chicken and fish (grilled or baked or broiled or fried), egg salad and tuna, even peanut butter and jelly. But no hot dogs.

My father hadn't asked for anything else that afternoon, so we didn't bring him a substitute, and he was asleep when we returned. He never got his final wish, the last thing in his life that he'd requested. A hot dog would have been his last meal, as he ate nothing after that day. I choked up remembering this; it was hard to swallow the hot dog, but in Schutty's parking lot, in the privacy of my car, I cried, finally, for the loss of my father.

I wonder why my father wanted a hot dog that day. I'd never known him to eat franks, nor did we find any in his freezer when we cleaned it out after he died. Aside from a sweet tooth for cookies, and apparently crullers, my father was health-conscious. He subscribed to *Nutrition Action News* and had lists of healthy foods pinned to a bulletin board in his kitchen. I'm sure he ate hot dogs at the places and events where hot dogs belong—football games, baseball games, cookouts. Maybe in my father's dream state, in that liminal space of being alive but on the cusp of death, he was screening the film of his life, his job at Boston Sausage Factory, or maybe he was reliving a Red Sox game, eating a Fenway Frank. Maybe he'd ordered a hot dog because it would be easy to eat. By then my father's hands were shaky from weakness, dehydration, and pain medication. Watching him trying to maneuver a forkful of food was heartbreaking, missing his mouth, food falling off the fork, his hand-eye coordination off.

As Memorial Day approaches each year, I still get a powerful craving for a hot dog, even now six years after my father's death. Perhaps my father is reaching out to me from the spirit world with his forever-unfulfilled lunch order. Or maybe my annual hankering for a hot dog is simply because I've made a habit of eating one in honor of my father, to memorialize him on Memorial Day, to enjoy on his behalf this small simple pleasure, nothing fancy, but something good.

DON'T FLIP THE PLOYES
Kevin St. Jarre

I HAD PLANS TO write an essay about ployes, an Acadian staple food, but I kept procrastinating. However, on the morning that I typed these first words, the woman who made ployes for me, and taught me how to prepare them for myself, died. It seemed a fitting day to finally start.

Ployes are neither pancakes nor crepes, but something in between. Thinner than the former, but more bready than the latter, they have a unique flavor and have been eaten by Acadians for centuries, or so it seems. They are a fantastic poverty food; many bellies can be filled for very little money with ployes.

I grew up in Madawaska, Maine, which was founded by Acadians, and our community clung to these cultural comfort foods long after we could afford something fancier. The recipe is incredibly simple, and the ingredients have always been readily available: buckwheat flour, all-purpose flour, baking powder, water, and a bit of salt.

Still, even with so few components, there are disagreements. I will stand with my mother when it comes to ployes. Everything she did was exactly right, and anyone who deviates from her method is sadly mistaken. You do not, as some claim, stir boiling hot water into the batter. The water must be frigid when added, not hot.

If you'd like to use a pre-made mix, Fort Kent's Bouchard Family Farms sells a tasty one. They transported, then rebuilt, a New Brunswick buckwheat mill to produce the mix's key ingredient. Simply labelled "Ployes," the product can often be found in local grocers or online. My mom would add a bit of salt to each batch, but she gave it two thumbs up, so clearly, it's legitimate.

Once mixed, you let the batter sit. It thickens and bubbles form, since baking powder is basically baking soda and cream of tartar, which when wet have a reaction not unlike soda and vinegar, though less vigorous.

Once the bubbles form, you gently stir and often add more cold water, because every recipe understates how much water one actually needs. I suspect this is to prevent outsiders from ever learning to cook them correctly. My mother used to say of the batter's consistency, "When it looks like paint, lá, like you would use on your house, it's good." It's perhaps the only recipe in the world for which the secret ingredient is water.

You then heat up the pan, and here's the next big controversy. Old timers will tell you that in order to cook ployes correctly, they must be cooked on an old, seasoned cast-iron pan, handed down for generations. As Mom would say, "Wayons, just use any pan."

This makes scientific sense, as long as the pan heats evenly, and while this was once an issue, today's $20 nonstick pan heats as evenly as any cast-iron pan. So, another win for my mother.

Once it is hot—and test this by dripping a bit of water on the surface to make sure it sizzles and dances before disappearing—add a ladle of ploye mix to the dry pan. Only a cheater would use butter or oil when making ployes.

Here comes the best-known secret of cooking these things . . . don't flip a ploye. Ever. You cook them on one side only. Bubbles will form, pop, and leave holes. These are critical for later. I say again, do not flip the ploye; one simply watches as the surface of the ploye changes from wet to dry.

Take this time to pull down a dinner plate and place a dishtowel on it. The towel should have half of its length on the plate, the other half on the counter top. When you pull the first ploye out of the pan, put it bubbles-side-down on the plate, and cover it with the remaining towel. The first ploye is never quite right. Don't be afraid to simply discard it; for me, this first ploye is to be split and shared with the dogs.

So you continue cooking ployes, and stacking them on the plate, until the batter runs out. You then serve the covered ployes in the middle of the supper table within everyone's reach.

Ah yes, supper. I forgot to mention something. Hipsters and marketing departments have suggested for the last few years that ployes might be eaten for breakfast, and of course this is true, but you must keep a few key items in mind. First, while they can be eaten for breakfast, they should not be cooked for breakfast. Morning ployes are leftovers from supper.

Next, the spreads used at the supper table are the only spreads appropriate for a ploye, regardless of the time of day, and we'll get to that whole topic in a minute. Just because it is morning does not mean that we should be applying grape jam or powdered sugar to our ployes. I sometimes eat leftover shepherd's pie (more correctly called pâté chinois, but that's a different essay) for breakfast, and you will not see me applying a layer of fruit jelly and powdered sugar to that. It's the same idea.

My mother loved cretons, as do I, and as does every true Acadian descendant. Cretons is a seasoned pork spread, made of the choice cuts of meat, not the undesirable scraps. It is made with garlic and onions, and is seasoned with a variety of spices including cloves, allspice, cinnamon, salt, and pepper. It takes hours to cook correctly and is served cold, as chilling is part of the preparation. It freezes wonderfully.

In some surrounding St. John Valley towns, which are a bit more distant from the Acadian center of Madawaska, they serve this delicious pork spread, but a visitor might hear it mispronounced as "cortons" or "gortons." Madawaskans, like Mom, are to be considered the guides here. The correct spelling is "cretons," the correct pronunciation is something like "kreh-toh," with the "n" serving to nasalize the "o" without being pronounced itself.

If someone tells you cretons is a Québécois food, walk away. This person is clearly not a source to be trusted. While the Quebecois eat our cretons, they mostly spread it on toast, which isn't bad if you don't have leftover ployes, but it's not how it's meant to be eaten. I mean, keep in mind it was the Quebecois who got people referring to French fries served with gravy and cheese curds as "poutine," which actually is a potato dumpling stuffed with pork. Ask any Acadian. The fries and gravy and cheese recipe is more correctly referred to as a "mix."

Cold cretons spread on a hot ploye is a dream. Folding the ploye in half is acceptable, but a bit odd. A ploye folded twice, into a triangle, is the sign of a ploye-eating expert, like my mother. A rolled ploye is the sign of a visitor from out of town, but don't say anything. If you've an outsider at the table who is willing to try cretons, let them do it any way they like.

The only other acceptable spread for ployes is butter. That's it. You can dip your appropriately folded ploye into certain side dishes, however. The most common year-round option is baked beans, preferably with a bit of real maple syrup splashed on.

At Christmas time, or in certain well-loved local restaurants, you'll often find ployes served with a thick, white chicken stew. It's usually chicken, potatoes, and dumplings. More recently, daring people added carrots, but I prefer the classic stew. When I was a kid, I used to love searching through the opaque broth for the chicken hearts my mother put in there.

The absolute best way to eat ployes is to climb off a snowmobile, half-frozen, walk into a warm house, sit with many loved ones, and dig one out from under a towel. Even better when everyone had two-stroke engines in their sleds, so the gasoline-oil smell hung in the air while you spread the cretons, but we have to let go of some things. As for me, I'm holding on to the memories of ployes, cretons, and my mother, Cecile.

WHAT'S HANDED DOWN
Gibson Fay-LeBlanc

M Y MOTHER LOVED a good farm stand and preached the gospel of fresh fruits and vegetables her whole life, and often made her casserole with fresh green beans. As a girl and young woman, she was steered by her parents and mentors toward an *appropriate* aspiration as a future mother and housewife but was also trained as a French teacher in New York and Paris in the mid-'60s. In those days, she had a Jackie Kennedy bob and was the homecoming queen at my father's college. But by the time I turned ten, she'd earned her real estate license, because her husband was an alcoholic who couldn't support our family. My mom was a smiling, lemons-into-lemonade kind of lady.

My parents' marriage didn't last to my teenage years. Green-bean casserole was a staple, though, through all the holiday seasons, with and without my father.

Green-bean casserole is not and never has been the height of culinary fashion. It's corporate comfort food. The recipe was created during the 1950s in the test kitchen of the Campbell Soup Company by a team of "home economists" led by Dorcas Reilly. Reilly was looking for a simple recipe that could be made with ingredients that families might have on hand: canned or frozen green beans, cream of mushroom soup, soy sauce, milk, pepper, and canned fried onions. All processed foods, not local. It was created in a culture focused on convenience and looking to sell more soup by helping out women increasingly likely to have professional careers on top of raising their children, like my mom.

The casserole became a particular favorite for my family on Christmas because of my older brother Leland. He was born a few hours after midnight on Christmas morning in 1970—my mom and dad had been upstairs at a Christmas Eve party in the apartment building where we lived on the North Side of Chicago when my mother realized that she needed to go to the hospital. As a kid, having your birthday on Christmas is the worst—no matter how much my mom tried to make Christmas both a family holiday and my brother's special day, it was always mostly Christmas with a few extra presents for Lee. But my brother chose the menu for most of our Christmases, and green-bean casserole was usually on it.

My brother did not live to see his fiftieth Christmas. Last April, the rollercoaster that was Lee's stage-IV melanoma, which had begun with a spot on his scalp that his doctor didn't think was anything, turned downward again. A line from a Gerard Manley Hopkins poem I love comes to mind: *cliffs of fall / Frightful, sheer, no-man-fathomed.* After years of experimental treatments, after special diets and setting a record for the most Gamma Knife radiation, after five surgeries including on his brain, Lee and his doctors had run out of options, and his body couldn't withstand the last-ditch chemotherapy. The fact that my brother had been told eight years earlier to put his affairs in order, that he had six weeks to live, made these years feel like a gift, like borrowed time. But it didn't make the last part any easier. He knew the end was near and wrote to me six weeks before with a list of things he wanted me to do after he was gone. He told me who might speak at his memorial service and asked me to slip a few Grateful Dead songs in if I could. He had written a blog for five years about his cancer journey—the title, *98 Brain Tumors: Um, I Better Write This Down,* hints at the humor and heart with which he wrote—and asked me to assemble and bind together printed copies for his wife and two teenage sons.

Lee died at home on Memorial Day after a weekend filled with visits from family and friends. He and his wife and two teenage sons were able to say their goodbyes, as was I. My father and stepmother were by his side, and I was lying on a cot in the corner of the room when he breathed for the last time.

My mother was there near the end as well—a few days earlier I'd bought us both tickets. I was on a flight two hours later from Maine to Chicago, where I picked her up, before we continued on to Denver, and then we drove to the hospital in Colorado Springs. My brother had collapsed and had a seizure and was in the hospital. My dad called to say he didn't know if Lee would make it through the night. On the flight from Portland to Chicago, I hoped I'd make it in time to see him, hoped I didn't catch coronavirus on the way, and wondered what would happen when my father, long since recovered and mostly reconciled with my brother and me, saw my mother. They hadn't spoken since my brother's wedding nearly two decades earlier.

While traveling with my mom, I quickly realized that she, too, was not well. My mother—who had been active her whole life, who walked, who played tennis, and who went to the community pool nearly every day in her eighth decade—needed my arm to walk more than twenty steps and needed to stop frequently and rest. She'd had an appointment with her doctor that she canceled to travel with me to Colorado. We focused on my brother, on being with him at the end. His passing was one of the few events I can think of that would put my mother and father in the same room together, would have them even express care for each other, and they did.

A month and a day after my brother's last breath, I sat with my mom as her doctor told her about the inoperable tumor in her esophagus, and she told her doctor she had no interest in the chemotherapy that might give her a few extra months. The hospice nurse came to visit that night. Twenty-nine days later, my mom breathed her last with my sister by her side.

So this Christmas I need comfort—that soft snap of well-cooked but not overdone green beans surrounded by a creamy sauce and the crunch of those fried onions—more than ever. I need a corporate casserole to connect my body—through my nose, lips, and tongue—to my brother and mother.

There's still a hole in my chest most days. I feel its edges. We make the green-bean casserole on Christmas, layering so many Christmases on this one. My wife, Renée, and two sons sit with me at the same long dining room table I ate at as a child—my mother shipped it all the way to Maine years ago—and I see my brother, sister, mother, father, and me sitting there. Mushrooms and onions, soft snap and crunch—my brother sneaks a punch in my arm, my sister laughs, fixes her hair, and rolls her eyes, my eldest makes a word joke my father would appreciate, my youngest rolls his eyes. Renée says my brother's name out loud, and I smile in the way I learned by watching my mother—my eyes brimming, my mouth and stomach on their way to being full.

TAKEOUT
Brian Shuff

D URING THE YEARS my mother was in and out of the hospital, and
certainly after she died, my dad and I ate dinner out most school
nights. He administered the counseling office at a junior high school in the
same district that I attended, and because our bell schedules aligned, he'd
arrive home in the late afternoons, not long after I'd shed my saxophone by
the back door and collapsed on the sofa for reruns of *Cosby*. I'd hear him
come in through his office off the garage. Shortly, he appeared standing at
the sofa's arm, tieless and staring at the screen. He watched along, holding
his keys, until one of us either needed to say something or else he needed
to sit, at which point he stepped in front of the screen, rubbing his chin and
asking in a voice meant to parody the broaching of a difficult subject, "I'm
a little confused. Do we eat in this family anymore, or what?"

Soon we were dropping onto the highway, merging with a flow of
commuters just starting to engage their lights. The Phoenix suburbs were
scattered across the East Valley then, separated by wide swaths of desert
and farm acreage, over which was being laid the infrastructures of a coming megalopolis. Hundreds of thousands of putty-colored homes like ours,
single-stories with gravel yards, had already been sold, and now a city was
being thrown together around them at a pace that felt like panic. Taking
exits at random, we drove frontage roads lined with bundled segments of
pipe, lots dug into quarter-mile craters. Along the canal ways, bulldozers
parked askew, far from worksites but signaling occupation. My dad asked
questions about school using my teachers' first names, while out in the dark
the exposed beams of half-formed structures grasped at the raisin sky. No
feature of their design revealed a future function, only that they would be
new—disconcerting at first, then quickly essential. I answered with due

dates and explanations of grading rubrics, a schedule for getting the work done. When we were both convinced, we let down the windows, and the rush of dry air lent our silence the aura of leisure.

We arrived at walk-up counters and strip mall take-out kitchens, sometimes the grill carts set up near construction sites to feed the night crews. Almost always there were strung lights, cooking on open flame, the smell of meat altered by smoke and fire.

Such evidence of food prep was absent, or certainly hidden from diners, at the family chains we still visited on weekends with my mother's parents. There, the hostesses carried urns of coffee and flirted with my grandfather on the way to the table. A parsley sprig and orange wheel came on your plate no matter what you chose from the Rolodex menu.

Our weeknight spots, mine and my father's, didn't have menus. They specialized in one or two items—gyros out by Papago Park, gorditas con camarones on Van Buren—items scrawled in grease marker on a tray or a piece of wood. Any regular knew them by rote. Still, waiting in line, my dad and I considered their merits, parsed any available decision up to the register—Fries or rings? Spicy or extra spicy? Coke or Horchata?—seeming to know that once we placed the order, all our tricks would be spent, and there would be nothing to do but wait.

The strain of those few minutes can sour my stomach to this day if I dwell on them. Had it been ten years earlier, my dad might have lit a cigarette; ten years later, we could have scrolled our phones. Instead, we kicked around by the truck, embarrassed suddenly by the other's presence. My dad rechecked our ticket.

A DISEASE HAD slipped our ranks, moved inside our home, rampant and already ravaging one of our own by the time of its discovery. My mother died from non-Hodgkin's lymphoma, and our anticipation of the cancer's terminus—none of the doctors gave firm timelines—instantly rendered us alien to ourselves and to each other. We had acquired new and inelegant forms, forms still in their shitting, screaming infancies and not yet ready for public display, despite the daily non-negotiables of school, work, debt, hunger. It felt indecent to be seen by anyone.

When our number came, we clawed at the wrappers, struggled to stomp loose napkins as we stole first bites. We told ourselves these were foods at their peak, fresh from the grease. Transport home, we said, cost the meal some of its brio. But we were not so epicurean. On the tailgate, we ate hunched over mounds of foil in our laps, tore off steaming mouthfuls of cheesesteak and al pastor that flushed our orbitofrontal cortexes with dopamine and deformed all speech. We ate like we were starved.

IN THEORY, I know more now than I did then. For instance, I know that grief, at the atomic level, is a panic response set off by change. And since change is a ubiquitous constant—no stone under heaven is fixed—the span of any one lifetime entails a succession of griefs both acute—accidents, diagnoses, disasters—and chronic—the creeping effects of age, a diminishing sense of potential, a growing catalog of unanswered questions. In both cases, the bereft laments what was and fears a lack of knowledge to operate in what is. My dad and I gorged ourselves on noodle bowls because a brutal transformation lay ahead. Fundamental institutions had been undermined—of family, of security, of partnership, of maternity—and reorienting ourselves to a world without these assurances meant bending to a force of change as unceasing as nature, enduring profound modification of Self, and accepting that by the time we regained existential equilibrium and could once again wait in contented silence for a couple of burritos, the contours of that future landscape would bear little resemblance to the one we'd mourned. The versions of ourselves inhabiting that new space would be unrecognizable, strangers we could not stop ourselves from becoming.

I know, too, that we were not the first people to stall this experience with chemical pleasure. Of the items people ingest to alter their states of mind—alcohol, narcotics, caffeine, nicotine—I know that food, besides having the advantage of being appropriate for a kid, holds an elite palliative reputation around grief. Unlike rosé or methamphetamines, the calories and nutrients absorbed from food contribute directly to an organism's daily survival, and their consumption—consciously or not—reinforces kinship with the living. A hot dinner is exactly what the dead don't need. Also, prepared food insists on pleasure. We can function on beans and boiled grain. Many do. Efforts toward a contrast in texture or temperature, to enhance flavor, to surprise, have affirmed quality of life since the first pinch of salt. The sensory and psychological experiences of certain food stuffs can implant in a cultural psyche to the point of shaping its history. Everyone knows about the blood shed over access to tea and spices.

What surprises me—what I did not know—is how well it worked, how thoroughly, albeit briefly, a carton of fried chicken with wax paper greased to translucence muted the fact of our dissolving convictions. For all their initial clumsiness, my recollections of those tailgate dinners—the time we actually spent eating, the fifteen or so minutes consumed by the task of breaking down proteins and plant fibers for digestion—play in my mind with a serene hum.

Those dishes deserve credit. If respite were only a matter of stuffing ourselves, then the post-Mass brunches that we had with my grandparents were the ideal environment for manufacturing relief. But the fare at JB's, Coco's, Perkins had nothing to offer but quantity. One Sunday close to Easter, waiting for my grandfather to receive his change, my grandmother drew me close by the sleeve. One of the women she volunteered with at the Paz de Cristo soup kitchen had a son who'd gotten something called email. The computer, she told me, was able to connect with other parishes just starting to come online, and some had agreed to include my mother in their weekly intentions. She clenched my wrist at the pulse, and she named cities where my mother's soul had been prayed for: South Bend, San Antonio, Tucson, Ann Arbor. I declined to have my Western scramble wrapped. Near the exit, a glass cabinet orbited pies named for candy bars. I wished for menudo on the way home, a broth made from beef tripe and heaps of red chili. Filiberto's made it on Sundays for hangovers.

I don't want to be too sentimental. My dad and my takeout binges were a means of dealing with pain, and like some of the most nourishing experiences, the agent of our relief dashed civil restraint and stripped us to our chewing, swallowing, membranous selves. As a home cook, I have watched with satisfaction as hungry tables go quiet when served a crackling roasted chicken. However, the older I get the more I understand that it's not always wise to indulge an appetite. Destructive tendencies thrive, too, in our coding, instincts to which we lose ourselves just as involuntarily—aggression, superstition, territorialism. The same year my mother died, Maricopa County elected Joe Arpaio to the first of his six terms as sheriff, following a campaign centered on migrant demonization and hostile budget reform. Gleefully, he informed the press of his plans to cut coffee from state prison cafeterias and to nix hot lunches for baloney sandwiches.

My father and I were eating largely immigrant cuisines, though I have no memory of acknowledging it at the time. More broadly, these were cuisines of scarcity, preparations refined over centuries of access to scant ingredients. Falafel is mashed bean. Pho Ga starts as bones, bits of cartilage, and leaf clippings. The tough cuts used for carne asada get broken down with lime juice. Why and how did these techniques develop? Under what socioeconomic and geopolitical forces did the dishes my dad and I used to hedge our discomfort come to be? And if these products could provide fleeting succor from grief, from even the specter of grim mortality, then where were the proprietors' franchised locations? Their mints for sale at the counter? Why did we have to drive so far from home to find these places?

The questions I never asked then embarrass me now with their salience.

Whatever *did* happen to the Golden Fortune, a Sichuan buffet on the fringes of downtown? We pulled into the lot one night to find a charred streak where the foundation had been a week before. An older woman who touched her thumb to a sponge before counting the till ran the place with a man of similar age who would poke his head out from the kitchen with a towel over his shoulder and who—I can't say why—read more like her husband's brother than her husband, despite what sounded like frequent bickering between them. We had come that night in the mood for their sweet and sour cabbage, slippery and warm with a hint of smoke from the chilis and bacon in which it was cooked. My dad noted a telephone pole at the far edge of the now empty lot. It, too, was almost burnt through.

MY STEPSON IS more conscious of his food than I was. I am the primary cook in the small apartment that we share with his mother. Another sequence of changes has recast this takeout stalwart as someone nightly at the stove—learning, experimenting, retrying, slowly becoming more capable, most so with the classic Roman pastas. When he doesn't have homework, my stepson asks if I need help in the kitchen, and when I decline, he'll often sit at the counter with his laptop.

He is only thirteen, with greater access to the world than many adults. He is often talking to his watch when we think he is talking to us. Before a food is a candidate for enjoyment, he must find the conditions of its procurement and preparation acceptable. He worries over GMOs, portion size, exploitation at all points on the supply chain, and he prefers we buy produce from farms within our county, where broccoli crowns and D'Anjou pears cost three times that of their supermarket counterparts grown in warehouses thousands of miles west. He peeks over the top of his screen to watch my hand with the salt, to request less butter.

These are good qualities. They make meals harder to enjoy, but meals should be harder to enjoy, or at least to enjoy with the same incurious license as when I was younger.

I feel cautiously optimistic that the shifts in culture rightfully threatening our most longstanding institutions are, for my stepson, simply the air
he breathes—at school, with his teammates and peers, in his two homes.
His conception of the world remains intact. It is his mother and I who are
adjusting.

Of course, what remains to be seen are the defenses he will employ, how
his future self will behave when cherished certainties require amendment.
He will not be spared in this life the panic of insufficient knowledge. But
it's hard to imagine him flailing and grasping to restore what was, insisting
that the dead are alive. Now, when he needs to check out, he goes for a run.
He tears through the woods, along the commercial waterfront of our small
port city. He takes difficult routes on purpose, tracks his mileages and times,
and refuses fancy Nikes, though we offer, refuses even a coat in the winter,
and returns wet-haired and gasping, standing in the kitchen with a look of
fierce focus across his flushed face, as if no frontier scares him.

Still, the pleasure receptors in his brain can be tripped by simple fat and
salt. While he cools off watching YouTube videos, I will make him a snack
of *cacio e pepe*. He is impressed by its four ingredients, two of which are
water and cracked pepper. If I get it just right—so that the pecorino emul-
sifies and oozes along the tangled noodles—he will hear the wet slap of
pasta tossing against the pan and appear at the kitchen counter. He tells me
what he has been watching, always short documentaries on hyper-specific
ways in which the earth is being saved or destroyed: Resistant bacteria in
Germany. Game-changing water filtration systems in the Himalayas. He
recounts the details, an outpouring that wanes only slightly as he begins to
devour the pasta. What he is saying feels urgent, is urgent, but the smoke in
the pepper distracts him, and as cheese gathers at the corners of his mouth
and steam from the bowl fogs his glasses, briefly it seems he will yield to
instinct. But he never succumbs entirely. His words stay just ahead of his
all-consuming body. This water system, it turns out, will save thousands of
lives if they can procure funding. When his mouth gets full, I listen closer.

A SUITCASE OF TOMATOES
Christina Baker Kline

M Y FATHER'S MOTHER grew up on the side of a mountain in northern Alabama. Quite literally dirt-poor, my grandmother, Ethel, lived with her parents, two brothers, and three sisters in a tarpaper shack with no electricity or running water. They raised chickens for eggs and meat, and made their own clothes out of flour sacks.

When my grandmother talked about those days, she didn't focus on the hardship, except to say that the life they led made people old before their time. Instead, she told stories about her brothers' rascally humor and her mother's determination to keep everyone fed and clothed. She talked about the large garden she planted and tended with her sisters, filled with corn, cucumbers, watermelon, okra, and tomatoes.

"We didn't have a lot," she said. "But we did have tomatoes."

My grandmother told me these stories about her life while I was sitting at her white-speckled Formica table in the cheery, spotless kitchen of the ranch house she'd earned as a hosiery repair worker at a woolen mill in north Georgia. As I remember it, she was always standing behind the counter, making dinner with ingredients from the large garden she cultivated just beyond the sliding-glass door. I never saw her use a recipe. The food she prepared nearly every day of her life was the food she'd learned to make on Sand Mountain: slow-cooked green beans with ham, creamed corn, cornmeal-fried okra, chicken and dumplings. And tomatoes: thick, unevenly rounded slices—deep red, dense as melon—that you sprinkled with salt and pepper and cut with a knife and fork, so mild and buttery they practically melted on your tongue.

When my father moved his fledgling family to Maine from the South in 1970, we were in for a rude culinary shock. Okra was impossible to get; nobody made chicken and dumplings. Even worse, the only tomatoes you could find came embalmed in cellophane—three uniform orbs, barely tinged pink, as bland and spongy as packing peanuts.

My grandmother only visited us a few times before she died. She found Maine too far, too cold, its customs altogether too foreign. I remember family trips to the coast where she would stand tentatively on the rocks, stepping gingerly over seaweed, sniffing the air. But most vivid is the memory of my father bringing her home from the airport to our Victorian fixer-upper with her two matching suitcases, one large and one small. The small one contained her clothing for the week, a tidy collection of mix-and-match polyester pantsuits. The large one was filled with tomatoes.

Packed lovingly in newspaper, these tomatoes, improbably large and ripe, were a visual reminder of all we'd left behind when we moved north. They evoked longings we'd tried to suppress: for the fertile black soil, the hot sun, culinary customs impossible to sustain in this new place. Even more, the suitcase filled with tomatoes reminded us that we came from a tradition of simplicity and resourcefulness—the kind of self-reliance that had allowed my grandmother's poor family of eight, with no money and few possessions, to thrive on the side of a mountain in Alabama.

Years later, I wrote a novel called *The Way Life Should Be* about a half-Irish, half-Italian woman named Angela Russo who, among other things, teaches a cooking class. Angela's grandmother, whom she calls Nonna, was born and raised in Basilicata, in southern Italy. She's a scrappy, salty-tongued matriarch who grew up poor—her village, Matera, was known as a place of *cucina povera*, the cuisine of poverty—and learned to make the most of what she had. I realize now that at the heart of that novel is my relationship with my own grandmother. Nonna passes on to her granddaughter an intuitive approach to cooking and a reverence for fresh ingredients. "Nonna doesn't use recipes," I write in the novel. "She cooks by feel, by touch and taste and sight."

And what does she cook? Tomatoes, of course. Served on a plate with fresh mozzarella and basil, drizzled with olive oil and a splash of balsamic; diced and slow-simmered into sauce; a main ingredient in dozens of soups and stews. Like my own grandmother, Nonna serves tomatoes fresh all summer and cans them at the end of the season. In the strange alchemy of storytelling, these two grandmothers, one real and one fictional, separated by continents and cultures, time and space, intertwined in my head—yielding a deeper understanding of my own family traditions than I could have imagined.

COOKING INTO THE EYE
OF THE STORM

Melissa Coleman

A FUNNY THING USED to happen to me in the kitchen. I'd be preparing dinner for my visiting mother and stepfather and family—measuring, mixing, sautéing, and . . . freaking out. The blood pounded in my temples. My eyes in the darkened window over the sink reflected back a crazed look. "It's going to come out terrible," said the refrain in my head. "Yet again."

"It will taste fine," my husband always countered when I voiced these fears aloud, but if I fiercely insisted otherwise, he'd carefully change the subject.

How could you ruin a quiche? I'd inevitably find a way. The distractions in my mind led to over-beating the eggs, forgetting the salt, and leaving it in the oven too long. Then there was the issue of the salmon. I could never remember the best formula. Was it 450 degrees for ten minutes, or 350 for fifteen minutes? On the few occasions when it came out well, in my glory I forgot to write it down, and Google never finds the same recipe twice. Before I knew it, the beautiful cut of fish was firmly coated in the white residue that signals overcooking. And blast it, the string beans left in the steamer had continued on from a crisp bright green to a dull overdone khaki. Cooking is all about timing, and my inner clock was seriously out of sync.

When I called everyone to dinner, we gathered around the table, my mother and stepfather, twin daughters, and husband, ever in expectation anew of delight, no matter how many times it had been denied. I'd smile and pretend everything was fine, that this was our happy family eating a fantastic meal, that the food was not overcooked, the cheer on their faces not forced. No one could understand the turmoil I faced around mealtime, not even me. But here's the thing about a less-than-delicious dinner, or a life—we forge through. At some point, we must ask, what is the point of a good meal wasted? At the heart of all failures is something vital—an opportunity to understand why.

THIS FEAR OF COOKING, I can now see, was a fear of things not turning out the way I hoped. Being blessed by an abundance of mothers, I had not only an abundance of examples but caution. Missing for me in the kitchen was the uninhibited passion my mother and two stepmothers put into giving it their all and not being afraid to fail, despite, or because of, their losses. Rather than relishing the simple act of mixing eggs and cream for quiche, I carried the weight of the many delicious meals made by my mothers over my lifetime, and the fact that those meals could not save them from divorce or death.

My mother, who gave birth to me at home, was heartbroken by the later loss of a child and a marriage. What good did her skill baking fresh bread on an off-the-grid homestead with only a grain mill and wood cookstove do against such events? My stepmother Gerry was diagnosed with a debilitating disease that first stole her balance and then her voice. Her famous roast chicken, with garlic tucked in the wings and salty-crispy skin, could not help her. And my second stepmother, Barbara, the time she lost a capped front tooth? We laughed when she smiled, despite the hint of mortality in the dark empty space where the tooth should have been. How could her exquisite lemon chicken soup, with its elegant melodies of citrus and cream, combat death?

These images pressed around me in the kitchen, distracting me with their warnings, preventing me from reveling in the simple act of creation. In the place of my mothers' passionate embrace of cooking and life, I was left with the fear that I'd burn the quiche, or lose my voice, a tooth, a child, my husband, my self.

IT'S TAKEN A NUMBER of gastronomic failures, or maybe just birthdays, but I'm beginning to reclaim my power around cooking and, along with it, life.

We lost my stepfather five years ago. My mother grieved him with her whole being, and while that did not bring him back, it has helped heal her many sorrows. She is becoming complete in herself. My stepmother Gerry also has left us. I think of her every time I roast a chicken, her kindness and grace, her acceptance of me in the face of failure. What more do we need of others? I've lost my husband, too, not to death or because of my cooking (though he might tell you otherwise), but we are finally becoming friends again, and that has made lemons into lemon meringue pie. What remains throughout is the cadence of my stepmother Barbara's meals, always slightly new, always delightful, the leitmotif of our extended family's comings and goings, joys and sorrows. In our family story, each of my mothers brings a unique dish to the table, and Barbara's has brought a serving of redemption.

It helps to remember that eating, that most basic act at the very heart of survival, is about turning calories into energy. Sea water into salt. One life force into another. All of us on this earth—animal, vegetable, and mineral—are continually consuming each other and being transformed in the process, just as our lives are reassembling themselves from joy to sorrow and back to joy again.

What I find now is that the act of preparing a meal, like loving, is an alchemy that turns the raw ingredients of life into gold. I catch my reflection in the darkened window over the sink and realize I can save this dinner, and myself. There's a grace that comes when opening the oven door to the smell of bacon and cheese and onion and the lovely dome of a perfectly risen golden-brown quiche, bubbling at the base. The salmon, timed exactly, tender, pink, and buttery, skin sizzling on the pan. Crisp bright green beans, julienned and lightly steamed, tossed with lemon and pepper.

A good meal is simply this—the introduction of fresh ingredients to the right amount of seasoning and heat. When I slow down and take it one step at a time, I don't worry so much about the outcome. The inner clock is magically reset in the present moment.

Then we come to the table, with family and friends and the spirits of those who never truly leave us, and take a divine bite that will be transformed again as soon as we swallow it down. In this moment it is perfection, but I cannot hold on to it. There will be no leftovers. Every day I must start anew.

UNITED OR LOOSENED
Georgia Williamina Zildjian

I T'S HARD TO CELEBRATE what you can't eat. Hard to be forced to eat
what you don't want. The only cure for that is humor. I am lucky that
while living on an involuntary elimination diet, I once had a partner in
crime. We were united in this milieu until he was loosened from this earth,
and I was the last one standing.

My body is incapable of hydration. As such, it is mandated that 50 percent of my fluid intake contains a high concentration of supplemental
electrolytes. The balance is in the blood. And my blood has no balance.
So I carry around electrolyte tabs, popping them compulsively like Perry
Smith's aspirin. The Pleiades are only half of the equation that holds the sky
aloft; hydration is only half of survival. I can drink, but I am hard-pressed
to eat.

There are seven electrolytes that sustain the human body, that race
through the blood on their own electrically charged current. Minuscule,
fairylike compounds that hold the balance of your life in the ring of their
light. They are like the seven sisters of the Pleiades who sustain their father,
Atlas, in the sky. The seven sisters are Alcyone, Maia, Electra, Merope, Tay-
gete, Celaeno, and Sterope. The seven electrolytes are sodium, magnesium,
potassium, chloride, calcium, bicarbonate, and phosphate. The word chosen
for these compounds of the body comes, like the sisters, from the Greek.
It is derived from the ancient Greek *electro*—the prefix related to electricity—and *lytos*—"able to be united or loosened."

Jack and I were never on the same diet, but we were always on one.
And, as such, we could commiserate and temporarily tease the misery away.
The week that Jack died, he said to his wife, Julie, "This must be how
Georgia feels," almost at the moment I was writing a letter to him that said,

"When I am at the very bottom of the pit, I think, 'This is but a tenth of what Jack feels.'"

We got sick around the same time. For him, a sudden diagnosis; for me, a steady decline. We alternately rallied and languished, living just around the corner from each other. We shared grief, strength, and, occasionally, "food." We were both cared for by women who believe food is part of medicine. (It is.) They took on the heavy mantle of mediator between us and food, knowing that what we would find treasonous might just help us heal.

These women practiced what they preached. In a time before this, they would have been considered witches for the culinary miracles they performed while cooking gluten-, dairy-, salt-, fat-, and lycopene-free at various points for two stubborn people with lavish palates.

It's equally hard to convey the indignity of suffering from a chronic or terminal illness, but it is an elimination—first of privacy, then dignity. And the true enjoyment of food depends upon these two elements of human life. We had to ask our mediators what we could or could not eat, beg for a diet holiday, and sometimes sneak past them some forbidden morsel that, beyond tasting delightful, offered—ironically—a moment of relief.

Jack and I shared loss and pain and the betrayal of a faulty body, and often found our humor when this manifested in food. At one time we shared a homeopathic doctor, who put us on a morning regimen of "nut mash." What on God's green earth this was supposed to achieve I could not tell you, but it did somewhat mask the taste of the myriad powdered supplements one stirred into it. "My clients love it!" the homeopath crowed.

"Julie says Jack doesn't mind this; she even eats it with him," my mother assured me. Knowing that "doesn't mind" really meant, "You probably won't throw up in your mouth," I adhered to the regimen until Jack and I both quit the homeopath. My faithful mother, like Julie before her, ate this lukewarm heap with me every day.

You will tell someone you can no longer eat gluten (the molecule that acts as a binding agent in wheat), and they will say to you, "Oh, I could never do that," or "I would just keep eating it," and then they will congratulate you on your willpower. That's a fun and privileged perspective coming from someone who has clearly never pooped their pants in public.

(But even I have said to myself, "If they take away cheese, I quit.")

JACK WAS IN the "foreign service," a world traveler with a cosmopolitan palate. As the radius of his travels diminished, so did his culinary choices. I wondered if, in the end, he would just eat what he wanted. I sometimes find a thrill in sneaking a bagel or brioche—for Jack, it was steak and red wine. But there is always a fall. To eat whatever you want becomes hubris.

(E.g., I will not compromise Jack's dignity, but I will say that I am writing this particular sentence on the toilet.)

JACK OWNED AN inn with a fine restaurant. Every evening he trolled between tables of gorgeous food he could not eat, doubtless answering questions he did not want to answer—

"How are you? And how is *It*? And are you feeling better?"

What a waste. To have a person like Jack at your table and not ask him about his take on the politics of the day or what he was reading or the innermost thoughts of Idi Amin, Somoza, or Prince Charles. It wasn't just their loss; it was his.

What the general eating public does not realize is that all time is borrowed. You live on the cusp of breakdown. You might be eating your last croissant as you read these words. Savor it.

Jack loved to come to my parents' house for dinner. He loved my mother's cooking, just as I delight in Julie's gluten-free baking. It's not their fault that we always wanted to trade—both women are excellent cooks and bakers, award-winning even—it's that someone else's cooking is a chance to escape the labyrinth. No more wending your way through the fool's errands and dead-ends of the diet du jour.

(E.g., When my partner, Brandon, and I were first dating, his parents didn't know I was gluten-free and served pasta for dinner. I *had* to eat it, to be polite, you see? *Best date ever.*)

BEFORE ONE OF our last dinners together, my mother said, "I want to make Jack something *really* good. I want to make him something he will love." At that point, it seemed that those were two mutually exclusive feats, but, of course, she pulled it off beautifully—save for the hot dogs. Now, this was a fancy dinner that somehow incorporated hot dogs. I actually don't remember what else we ate, but I remember the night because my mother made "normal" hot dogs for the "normal" people and tofu hot dogs for Jack and me.

Tofu.

Hot dogs.

I would not touch them. But Jack, ever the diplomat, took one on his plate. We're eating and passing dishes and talking, but somehow (it's always the way), as Jack lifts his fork to his mouth, everyone is watching. I already know what this is going to be. There is no Venn diagram for tofu and hot dogs. But intrepid Jack puts it into his mouth. Chews, swallows—and roars with laughter. I am already giggling; my mom bursts out laughing: "I'm sorry, Jack; I'm so sorry." My father, sister Phoebe, Julie, Brandon—we are all laughing at the absurdity. As the laughter finally subsides, Julie says, "Go ahead and have a real one, dear."

"Yeah?" Jack says, all the phases of the moon contained in that expression: The full moon of the boy who rowed across the bay to Gloucester, dreaming of a deeper sea, a bigger ship. The quarter moon of the man who rode a barge down the White Nile on an aid mission for the World Food Programme. The crescent moon of the man who sat before us—and perhaps the new moon too. When he would stroll the streets of Yerevan with Phoebe and me on that oft-promised trip. Comparing *lokhum* flavors and feasting on *soorj* and *lahmajun*.

Julie repeats, "Yes," and I silently cheer for his success. And we all keep laughing. Because if we don't, we will cry.

A FEW DAYS before Jack died, he was still drinking water. He had run out of electrolyte tablets, and Julie asked to borrow some from me. There were only a few left in the tube, but I wanted to give them all. Jammed in that little tube were some sparks. And I thought—*I will give my electricity, so I can see you again.*

THINGS MAKE MORE sense in Ancient Greek to me. They call it tragedy, or "high drama," and yet it is my lifeline to weather the everyday—Seven Sisters, seven electrolytes.

The Seven are slippery—

Mythologically, they share their names with other women. They are daughters of the man who holds up the sky, and yet one of the stars slips in and out of focus, and no one can decide who it is, or why. Is it Merope, because she broke the code of the sisters and married a mortal? Or is it Electra, who hides her face from the burning of Troy? Is it potassium, missing because my adrenal glands are failing? Or is it magnesium that dwindles and keeps me awake until my brain burns?

ON THE DAY Jack left, my mother was with Julie at his side, helping to ease the loosening. It had just struck noon. I knew it was a hard day, so I headed down to his house with a basket full of Gatorade—more electricity. I thought I would just drop the bottles off, but my mother came outside. She said what I had known when the clock struck: "Jack got away." Later that day, somewhere between the washing of sheets and gathering of flowers, my mother handed me back the tube. He had only taken one.

I used the rest, but I kept the tube, shaped like a miniature time capsule. Blue and white, mixed-berry flavored—the best flavor. My mother keeps her father's Kleenex in her coat pocket. I suppose this is the same, nestled between my pills in the pill basket, sustaining me because he touched it.

IN GREEK MYTHOLOGY, there is a concept called *catasterism*. It is the transformation of a human body into a celestial one—a soul into a constellation. The opportunity to trade the seven small electricities in our body and join the seven blazing ones in the sky. No longer burdened by holding a body together, we are only enthralled to "the wonder that's keeping the stars apart."

The night his soul slipped his body, the moon shone bright and full, reigning supreme amongst the constellations—Jack's joyful face. He could eat whatever he wanted. Seven sisters welcomed him, while I stood on the ground as my grip on him loosened.

And here I stand, until we feast together again.

PROSPECTORS
Martin Conte

COFFEE

It's 7:30 a.m. on a Thursday morning, the start of my workweek. Portland, outside my window, is a chilly gray, a February gray, a gray that feels indisputable. I step quietly past Meg's bedroom, down the stairs past Dan and Mia's, emptied for the day since they leave for work earlier than the rest of us, and back across the house toward the kitchen. Marley, the household hound, pads along behind me. There are familiar rustlings coming from the kitchen, and I step across the cold floor to the hooked rug by the sink, ducking around Corey, Meg's beau and a now incorporated addition to our household of roommates. He pauses from making toast to kiss my cheek good morning, fuzzing our beards together in our daily ritual.

My mornings are slow, not because I'm groggy or a snooze-button person. Quite the opposite. Morning is a time I relish, a time I want to take at an even, agreeable pace. I sit at the breakfast table, pulling my feet up a rung on a chair to avoid the cold tile, and watch Corey: quiet, efficient, satisfied in his breakfast labors. Corey offers me bacon and eggs, but I pass; I'll make some after he and Meg leave. He fetches a bag of coffee beans from the freezer. The little dusty pits have a comforting scent. With one hand, he presses the lid of the grinder down and the loud whirr fills the room. Each time I hear this whirr, I think back to my childhood best friend's house, where I spent many nights (usually crying to go home because I was afraid of the dark) and would be woken just after dawn by her mother grinding coffee. With his other hand, Corey fetches three mugs: the hefty mustard crockery-ware one, the delicate Pantone one with the bright turquoise stripe, the white square one that everyone except me hates. My arms hang weak with gratitude, as he deftly pours hot water over brimming filters, then eyes the drip with satisfaction.

I can't locate when mornings began to begin this way, with Corey preparing me coffee. I do not know how many mornings actually resembled this one, and how many I woke alone, or woke and left before Meg and Corey rose. Events lose their singularity; they take on the semblance of all things. It is a strange thing to make home as a young person. Dan, Mia, and I had known each other since high school, had traveled and played music together. Meg was someone I had only come to know the summer before we moved in, when we acted together in a Civil War play. Dan and Mia didn't even meet Meg until she was signing the lease with us. It is this time of our life—fresh out of college, not quite professionals, not yet creating our family units—when no one is *expected* to provide for us, and we are *expected* to provide for no one. It is the providing we *choose to do* that shapes us the most.

In a moment, Corey will hand me a cup, and I will thank him. I will feel like a child, like no amount of cold in the February forecast can snuff the warmth that Corey passes to me. In a moment, Meg will join us, and we will trill our good mornings, kiss cheeks, clasp hands. I will watch as Meg's love for Corey writes itself in the air over the toast he hands her. We will sip our coffees, and then we will go, facing the muffled cold, to work.

TOAST

Meg came to us with two Dutch ovens, cane proofing baskets, and dog-eared bread books. She works as a set designer and prop master for theater but her professional bio always notes that she is a bread baker. Her bread rises tall and crusty and satisfyingly pulls apart to reveal an airy and elastic inside.

On a September Saturday afternoon, coming home from work, I am met with the haze of flour sifting through the window light and find both Meg and Mia concentrating on the dough between them, plumped and stretched on the powdered kitchen counter. Mia laughs—a waterfall of energy—as she digs and rolls the clingy dough. Meg's cheeks are red with hilarity. While Mia looks up, around, anywhere but her kneading hands, Meg assures her she's doing a "great job," which only makes Mia laugh harder. This is their second knead, a brief turning of the bread before it sits for a second, hour-long proof. The kitchen is hot from the preheating oven. Bread baking, like most Saturday afternoon activities in our house, is accompanied by glasses of loamy red wine.

Home means many things. I remember my mother and me having after-dinner snacks of toast and Sleepytime tea. The house where my four siblings, my parents, and I lived has been replaced by this rented house next to the train tracks, with its tall windows and curving staircase. It is difficult, leaving a home meant to *be* home, and entering first a shared dorm room, then a closet-sized apartment with sloped ceilings and only three windows, and, after, a big, echoey house without enough furniture. The memory of this day of bread binds what was to what is: from my mother's hands carrying me the plate of toast to Meg's hands deftly cutting me a slice. In the sound of crunching toast, I hear the cackle of Mia's laughter and the murmur of my mother.

Some of my friends in Portland struggle with the "imposter syndrome" of *adulting*, as we now call it. They lived in housemate situations with strangers they never saw, or with walls empty of art, or in kitchens reserved mostly for take-out containers and frozen pizzas. Our home on Prospect Street became not just a home to *us* but to these friends as well. This was not without intention and effort. Dan, Mia, Meg, and I discovered that the greatest bond we had with each other was a shared *belief* in home, in home as a practice and a method, a way of being. One of those ways was the constant cooking, baking, preparing, and sharing of food.

CHOCOLATE

Marley the dog was old when he joined us, six months after we moved into the Prospect house. He was skinny enough we could see his rib cage, eyes caked with grime and snot. Dan and Mia figured he would last maybe a month, but he bounced back, made a real show of it, and had a great year of life with us. We quickly learned he had an insatiable appetite. Anything might disappear into Marley's iron gullet. He was particularly fond of whole loaves of bread, crumbs scattered across our rugs, or any ounce of chocolate he could snag.

And it didn't stop at food. Mia's underwear dwindled and disappeared. Then our socks. We didn't know how Marley survived these gastrointestinal expeditions. In one single week, he ate half a chocolate cake, a loaf of fresh bread off the counter, and then—what we thought would be a clincher for his system—a container of chocolate-covered espresso beans.

We woke up one March morning, and he was standing, unmoving, in the kitchen. We knew his condition was critical because he hadn't touched his breakfast. He died just about a year after we adopted him, lasting a solid ten months longer than we ever expected him to.

We rarely speak of Marley or tell a Marley story that doesn't involve him devouring something that belonged to us. I wonder if Marley had more of an understanding of his own death then we might give him credit for. Marley ate the underwear, the socks, the scarves, the places of sweat and odor, to keep us as close as he could. This thought is somehow strangely comforting. He was gross, we readily admit, gross and old and so kind. Now, Marley has become food. Ants and earthworms will digest him, transform him into earth, which will grow grass and flowers and herbs and the food that Marley himself so loved to steal.

CAKE

For two years, Dan, Mia, Meg, and I made our home on Prospect Street, off-peninsula, just above the railroad tracks. I do not take this term "making home" lightly. How does one make home? In what way does a house you live in turn into a home? Bickering and needling made the Prospect house a home. Our willingness not just to love each other as friends but also to get frustrated with each other, to tease and mock, to wound the fragile threads of acquaintance into the firm rope of family.

One day, Meg prepares a cake for a friend's birthday party. She had to do the cake in two gos. The first iteration stuck in the pan, and she pried it out into chunks, which she piled on a plate on the counter, with a note: "Sorry this is such a mess! I don't know what happened! I hope it tastes ok!"

I snag a piece, then a few more. Dan, deft vulture of any potential food scores, joins me. Dan scribbles below Meg's note: "Meg, the cake is fine."

When Meg comes home that night and finds his note (and most of the cake gone), she needles Dan: "Fine, huh? Not good, not tasty, just fine? Oh, I see, Dan; it's adequate, huh?" We laugh, as Dan stutters to explain himself: "No, no, I mean, it wasn't bad like you were worried about!"

"Oh, so you expected it to be bad, then?"

"No, no—"

"Well, thank God, it's FINE!"

The word became a joke, a catchphrase, and the story became synonymous with Dan's character. When we returned from a show or trip, we'd tell each other it was fine. When we went out to eat, we'd describe our mussels or ramen as fine. When I introduced Dan to new friends, I told them, "This is Dan. He's fine."

BACON

Dan and Mia find a South Portland apartment for just the two of them. Meg moves in with Corey. Meanwhile, I will soon return to my parents' home, back up the coast to the Blue Hill peninsula, to start my graduate degree in English literature. After three years, our time at the Prospect house is coming to an end.

A party is in order.

We had discovered the joy of partying in Prospect two months into living there. The first floor was wired with speakers; the small backyard could be lit up with lamps on extension cords and Christmas lights strung from the bathroom window. Street parking was ample. A waffle bar became expected at our parties, as well as all manner of bizarre and not-exactly matching appetizers and finger foods. Dan did the cleaning. Mia appeared with arms filled with rosé.

The night of the farewell party the house fills slowly. Familiar faces first: the writing workshop I'm a part of, a few choice friends from the restaurant where Mia waits, our steel-band crew, Meg's theater friends, the science center attendants with whom I used to work, professors, and, yes, a few people who we don't precisely know. One energetic young man appears, apparently a friend of the husband of one of my friends, and begins mixing cocktails at the kitchen counter.

The "theme" to my appetizers is bacon: bacon-wrapped asparagus, bacon-wrapped dates, bacon-wrapped water chestnuts marinated in soy sauce. When Corey first started spending nights at the Prospect house, Meg had asked him what he thought of us. His response was: "Martin and Mia eat a lot of bacon." (It was true, and particularly true at that time, while Mia was between day jobs, and we had lazy mornings off where we cooked big breakfasts and then Mia would quietly stress out about finding work; the bacon was a saver of our spirits, even if it was a danger to our hearts.) There is a general consensus that the bacon and asparagus is delicious, and the bacon and water chestnuts is "weird."

An essential part of *making* home is *sharing* home. It is nights like these that reveal how the Prospect house is not just a home to us but to all those who dine at our table. To see all these happy faces (and full stomachs) at once is to see the physical results of that essential pleasure of making home.

When I reminisce about living in Prospect with my Portland friends, I'm not the one who tells the story of Marley eating everything; it's our friend Jess. It isn't me who reminds everyone that Dan is FINE; it's Olivia. It isn't me who recalls the comfort of breakfast rituals in Prospect; it's Shannon.

Prospect will soon become a home to the memories of this time in our lives, when our days intersect and overlap, when we experience the rhythm of the city together, and when our house feeds, comforts, and holds not just those of us fortunate enough to live here but all who cross our threshold.

POT BROWNIES
AND DINER BREAKFAST
Shonna Milliken Humphrey

J OE ORDERS THE egg-white scramble with tomatoes and mushrooms, and I like the spinach and feta. Dry toast for Joe, sometimes bacon for me. We drink the bitter coffee, his with milk and mine black. The mugs are yellow and thick, and they feel heavy and right in the way diner mugs should. We know the servers by name. Katie is our favorite—a singer by profession, I hear her voice sometimes when I walk downtown at night.

The topic is never off-limits, but we don't often talk about Beth. I do wonder what she might say though. She requested different things from her friends: watch out for my boy, help write an obituary, sort belongings.

"Make sure Joe is OK?" she asked me, after the pot brownies.

BETH RECEIVED HER first diagnosis during the summer solstice, details emerging throughout the upcoming season in clipped or hissing syllables: stage four, metastasis, inoperable, two years, maybe. A doctor would eventually say with certainty, "This will shorten your life," but that first day when Beth knew "bad," just not "how bad," I did what she requested.

I brought the weed.

"To smoke or to eat?" I asked.

"To eat, please."

Because Beth did not regularly use marijuana, I arrived an hour later with two dry chocolate brownies pulled deep from my freezer. She sat on her bed, propped up with pillows, while Joe puttered in the kitchen. She tucked the foil-wrapped package discreetly under her blanket because she was not quite sure how Joe might react.

The tiny subterfuge seems funny now. During the Miss Portland Diner breakfast that has become our weekly ritual, Joe insists he would not have cared. He suspects Beth got a thrill from the secret.

ON THAT FIRST day, though, before Joe became as much a friend as Beth, when she hid those pot brownies under her blanket, she said it felt like her belly had been punched. Colon for sure, the tests confirmed, and lungs likely. She was waiting to hear about her uterus.

"I keep thinking this all must be wrong," she whispered, and I agreed.

On that longest and brightest day of the year, with the sun not scheduled to set for several more hours, any unexpected tilt toward darkness seemed impossible. Any return to light, unnecessary.

OF HER MANY FRIENDS, I was not surprised I got the weed call. My musician husband often found homegrown at the bottom of his tip bucket or pressed into his hands by appreciative fans. After shows, he counted crumpled bills on the coffee table and placed baggies into a glass jar. One jar filled, and then another.

Too frugal to throw the pot away but unable to ever smoke that much, he gave it to me, because I dabbled in homemade edibles. An accomplished home cook and occasional food writer for the local newspaper, I knew my way around a recipe, but marijuana baking requires journeyman chemistry skills. Cannabinoids, the chemical compounds secreted by the cannabis flower, if not directly inhaled, require an oil conduit for release. Temperature affects the release too. Sprinkling marijuana cuttings into brownie batter has little effect.

With practice, my brownies tasted quite good, but it took a while. The early attempts were grainy and burnt. The kitchen smelled foul. As I pulled Beth's first brownies from the far corner of my freezer, I remembered scraping early batches into the garbage bin and wondering what I had done wrong.

BETH, TOO, WONDERED what she had done wrong. At forty-six, she exercised and ate a mostly vegetarian diet. Her family were healthy, long-living types, and she dreaded calling her vibrant, horse-riding, eighty-year-old mother with the news.

I nodded down the hall and asked if her young son knew.

"Not yet," she said. Her son was smart, though, and Beth had already caught him searching "How to stop a bad cough" on the Internet.

I watched her son's bedroom door and recalled a story about his pet lizard, Twister. During a particularly brutal Maine ice storm, the power went off in the middle of the night. With no electricity for the heat lamp, Twister would freeze, so Beth gently pulled Twister from the dark and cold terrarium and snuggled the bearded dragon like a newborn baby between her chest and blankets while her husband and son slept.

"You do what you've got to do," she told me the next morning. "You know?"

I knew.

AFTER LEAVING BETH'S bed on that first day, I did laps in the grocery store with an empty cart. Her diet would now be sugar- and gluten-free, and rather than contemplate a world without Beth in it, I focused on developing a pot brownie to accommodate the food restrictions. However, when the shock of a fatal diagnosis swirls in big, painful, existential circles, it is difficult to concentrate on wheat flour substitutes. While trying to process Beth's news, I filled two bags with random ingredients. Once home, I stacked cookbooks on the countertop, pushed emotions to the side, and got to work. This, I reasoned, was something I could do.

Each batch improved, and here is what I learned: Grind the ingredients super-fine. Double the oil. Use almond butter. Mint and cinnamon too. Avocado adds extra calories. Bean paste makes the best base. Try coconut sugar. Stevia tastes funny. Four eggs are better than two. I studied cannabis varieties and their differences. Sativa, indica, and hybrid each have different properties. Sativa can lighten a mood, and indica can relax a body. The nameless, cheap, and sticky buds I smoked as a college student seemed quaint now. The baggies from my husband's tip jar, elementary level, and I frequently found myself driving a car loaded with a felon's worth of upscale marijuana varieties to my kitchen.

With time and practice, I developed a potent and delicious product, as rich as any professionally baked confection and as mellow as two glasses of wine. The dosage was simple: take a small bite, wait an hour, then go to bed. I instructed taste-testers to not get cocky and eat the whole thing. "Blend a brownie into almond milk for a hot or cold beverage," I advised while imagining a Nobel Prize speech or medical school acceptance letter if only I had learned chemistry like this in high school.

As municipalities legalized medical marijuana and decriminalized recreational possession, word got around, and friends began making requests. Entrepreneurial friends suggested I start a business for profit. I never accepted money, but I often presented neatly wrapped packages as gifts. A friend sent me a cheeky "Chocolatier" T-shirt, but it was a misnomer because in addition to chocolate, I offered gingerbread, pumpkin, and banana brownies.

"I shall not go gently, Mrs. Humphrey," Beth whispered in her throatiest Katharine Hepburn from her bed as she patted those first brownies.

"I should never doubt it, Mrs. Lombardo," I answered, trying to replicate Maggie Smith.

Many years prior to her diagnosis, Beth and I perfected a *Downton Abbey*–style dowager countess schtick in the manner of Edina and Patsy from the British television show *Absolutely Fabulous*. As Mrs. Lombardo and Mrs. Humphrey, we affected accents, riffed on opium dens, and recalled imaginary Eastern European lovers. We invented a pool boy. "Of course," we always nodded, "that was before the War."

We exchanged text messages and left voicemail recordings from the perspective of ironic, impatient, imperialist bigots. Together we crammed double entendres and literary references into these daily exchanges. It was our middle-aged version of playacting, and we giggled like teenagers.

Beth did not go gently. After the confirmations, she asked not to see the Bell curve. When the doctors suggested her disease's likely trajectory, Beth focused harder. She wanted all energy directed toward her health and healing, and there was no space for doubt or negativity. When presented with bad news, she challenged her team to describe the aspects in her favor.

Still, when Joe took her son to run an errand one afternoon, I warmed our marijuana smoothie mugs and rubbed her back while she sobbed, bent forward into my neck. As I tightened the blanket on her shoulders, it occurred to me that I had never held a grown woman before. It felt as foreign to me as a newborn or a lizard named Twister.

We swapped stories about old boyfriends, stupid decisions, and the sum total of experiences that make a life. Both of us grew up in small rural towns and found home in Maine. She described her years as an expatriate in Japan, telling me again about the children's television show *Betty's English* that she hosted and how her recorded voice once welcomed visitors to a terminal at the Kansai airport. During one particularly wild night, she made a bartender piggyback her through the streets. She pretended he was a pony, she told me, and this reminded me of the parable of the optimist and pessimist child each placed in a room filled with manure. The punch line has the optimist child noting that with all the poop, there must be a pony hidden somewhere.

Later, Beth thanked me for sitting in the dark places with her. I still have the text message exchange. "Much shit, many ponies," she offered, and I cheekily asked if that was Rumi. "No," she deadpanned, "Chief Seattle."

She called me while I was still laughing. We were both a little high.

"I do not wish to leave my boys, Mrs. Humphrey."

BETH DID NOT want to die alone, and we all promised that she would not.

The home-based hospice nurse answered questions while I took notes with a pencil, trying to be helpful. She explained the process—what Beth might feel, how to conserve energy. I sat on the corner of the bed with Joe, the three of us making an awkward triangle.

When Beth said, "I do not want to suffocate," I realized my pencil notes were useless. By this time, Beth had no need for my brownies. She had moved on to stronger painkillers, and I held her pale hand during the barely conscious ambulance ride to the hospice center. Another friend rode in the ambulance, too, and still more followed in a Joe-led caravan. There were seven of us, total. She did not suffocate, and she did not die alone.

BETH RECEIVED HER diagnosis during the summer solstice, and her funeral happened on the next year's Lammas. She would have smiled about the impropriety of a gluten-free cancer diet aligning with a wheat harvest celebration. The church ladies laid out a potluck. Finger sandwiches. A berry cobbler. Cheese and crackers. Brownies, but not the marijuana kind. I imagined her Katharine Hepburn nasal voice noting the vulgarity of such abundance.

Before Beth, the closest I ever came to a friend's death were acquaintances or high school classmates. Tragically young or mercifully old. Sad, but with layers of distance—often just newspaper obituaries mailed by my parents. Suicide. Car accident. Heart attack. War.

Before Beth, I had never taken the first shift of a hospital stay and adjusted a friend's incontinence pad. I had never coached anyone through an anxiety attack or watched them vomit from stress.

Before Beth, I sent condolences.

I never grieved.

When the third Valium had no effect on the day of her funeral, I sat down on the church bathroom's floor and swallowed a fourth, wishing I had packed a brownie, the tile cool against my bare calves.

IN THE SPACE following those final moments, there is so much I want to tell Beth. Joe and I eat breakfast almost every week. He often orders home fries packed to-go for their son, who is off to college soon. Their son is much taller now, handsome and lanky with adolescent swagger. A smart kid. Funny. I see Beth's features in his face. She would be so proud. Twister still lives in his bedroom.

On that first day of her diagnosis, when Beth knew bad but not how bad, Joe existed as a sort of peripheral presence—the husband character in the stories Beth told. He was a man waving from the porch or offering to toast bagels, not a friend sitting directly across from me. As Beth declined, Joe became more of a presence. I learned cheesecake was his favorite when, unable to drive, Beth asked me to deliver one for his birthday. Throughout her illness, Beth requested foot rubs from each of her visiting friends. She ranked Joe and me both as the very worst foot massagers, dead last on the list. It was the first time he and I laughed hard together.

"I really loved her," he said when he let her ashes go.

ONCE IN A WHILE, he says the same words at the diner. Usually, though, we talk about ordinary days. Salmon on sale at the grocery store. Olive oil imports. The election. We like the same hot sauce. He worries about his dad. We both stress about money. Joe offers good advice and tells funny stories. He listens. He thinks he might want to fall in love again someday. He says he is okay with me writing about Beth dying and the brownies I made for her.

We nod when Katie asks if we want a coffee warm-up.

HEIRLOOMS
Stuart Kestenbaum

I T FALLS TO my sister and me to sort through the household items. We're kneeling in the living room of my mother's small apartment in the assisted living complex. She has already been moved to the adjacent nursing home and will survive there only a while longer. Even though these things are the touchstones of our childhood, there is not much of material value. We spend the afternoon dividing household items. Some things will go to Goodwill, others to our children or nieces and nephews, and some to us. My mother made provisions for a few pieces of heirloom jewelry years ago. For the rest, it's up to us.

Making these decisions is humbling. What is the meaning of what we've accumulated? When an object reaches the thrift store, it becomes only stuff; if we hold onto it, it may continue to hold meaning. This afternoon we're sorting objects and listening to the stories they tell. Our mission comes at a time when I don't need to add anything else to my life. My children are mostly grown and out of the house, and I've got enough stuff of my own that needs sorting. What I'm looking for is what I want to remember.

Most of my mother's pots and pans have survived four moves and over sixty years of use, as have many of the kitchen utensils that I remember from childhood. And I remember my mother in the kitchen, where she cooked every meal and where we ate most of the time. Our dining room was used only for larger family gatherings and holiday dinners. I remember particular meals, like a Friday night dinner featuring a chicken soup I still try to emulate, or the sponge cake soaked with orange juice and layered and topped with whipped cream, which is still the cake of choice for my birthday. But it's the simpler things too—the way that she could make the perfect scrambled eggs with the butter browned, or put the extra frosting from a cake to harden in a small custard dish for a surprise treat.

In the commotion of getting four children out the door on school mornings, I, the youngest, could keep an eye on the coffee pot and turn the flame down halfway on our gas burners when it began to boil over. Inside the coffee pot was the mysterious world of percolation, the water in the bottom, the grounds in the basket with the perforated lid, water boiling up into the glass bubble on the lid and transforming itself. The aroma of coffee brewing is always the scent of a new day. And after dinner I could help clean the stove—a big white O'Keefe & Merritt—which had four burners and a griddle in the center, and an oven and broiler side by side. Under the burners was a chrome-handled tray that would catch whatever may have overflowed during cooking, and I slid them out and wiped them off. Some evenings my mom would let me clean the bottoms of the copper-clad pans with a cream cleaner called Twinkle. Rub it on with a sponge and rinse it off, and the copper magically loses its tarnish and looks new.

I choose two things: a green plastic measuring scoop and a large Revere Ware frying pan. I imagine the tool was a give-away at the A&P, the old store with the wooden floors and display of coffees (Red Circle, Eight O'Clock, and Bokar) next to the bean grinder. On the bottom, stamped in a semicircle, the words "ONE HEAPING TABLESPOON" and in the center "A USEFUL KITCHEN AID." I remember it having a long handle, but to accommodate a new cannister, my mother cut it. I can see the marks from the scissors.

Every morning I will use it to measure out my coffee. One scoop at a time, I will remember my mother with this small gesture. She is gone, and I am measuring out my own life, one morning following another.

The skillet is the perfect size for larger dishes of fish or chicken. At Hanukkah, I use it to fry potato latkes. After the meals, when I wash the dishes, I clean the copper bottom and watch the transformation from tarnish to shine, renewing one small part of the world with a small gesture.

This is what I have inherited or chosen to remember. Two humble objects from the kitchen of my childhood. I would be bereft were I to lose them.

I TELL HENRY THE PLATE IS RED
Annaliese Jakimides

ALTHOUGH HENRY AND I have been eating together for years—Brazilian and French, Cuban, Filipino, Turkish, and the twenty-four-hour mashed-potato diner near his place in Brooklyn that stays open every holiday—he has never eaten in the place where I live, until now. He has never even visited.

Henry is my love, my late-in-life love, the impossible love who crossed my path about twelve years ago, after my twenty-seven-year marriage was over, and the three children were grown and gone. (One really gone like my love will be.)

We met when he was performing in Orono—Charlie Musselwhite, Deborah Coleman, Corey Harris, and Henry Butler. No food involved.

When I pick him up at the airport, he is surprised that almost everyone knows me. I remind him that this is a small place. I could walk to the airport or the bus station. Bus is how I usually travel when I go to visit him: take the Concord to the Greyhound, then to Port Authority, where I catch the Metro, three changes, many stops. A stroll down the street, past Collado's, the family-owned Dominican fast-food place with community tables that we love. The el rattles overhead, flecking daylight through the grime-crusted rails. Finally, key in the door. Of course, getting a key to Henry's didn't happen immediately. It might have. It could have. If I'd realized that all I had to do was give him the key to my world—no strings attached, meaning "You're always welcome; you will never find me being anyone but me—the me that you know and trust."

When we enter my building, he immediately perceives that I live in an old high school—the broad, high-ceilinged hallway and the faint must of old wood and plaster make it clear.

Sun glitters through my twenty-foot-tall living room window, revealing the patinaed copper dome of the library next door. With the bowl of sky over the dome, it looks as if I could be living in a European—maybe Portuguese or French—city instead of Bangor. Although Henry's performed in those countries, it's not the look of my place that matters to him. He has never "seen" any of it, although I often forget that he cannot see. (All right, let me get this out of the way. I know it will linger if I don't. Infant glaucoma. Untreated. So shortly after birth, totally blind, no light. Eyeballs removed.)

He can identify everything by scent and taste, texture—and sound.

For days, I have been making lists:

> peppermint leaves
>
> long-grained organic brown rice
>
> unripe bananas
>
> granny smith apples
>
> bulbs and bulbs of garlic
>
> scallops from MacLaughlin's Seafood down the road

and planning meals:

> CABBAGE SALAD: purple and green, with wine-soaked raisins, toasted sunflower seeds, diced apples, onions
>
> NUT LOAF: cooked rice, cottage cheese, walnuts and cashews ground in the old hand grinder
>
> TOFU PIE: chunked, with carrots and eggplant, nutritional yeast and tamari, ginger, Mom's pie crust, still unmastered but acceptable
>
> ALL WITH BREAD: not mine. I no longer bake.

I've stocked the refrigerator as much as I can. Usually the interior is cavernous, with open spaces and an easy view to every corner; now it is so full I hold a map in my head of where, and behind what.

I know that these are the only days I will have to feed him. I will chop and season and cook in the tiny galley kitchen. I haven't fed anybody three meals a day for five days straight since I moved to this apartment, almost twenty years ago.

I'm not saying *have to* like it's an obligation, a weight, as in "Oh, damn, I gotta feed this man, every day. Shit!" No, it is literally all I will have, this one time in which to cook for and serve him. I can't say how I am so convinced, so sure that this will be it, that he will never be in my apartment again. Perhaps it's because it's taken him all these years to free enough days to come to a small town with no music, even if his love lives there. Perhaps it's the rumble of rapidly expanding cancer cells I can hear, and he can't.

A FEW YEARS AGO, we met three other couples at Chez Josephine on West Forty-Second for dinner. I was the only sighted person at the table and read the entire menu aloud, and loudly, in the crowded restaurant. I am convinced food has a language—is a language—beyond its spoken tongues of *escargot à la bourguignonne* and pissaladière. It comes out in your choices, your offerings and awarenesses, reactions. You don't get to know someone because of what they tell you about themselves. That's a façade or a shroud, a strange covering. The surface.

I am New England, not fancy. He is Southern, New Orleans.

Henry and I were born days apart. Worlds apart. Foods apart.

I went to public school. He went to boarding school for the blind. Neither of us cooked at home.

While Henry was playing the piano in St. Petersburg and Paris, developing his palate, I was a back-to-the-lander learning how to boil water on an old King Kineo wood cookstove in Mount Chase, Maine, population 146, in the shadow of Mount Katahdin. Dirt road. No electricity. A red Deming hand pump.

Growing up in Boston, I had no interest in knowing where food came from or how to prepare it. When I married and moved north, I never envisioned that we would grow or gather almost everything we ate, including borage and pigweed, wild mint, dandelion root, and thistle.

Nikki Giovanni says that you take what you have and make what you can. It's how I learned to cook. To write. To make art. No instructions—except to not waste what you know, what you feel, what you have. I learned I could always make something from nothing.

HENRY IS CHECKING out the old crock on the kitchen counter, filled with my cooking utensils. He runs his palm along the hand-carved donut stick I no longer have a need for but still love—the shape, the smooth maple. He fingers the old wooden spoon with the singed bowl. I know he's building a story of what they are, where they have been—before he asks, or not. Sometimes looking is enough. Like today.

For a moment, I wish he could have experienced me up north in the old kitchen big enough to hold both this living room and the galley space. The room with southern light and a table made from an old bowling lane, with plenty of room to measure, roll, chop, and mix. Food from the land. Immediacy. Freshness. And music flooding from speakers mounted in the high corners of the barn-beamed ceiling.

Luciano pavarotti said, "One of the very nicest things about life is the way we must regularly stop whatever it is we are doing and devote our attention to eating."

Still, I often skip eating, waiting for hunger itself to drive me to food, often just food at hand.

Today, I am neither hungry nor casually at-handing. I am purposeful, and happy to be feeding someone I love, this particular someone I love. Breakfast already in motion, I pre-chop extra onions and green peppers to go with my cheese soup later. I say "my" because nothing I make ever turns out the same. Another go at it, and I will have a new version.

Henry is waking hungry these days here with me—unusual for him. He sits at the early-morning table in a soft ocean of thin light leaking through the east window. I only have east windows, morning windows, windows that are today channeling a fierce winter wind. I watch his face— his whole face, glasses off—and his straight back. He was shocked one night at Dizzy's when I told him how a certain pianist was almost lying on the keys when he performed; he always thought everyone played sitting straight up as he did.

I can see him easily through the rectangular opening over the sink be-tween the kitchen and the living room. For the first time, I wonder why we don't call them "cooking" rooms, like "living" and "dining" rooms. I realize my chairs are not quite enough for his large ass and deep chest capable of rolling out thunderous notes, a moving baritone.

I've cooked eggs, large and fat-yellow scrambled. I have never mas-tered over-easy or sunny-side-up, a perfect omelet. He uses Louisiana hot sauce. For me, it's that wicked-hot Deer Camp 12 Gauge Ginger made in Waterville.

"You *can* cook," he says. There's almost an exclamation point at the end. He looks right at me. His smile opens the world.

We have eaten. I have made breakfast and lunch and dinner. Washed all the dishes.

He is listening now to Tyshawn Sorey. It is like dessert to me, the sound of Sorey swirling in the room, licking into his ears and mine. Sometimes he doesn't like to listen to music, but I'm hell-bent on playing some while he's here, on his knowing that I have a deep and diverse sound bank in my head, my heart. I don't know how to talk music any more than I know how to talk food.

I can only show you, and that requires you to be in my world—even just this once—so I can show you, Henry My Love:

> —How I set the table. Cloth napkins, some from my mother almost thirty years gone. The square plates with the tilted edges, food safe in the middle. I tell you they are red.

> —How I scrub the carrots and the apples, vinegaring them just as you do.

> —How my landscape is shaped. The long community tables at Bagel Central around the corner like at Collado's and the tiny halal place on your street. The people, the conversations, the love.

> —How the earth shifts—tectonic plates adjusting to apples and sauce, coriander and cheese, tofu, peppermint, and potatoes from the fields up north, food made by my hand, placed on your plate, at the little square table, our faces inches apart, feeding each other in unimaginable ways, sustenance and salvation, over and over again—in this cluster of days in the February before you leave.

TOLEDO
Susan Kenney

WHEN I WAS SIX and my little sister was six months old, we moved to Toledo, Ohio. The Sun Oil company had promoted my father to the position of land manager in charge of negotiating leases for pipelines in the northwest Ohio region and southern Ontario, and Toledo was where the refineries were. He had a nice office in the city and didn't have to travel so much anymore. We lived there for five years, and what I remember most about our time in Toledo is that my father came home for dinner almost every night and was home on weekends with the rest of us—my mother, me, my little sister, and my baby brother, born in Toledo a year after we got there. Soon registering the fact my mother had her hands full with two energetic kids in diapers and another one in elementary school, plus all the housekeeping, my father willingly took on the role of chief cook and bottle washer. The only thing he refused to do was diaper duty.

Raised in a traditional Scots-Irish household with a martinet father and a complaisant but secretly jovial and spirited mother, my father soon established routines for all of us for when he got home in the evening.

He and my mother would sit down in the living room and have a highball while I did my homework and the little kids played with their toys. Then my mother would feed them and take them upstairs to bed. Meanwhile my father would start dinner while I sat in the kitchen and told him about my day. Dinner was invariably meat or chicken, broiled, roasted in the oven or fried, mashed potatoes, a vegetable or salad greens doused in vinegar and oil. There was the occasional macaroni and cheese casserole, but never anything fancy that took too long or required looking at a "cookery book."

For me, these meals and their makings all merge together as much the same, but there is one ubiquitous menu item that stands out in my memory: Daddy's Welch Rabbit. Without fail, every Sunday after church we headed straight home, and he would make our special Sunday brunch: a savory dish he had learned by heart from his bachelor days in the city.

BECAUSE I AM THE OLDEST, while Mom and the little kids sit around the table in the dining room, I'm allowed to stay in the kitchen to help. I hop on a stool and watch as Dad gets cooking.

First, he starts up a double boiler on the stove, then pops open a glass jar of Kraft Old English Sharp Cheddar Cheese Spread and with a dinner knife scrapes the contents into the top of the double boiler while the bottom half keeps up a rolling boil. While the cheese melts, he gets out the sliced bread for me to toast, two pieces for each of us. When the cheese is completely melted, he opens up a can of Campbell's Condensed Cream of Mushroom soup and pours it in with the melted cheese. He stirs it all together until it is smooth and creamy, a nice golden color with the little chunks of mushrooms that I can't stand to eat, but it's all part of Dad's time-honored recipe, and I will take care of that later. Lastly, he shakes a few drops of his ever-present bottle of Worcestershire sauce and stirs it in. "All done!" he says, turns off the stove and licks the spoon. "Mmmn-umm! Okay, Susie Q, time to make the toast."

I pop the bread slices in and out of the toaster as fast as I can and put two buttered pieces on each plate. Dad ladles the Welch Rabbit onto each plate, except for my brother's, as he only eats the toast and will throw the ones with sauce from his high chair onto the floor. We take the plates of toast and sauce into the dining room and pass them around. Mom reaches across the table and cuts my sister's into several pieces so she can manage better.

I sit down in my place next to my sister and we all dig in, except for my brother, who is putting a piece of toast on top of his head with both hands. While Dad is dealing with that, my sister is eyeing my plate. With my fork I quickly pick the mushroom bits out of my sauce, push them onto her plate, and she gobbles them right up. I finish mine up mushroom-free.

And that is how in all those Toledo years we had brunch each Sunday with our unforgettable Daddy's Welch Rabbit.

And I never even thought to ask which part was the rabbit.

Some years later I happened to mention my dad's Welch Rabbit recipe to a culinary-wise friend, who immediately corrected my pronunciation: "Oh, you mean *Welsh rarebit!*" and directed me to a recipe that included thick-sliced hearty whole-grain bread, cheese sauce from scratch, mustard, and hot pepper flakes mixed with either dark ale or stout, open-faced sandwich broiled or torched to brown the cheese and there you have . . . Welsh rarebit. Definitely not quick and not child-friendly. Like my father's simple recipe, it did call for a splash of Worcestershire sauce, but that's it. Still, I will be sticking with my father's version.

Either way, there never was a rabbit.

ALMOST FIVE YEARS to the day after we moved to Toledo, my father died suddenly of a heart attack away from home, one week after he turned forty-eight. He left the house in Toledo on Wednesday, drove to Sarnia, Ontario, on business and died at 4:20 a.m. on Friday, June 19.

The phone ringing at 5 a.m. woke me up, and I hurried into my parents' room with a feeling of dread. Even as a child, I knew that no one calls that early in the morning with good news.

My mother was sitting on the end of the bed, staring out the window, the phone in her lap.

"Daddy?" I said.

I remember my mother's profile, the slow, precise movement of her hand as she carefully placed the phone receiver back into its cradle. Then she turned to me. "Yes," she said. "He died an hour ago." Then she corrected herself. "Actually, forty minutes." She turned back to stare out the window, her figure as pale and silent as porcelain in the dawn light.

My mother was forty-four years old; I was twelve, my little sister was five, and my brother was four.

"Go back to bed," she said. "No crying. I don't want to wake the children. If you need to cry, you can go next door and stay with Mrs. Smith for now. She'll know what to do. I just have to think."

I didn't want to go back into my room or go next door, so I asked if I could stay with her. She sighed, then nodded, and we both crawled back into her bed. She waited until it was around 7 a.m., right before the little kids usually got up, and went downstairs to call the family. The sky brightened into daylight, my sister and brother tumbled out of bed as usual, but my mother told me not to say anything to them just yet. "Just let them go on with their day," she said. "They'll find out soon enough."

They probably knew something was up, because as soon as the word got around, by mid-morning, the food began to come in. Food was comfort in those days, and it started coming in from neighbors and friends both on foot and by car well into the afternoon and evening. Food in trays and casseroles, both baked and unbaked, soups and breads, buttery sweet rolls still warm from the oven, fruit pies and vegetable pies with cheese and egg, baskets of fruit, cookies, cupcakes, even ice cream. Some were food items I had never seen before and couldn't name to this day. Our refrigerator and cupboards filled up, and so did the dining room table, until our next-door neighbor took charge, stood at the front doorway, and began diverting contributions to her house to save for later.

A friend with children the same ages as my sister and brother drove up the driveway and took them away to have breakfast and lunch and play at her house for the day. Someone else took the laundry away and brought it back clean and folded next morning. The parents of one of my sixth-grade classmates came and picked me up at noontime and took me to their country club to have lunch and swim.

Through all this, my mother made a brief appearance, then went back to her phone calls, arrangements to be made, my father's car in Canada, *my father* in Canada. Except he wasn't, he had been taken from his motel to a hospital in Port Huron, Michigan, and that is where he died.

Meanwhile, my grandmother in Skaneateles and my grown-up cousin Charles had gotten right in the car and were on their way, even though it meant they had to drive all night.

All this flurry and bustle was exhausting. Also distracting, glossing over the hours of this long sad day with a feeling of unreality, a sense that the bad news was really all a dream. So my mother and I slept hard that night, as did the little kids, as though everything was just the same as yesterday. Tomorrow would be another day and then it would be time to cope. And we wouldn't have to worry about our next meal for quite a while. What the friends and neighbors had given us was not just food and comfort, but time.

FATHER, FORGIVE ME
Hal Crowther

NOVELIST AND COLUMNIST G. D. Gearino wrote a graceful tribute
to his father, and admiring it, I realized I'd never written anything
about mine. Maybe every father with a son in the writing trade deserves
at least one of these family portraits, especially if the father's no longer living and the son has something nice to say. What occasion would be more
fitting than the close conjunction of Memorial Day, Father's Day, and the
anniversary of my father's death? And of course, I'd been grilling out, and
grilling out never fails to make me think of my father.

I was working on the expensive gas grill my wife gave me for Christmas, a formidable machine that produces, in a matter of seconds, enough
heat to barbecue a small heretic with some baked potatoes on the side.
How this high-tech monster would have amazed and probably disgusted
my father. He worked for years with a wretched little grease-caked hibachi like you see at every garage sale, and never graduated beyond a $25
charcoal grill. He never owned one with a cover, which he would have
regarded as effete.

The alarming thing about my father as a grill chef was his impatience
with slow briquets and his willingness to goose them with anything flam-
mable. I saw him use gasoline, kerosene, transmission fluid, and sludge from
someone's oil change he found in his shed: every petroleum product the
instructions on the bag of charcoal tell you to never, never try. We ate beef
seared with everything but napalm. Sometimes I'd find a little pellet of
poisonous-tasting carbon stuck to the underside of my T-bone.

There were tremendous bursts of flame when he tossed in his match, or
sometimes a lighted cigarette. One Sunday, he smeared the charcoal with
an unidentifiable mess from a rusted can, and the blast singed his eyebrows

and chest hair. The trick was to toss the match and spring away back-pedaling; in his fifties, he was still surprisingly quick.

When he'd fire up, I'd cower by a lilac bush twenty feet from the flash zone, counseling caution. He was not a man of action or a man who courted risks, my father. But he had a great misplaced confidence that nothing in the physical world could defeat him, or at least nothing so humble as a charcoal grill or an outboard motor. Of course he never cooked or prepared anything indoors. Men of his generation got away with the self-serving myth that the kitchen contained mysteries beyond their grasp. My father could operate a thirty-foot fishing boat but not an electric can opener, and he found it impossible to manufacture a sandwich.

Something of a dandy for an academic, he usually wore a coat and tie, often a vest as well. But when he grilled, in the privacy of his backyard behind a fifteen-foot hedge of wild roses, my father went topless over a pair of Navy-issue khaki shorts that hung below his knees, NBA style. On hot summer days, he'd sweat them through till there was no dry patch visible. Fierce perspiration was another genetic legacy I'd have passed up if I'd been given the choice.

He taught me to enjoy steaks the way he prepared them: bloody inside a rich crust of carcinogenic carbon. He loved to bait "the peasants," usually members of my mother's family, who took their meat well-done. As a child, I was an awed spectator at the grilling ritual. But when I reached my late teens, he began to share his martinis with me and put me to work as a sous-chef, usually wielding a hose or a watering can to keep the flames from consuming the meat and half the shrubbery.

Those were the best of times for me, the best I can remember with my father when he was still in his prime, and I was old enough to amuse him. For me, a dry martini was always the shortest distance between a malignant universe and a benign one. Martinis made my father expansive and approachable, which he was not as a rule. He laughed in two frequencies, a rib-rattling bass rumble and an incongruous high-pitched giggle. Sometimes when he drank, he'd speak in tongues, dazzling me with words and phrases from a dozen languages he couldn't actually speak. He collected them because he loved the way they sounded. We talked about sports, religion, women, and politics. And more seriously about money, work, and ambition, of which both of us have been charged with an insufficiency.

Picture a tall, underdeveloped-looking white boy with a Ricky Nelson brush cut, a nearsighted boy wearing thick glasses with geeky black plastic frames à la Buddy Holly, only geeks weren't cool in 1962, and I'd never heard of Buddy Holly. Picture a small, trim bald man in his forties, known for his good looks when he had hair, a man somehow dapper even half-naked in droopy, soaked Navy shorts; a man from the prewar generation for whom a cocktail in one hand and a cigarette in the other were accessories as natural as a fedora and two-toned shoes. I don't know who ever saw us out there drinking—my mother and brother rarely ventured out—unless it was the Kaufman kids from next door, peering through the hedge in bewilderment to see if Dad's towering inferno was a threat to their home.

Father and son. Senior and Junior. There's something especially intimidating about carrying the same name as your father, a burden that Roy Blount Jr. explores at chapter length in his memoir *Be Sweet*. A son so closely identified with his father tends to get a mixed message: He can't fail life so miserably that he embarrasses the old man, but he shouldn't make such a success that he eclipses him either.

Even if my name had been Hector, my father would have been a tough act to follow. Disapproving women say of such men, "He's in love with the sound of his own voice." And a rare voice it was, a full pulpit baritone with a fine singing range and room-shaking volume when he chose to turn it loose. I was never so mortified as when he sang his favorite hymns so loud that the Methodists turned around in their pews to stare. On the other hand, I was never so impressed as when he stood silent during the Apostles' Creed, so conspicuously silent with his big voice, silent because he was raised a Universalist and wouldn't recite anything he didn't believe.

When I first understood what he was doing with his silence—legitimizing nonconformity, rejecting peer pressure, making a public show of dissenting principle—it probably influenced me as profoundly as anything he ever offered me. My father had no time for public opinion or group-think of any kind, and on this score. I'm sure I've never disappointed him.

Of course, there's a downside to a father like mine. He was a great big voice that issued judgments, swift and stern, from a swirling cloud of smoke. In my Bible School days, I must have confused him with the God of Moses. Whatever doubts he may have had about himself or anything else, he did not wear them on his sleeve. An over-confident father rarely raises confident sons. On the few occasions when I take myself into the shop for a psychological tune-up—just light maintenance, really, anger management, attitude adjustment—the counselor always diagnoses me with a violent aversion to authority, and my father is always the scapegoat.

When you open this door, as Gearino and Blount must have discovered, the stories and associations just tumble out and start racing in all directions. There's no closure, as the psychobabblers call it, when the subject is Dad. No matter how long he's been gone. A friend of mine in his seventies told me that it was hard to focus on his relationship with his son—age fifty—because he'd never resolved his relationship with his father, who'd been dead for thirty years.

In Ethan Canin's story "The Year of Getting to Know Us," a father tells his son, "You don't have to worry about getting to know me, because one day you're going to grow up and then you are going to *be* me."

This is the last laugh all fathers, beloved or belittled, will have on all sons. There are time bombs lurking in our chromosomes, genetic traps that were set before we were born. Sometimes it's scary. We resist by parading small victories that prove we're not clones. Of all the milder forms of stupidity, I suppose I hate cigarettes the most. I've never smoked one. I hate them because my father's smoke screen kept us even farther apart—I'm allergic to the stuff—and because they killed him and I miss him. But in a hundred other ways he's creeping up on me, and there's no way to distinguish what he taught me from what he buried in my blood.

Once, he was the dude with a hundred suits, and I was the hippy with one ratty blazer who mocked him. Now my closets are filling up mysteriously with clothes I don't need. When I'm not working I read all day, every day, just as he did back when I was trying desperately to get his attention. I'm starting to pull away from people a little, the way he did in his fifties. Even some of his famous eccentricities—like his rule that no one but blood kin was welcome in our house after sundown—are beginning to make sense to me now.

I still like to drink martinis, though not as often or as many as we used to. And when the sun gets low over the crape myrtles, I still go out to the back fence, as often as I can, and start my fire. The backyard grill is the one middle-class, wholesome, suburban all-American habit I've kept all my life, even when my hair was so long I had to tie it back to keep it out of the coals. I'd hesitate to say this about anything else, even now, but I'm better at it than my father was. And I never use diesel fuel.

COMFORT, CONNECTION, CONSOLATION

Mary E. Plouffe

F OOD IS NOT about the *s*'s for me: salt, sweet, and savory. I'm not even sure I know what savory means. Ask me about food and my mind goes to *c*'s: comfort, connection, consolation. These are the meanings I know best; the only ones I can try to explain.

COMFORT

One moment we are floating, serene and secure, surrounded by warmth and umbilically tied to every nutrient we need. The next, the comforting warmth drains, and we are pushed, pulled, muscled free into a new world. We know instinctively to do two things: breathe and root, our tiny mouths turning toward warm skin, searching for food, desperate to be held. From that moment on, food means survival and comfort.

The survival piece never changes. No one can live without food. But the comfort piece shapes itself around each person's story. What are the foods we crave, the ones that trigger long-buried images of being held and soothed? The ones earliest attached to endorphin release and cortisol reduction and all those complicated, unnamed chemicals of contentment? Comfort foods are the foods of regression. We return to them under stress, or in moments of loss and upheaval. This story of comfort food is unique to each of us.

"Mary Beth, put the potatoes on while I decide what we're having for supper." By the time I was ten, this was my 5:00 p.m. chore. A pot full of boiling potatoes was essential, no matter what else was on the menu. In my Irish American family, the word was pronounced with more *d*'s than *t*'s, but the message was clear. Potatoes first and always. It was our tie to the old country, the Ireland that all four of my grandparents left as young adults, because there were no jobs, not enough farms, and no future after decades of famine that their parents and grandparents had endured. Like the passing of genetic trauma, this story lived in us, and each night one simple Irish reenactment soothed us all, especially my grandfather, at eighty-five the only one left at the table to remember.

Simple foods, simply prepared, are still my first choice. Complicated recipes are fun to try, but I need energy to do so. There's a space for me between hunger and adventure. My children have crossed that space, long since expanding their palates beyond the foods I cooked for them, because familiarity is only half the comfort story. Something more primitive is needed to lock sustenance and security together. Something that feeds more than your stomach.

My real comfort foods are remnants of the sweet tooth I indulged when I felt weird and different. The days I wanted more solitude than my friends did and my mother's expression suggested concern. A nickel's worth of penny candy gave me comfort then. Now, that pure sugar is easy to avoid until I'm exhausted, or emotionally drained. Most times, I just breathe deeply as I drive by the drugstore, aware of the temptation. Some days, I take the other way home.

Comfort foods are usually simple foods: carbohydrates and sugars, pastas and pizzas. The biology of how they trigger our pleasure centers is easier to understand now, its chemistry revealed. But the psychology of comfort food remains mysterious because it is unique. It can take us back to the hot dog at our first baseball game, excitement its most powerful seasoning, or the ice cream cone salted by tears on the day a grandparent died; a parent's pure belief that we could do anything, and their protective shelter when failure came. Food shared in these moments built more than muscle. It built identity, self-esteem, and resilience: strengths we reach for when the world knocks us down. Our taste buds pull us back to the intersection of food and nurturance and love.

The tapestry of food and feelings is woven of moments seared in our memories. A hundred stories of food and family, frustration and fear, and how we found our way.

The story of comfort food is the story of our lives.

CONNECTION

When my daughter-in-law had cancer, her extended Jewish family sur-rounded her. Whenever she was home between surgeries or clinical trials, dozens of cousins, aunts, and uncles arrived on the weekend, and her New York City apartment was filled with laughter and gossip, teasing family stories, and roughhousing on the couch. It was loud, it was festive, and she loved it.

Mid-afternoon, the doorbell would ring. "Let's see what he sent this time!" someone would yell, and the unwrapping began. Meats and cheeses, bagels and lox, platters of 2nd Avenue Deli cookies and specialties poured out onto the granite island, ordered by an uncle at home in Los Angeles. "He must have known you were here, Ben. Remember these?!" or "What, no biscotti?" added to the din. The foods of a hundred family celebrations required no menu, no order from the guests. They simply arrived, filling the house with the smells and tastes and the stories of her life.

Food is the connection that forges our families, deepens our friendships, and speaks the language of affection. We know you. We see you. We are with you.

Sometimes this language spans generations, like the worn brown recipe boxes in my cabinet, filled with index cards stained with age. No matter how rarely used, they can never be thrown away. They are the daily written record of the way our ancestors loved us, cooking what food they had, meager or rich, and feeding those who would give us life. Notes in the margin, written in a penciled hand we never knew, speak warnings ("350 too hot, try 325"), or suggest a secret variation ("Mom adds raisins . . . ?"), and we listen. Voices from the past, teaching us today. Loving us with food. Offering a foundation stone, so we can add our own food connections and build our own stories.

Last week, I sent three orange Tootsie Pops to my oldest friend. No note included, no words required. Just something to hold onto as she sat, waiting for test results that could upend her life.

Food is how we know one another, and how we connect in love.

CONSOLATION

"If one more person brings me food, I'm going to scream. I've flushed soup down the toilet three times this week already!" the young widow raged in my office. "For God's sake, tell me why they think I want food?"

Food speaks the language of compassion. In almost every culture, consolation and sympathy come packaged in a casserole, cookies, or homemade soup. On the surface, it's a simple message of caring. You are too sad, too distracted, too upset to worry about meal preparation, it says. We know you are hurting. We will feed you.

But the woman in my office knew this. Her rage was deeper. "They keep saying, 'You've got to eat something,'" She paused and glared at me defiantly, "Really? Do I?"

That was the question stuck in her throat, the implication in everyone's kindness. For underneath compassion, beneath caring, lies an invitation to courage. You will survive this, you can get through this, we want you to try.

Most of the time, we find this reassuring. Others have felt the shattered dislocation of an untimely or devastating death. Others have survived the frozen panic that surrounds us now. In deepest grief, we lap up their courage, hoping it will take, hoping it will help us find our own.

But not that morning. Not the day this young woman sat across from me, torn with guilt, fractured with fear. Her husband's suicide sat between us like a raging lion. Consolation had no place in the room.

"They want you to live," I said softly, almost afraid to speak the words aloud.

"Well, they're going to have to wait," she hissed, and turned away, " . . . until . . . I can decide."

And so, they did.

A friend arrived each evening, bringing dinner for one, and ate it while she watched. Night after night, without comment or cajoling. They listened to her silence, nodded softly when she cried. They sat and ate, one slow, small bite at a time.

Months late, she told me the story. How no one pushed her to join in the meal, how leftovers went home with her guest. "All they asked was that I sit with them and watch them eat. I could do that, couldn't I?" Nights became weeks, and still one by one, they came. Without judgment or explanation, they continued the vigil, bearing witness to her pain.

I listened silently to her story, not sure how it would end. She shook her head, struggling to explain. "It's like they showed me how to live, one tiny bite at a time. One night I felt I could try that, one step and then one more. I didn't know how, but I wanted to survive."

The food of consolation can take us full circle. Beyond courage and caring. To that liminal space between a world we've lost and the unknown. To the threshold where, first, we must learn to breathe.

Food is how we hold each other up, and how we begin again.

PART IV

FAMILY AND COMMUNITY

THE TRANSIT OF MEMORY
Jane Brox

M Y CHILDHOOD WORLD was a hundred acres of fields, orchards, and woods in the Merrimack Valley of northeastern Massachusetts. When my grandparents settled there as recent immigrants early in the twentieth century, dairy farms were just scraping by, supplying milk to the tenement neighborhoods in the nearby mill city of Lawrence. The old Yankees were ready to abandon farming, but for my grandparents the prospect of life on the land looked promising. A house, a barn, and a small herd of cows were enough to give them hope of establishing security for their children and maintaining a little of the rural life they left behind in the dry vineyard region of Lebanon. They spoke Arabic, then broken English. Their children heard plenty of Arabic but spoke only English, and all save one would never see the world their parents left behind. But when they sat down to a meal, my father and his siblings lived in the memory of another country: Stuffed eggplant, stuffed kousa, stuffed grape leaves, hummus, za'atar, shish kebab. Eggs fried in olive oil.

In time, those Lebanese dishes, all handed down the generations, were joined by ones my grandmother and aunts picked up from neighbors or cut from newspapers, which they stuffed into the pages of their copy of *The Modern Priscilla Cookbook*, published in Boston in 1924. I still have recipes my aunts copied out by hand—doughnuts, cream cake, Indian pudding, bread and butter pickles, corn pone—from a time before elaborate and detailed instruction, before precise weights and measures: *Use a piece of butter the size of an egg. A little nutmeg. A pinch of salt. Bake in a slow oven. Serve with any desired sauce.*

WHEN MY FATHER took over the farm, around the time of the Second World War, he sold the dairy herd and turned to growing the usual New England vegetables: sweet corn, green beans, cucumbers, tomatoes, winter squashes. He planted an apple orchard typical of that mid-century: standard trees bearing mostly McIntosh, Cortland, and Northern Spy. He'd graduated from the Stockbridge School of Agriculture, and I remember him being as proud of Waltham butternuts, which were developed at the nearby Massachusetts Agricultural Experiment Station, and Northern Spies—"a New York apple," he'd say brightly—as he was of kousa, a pale green Middle Eastern squash that we ate stuffed with lamb and rice, and that he grew for us and for other descendants of Lebanese immigrants in Lawrence.

My grandparents had died by the time I was born, maybe even before the first Spies began to bear, though I can't be sure of that. Although the family gatherings of my childhood always began with hummus drizzled with olive oil, scattered with red onions, and served and with small wedges of Syrian bread on the side, I rarely heard Arabic except when my father talked a kind of pidgin with his brothers: it had become their secret language. If I remember rightly, our everyday meals were more or less evenly split between American fare and Lebanese dishes. One night we'd have grape leaves for dinner; the next, hamburgers. We ate sweet corn with our shish kebab wrapped in Syrian bread. Marinated black olives shared the center of the table with ketchup and mustard.

NOW HALF A CENTURY LATER, I can't tell you which means more to me: a pie made with Northern Spies or flatbread sprinkled with that pungent spice mix za'atar—which is what we called the bread itself, and the only way we ate za'atar. The fruits and vegetables my father grew and those traditional Lebanese dishes live side by side in the province of my memory even though I've long inhabited a borderless world of food. I eat, and often cook, things that would have been unthinkable around our table on the farm—corn tortillas, jalapeños, *bánh mì*, *cacio e pepe*, bouillabaisse, artichokes, avocados, socca. My store of flour alone goes far beyond my mother's bag of Gold Medal: chickpea, buckwheat, whole wheat, semolina, rye. I own several dozen cookbooks, and among them are Sicilian, Northern Italian, French, Mexican, and Chinese. There's a Lebanese one, too, because I didn't write down those recipes, and though I can easily conjure stuffed kousa simmering on the stove, I don't remember precisely how to make it. Almost all the recipes in that cookbook—as they tend to be these days—are elaborately prefaced with an anecdote from the author's own life. Her version of stuffed kousa tastes a little different from what I remember. I think the author goes in for more tomatoes and garlic than my aunts did. But it's close enough. She also notes that I can substitute zucchini or yellow squash for kousa. I'm not sure what my father's sisters would think of that. They both lived their entire life surrounded by the farm, as did my father and several of my uncles. They would be the generation for whom that land turned out to be a lasting home. Their immigrant parents were determined to make it so, but they could not stay time entirely. Almost all of my generation moved away. I can clearly remember my Auntie Del, the eldest, turning to me as I was about to leave for college. I'd never seen her so serious as she said: "Remember who you are." She must have known that I was already feeling I had to try very hard to forget in order to move forward.

DID SHE FORESEE how much my life would become a patchwork of the long familiar and the newly strange? How many islands, cities, and towns I would light upon and then leave? How each would come to have a tug of allegiance in my heart? I now live over a hundred miles north of where I was born. During the more than fifteen years I've called the coast of Maine home, the last of my parents' generation passed, and I have little reason to return to the farm of my childhood. The winds here are more bracing than they ever are in the Merrimack Valley and are also tinged with salt. But they toss the white pines and maples I've always known. The slopes of these hills aren't quite as pronounced as the ones I was born among, but I see in them a shadow of recognition. They are and they aren't familiar.

I could say that the memory of the foods of my childhood, both of the farm and of my Lebanese heritage, provide a sliver of constancy in my life. But even those borders are hazy. What is hummus now? Supermarket shelves are stocked with myriad flavors, including Thai coconut curry and dark chocolate. And none of them tastes like my aunt's. As for za'atar: its flavor is so intense that I never imagined it could be other than ours alone, or used in any other way besides topping flatbread. These days the *New York Times*, *Food and Wine*, and *Food52* publish dozens of recipes where za'atar is added to zucchini or roasted chicken. Stirred into greens, strewn on tomatoes, mixed into a purée of beets and yogurt. I've gamely tried most of them and especially like the beet recipe. Sometimes I even fry my eggs in butter and sprinkle them with za'atar.

While the privacies of my Lebanese childhood have spilled into the world, other things from that time have become rare. Macs and Cortlands always show up in the supermarkets in late summer, but Northern Spies are known as an heirloom apple now and are more difficult to secure than a bag of za'atar. Of all the crops my father grew, apples hold the most stubborn share of my memories. You plant apple trees and then you wait. For Spies, you wait a long time. They can take a decade to bear fruit, and they are the last lingering crop of the year to bring in. I can see them now, hanging on alone and weighing down the branches in the resounding silence of the frost, while the other trees in the orchard are all sprung and light with just a few yellow leaves clinging to them. Only during the final short days of the season did my father haul bushels of Spies to the apple cellar where they'd keep even into spring settled among the boxes of softening McIntosh.

It gives me inexplicable pleasure to come upon Spies now, and sometimes in October I roam the surrounding countryside looking for them. What am I searching for? What Spies meant to us snugged in that valley together? Or what they've meant to me since I left my first home? I think of what my friend Esther Weisslitz, now gone many years, wrote about Canada geese: *They are still all about always to me.*

THIS PAST FALL I drove a little inland to Sabattus along a high stretch of road with the Western hills in the distance, far beyond the quiet farms neat in their late season. When I saw the orchard set behind the modest roadside stand I'd been looking for, my throat tightened with recognition. The old trees had the same broad crowns as my father's orchard. They were spaced in the same way. I'd run through such trees a thousand times. Climbed them. Stood in a rain of their spent blossoms. There and then I almost forgot that they, too, are fleeting, prone to weather, circumstance, and human wishes.

I only need to go back to Henry David Thoreau to remind me of just how much those orderly rows of trees are part of a created idea of place in time. In the middle of his own century, he railed against the carefully plotted orchards of my memory. He had no patience for them nor likely for Northern Spies, which had been discovered in an orchard in 1800 and then moved into general cultivation in the northeast around the time Thoreau was writing "Wild Apples," his song of praise for scraggly, waning cider orchards. "I love better to go through the old orchards of ungrafted apple-trees, at whatever season of the year—so irregularly planted," he wrote, "sometimes two trees standing close together; and the rows so devi-ous that you would think that they not only had grown while the owner was sleeping, but had been set out by him in a somnambulic state. The rows of grafted fruit will never tempt me to wander amid them like these. But I now, alas, speak rather from memory than from any recent experi-ence, such ravages have been made!"

There, in Sabattus, I wanted nothing more than to wander among the orderly rows of grafted, pruned Macs, Cortlands, and Northern Spies of my own time, even if just for a moment, even as the passing migrant that I am.

ALL THE WORLD LOVES
A GOOD COOK
Deborah Joy Corey

I N MY CHILDHOOD HOME, food was the maypole that we danced around, morning, noon, and night. While enjoying pork-fry and biscuits with home-made strawberry jam on a crisp fall morning, our parents might discuss current events or listen while we children practiced a new accent or a skit, but without fail, they always discussed the lunch and dinner menu to follow that day. It was as if the present meal could not be fully enjoyed without glimpsing the ribbon that would lead us to the next.

Our large kitchen was set in the center of a rambling house, which my paternal grandparents had built. There were two rocking chairs and a large oval table surrounded by a bevy of wooden chairs with an antique bench along the back. Above the table, which was often covered in a tablecloth to match the flowered wallpaper, a cuckoo clock reminded everyone of the new hour and of mealtime. There were shiny maple kitchen cabinets and a window over the sink that faced a hayfield. Another window on the opposite wall faced our driveway and beneath it was an antique day bed covered in crushed blue velvet. Our family kitchen was bright and warm, and it was where we gathered.

I don't believe the word *sustenance* was ever mentioned, nor for that matter was the word *nourishment*, and no food was ever restricted for its calorie count. No attention was paid to the amount of butter or cream used. Our kitchen was a place of entertainment, comfort, and healing that often smelled of brown bread rising and berry pies baking, of braising roasts and simmering stews, of gingerbread, and nutmeg and cloves.

For the ill or injured or recently bereaved, it was base camp. Our mother made mustard-seed poultices for chest congestion, milk toast for anyone recovering from nausea, and a rich beef marrow broth to help heal broken bones. When we lost a beloved relative or neighbor, Mom would bake a ham or two chicken stews with dumplings shaped like heavenly clouds. One for the grieving family and the other for us. Never a heartache passed without our father saying, "Everyone has to eat."

DAD WAS THE main food gatherer and Mom, the star cook. She had learned from her Scottish aunt with whom she lived after the early death of her parents. She called her "Mama." Evidently, Mama's shortbread would make a queen cry.

"Her shortbread melted in my mouth," Mom said, "simply irresistible. And Mama's warm chocolate pudding was often waiting for me when I returned from school. Oh, how I loved the skin on top. A recipe today would tell you how to avoid that by pressing plastic wrap down before it cools, but then it is just pudding. It won't have that intense topping of chocolate. And it is best eaten warm with a little cream poured over it."

MOM ALSO LEARNED to cook from two older sisters, who had left New Brunswick after the death of their parents to work in the pantries of wealthy Bostonians. Each summer, when they returned by train to Canada for their holiday, they passed along their pantry tips: Always slide fork tongs down the flesh of a peeled cucumber to keep it from tasting bitter when sliced. Hollandaise sauce must be made slowly in a barely warm pan. Unsweetened heavy cream, rather than whipped cream, is best for pouring over bread pudding.

GROWING UP, MY siblings and I followed my mother from task to task like pheasants. We watched her roll, beat, stir, fold, whip, cream, glaze, pinch, crimp, sear, steam, and sauté. When she kneaded bread dough, she engaged her entire body in a gentle back and forth motion, as if swaying to a hymn, her lovely hands corralling and pushing the baby-size mound of smooth dough.

"How do you know when to stop kneading?" I once asked.

"You feel it."

"What do you mean by that?"

"Well, the dough will expand and resist your hands just the right amount. Then you can butter it and put it in a bowl to rise."

You feel it.

———

ONLY A FEW COOKBOOKS were stacked in the cupboard over the fridge. The largest one was Irma S. Rombauer's *Joy of Cooking*, but Mom didn't often retrieve a cookbook. Instead, she might peruse her plastic turquoise recipe box, jammed with index cards of handwritten family recipes and clippings from magazines and newspapers. Flipping through the cards, Mom might pull out a recipe, glance quickly, and then return it to its spot.

Perusing the recipe cards with Mom, I noted the ones written in her handwriting often only listed the measurements of ingredients without instructions. Later, I would realize these were recipes that she had invented. Other recipes, the ones coveted and requested from aunts or friends, were neatly printed out with edits by Mom:

- Ruth's Family Reunion Coleslaw (*a touch more salt*)
- Edna Corey's Sugar Cookies (*shorten cooking time by 3 minutes*)
- Verta's Goulash (*add sugar to tomatoes*)

Some of the recipes were in our grandmother's handwriting, but none of those had been edited by Mom. She spoke of Gram Corey with admiration. Gram could make several pies at a time, all with an exalted buttery crust.

Once, when Dad and I were sharing a last piece of raspberry pie, I asked Mom how to make Gram's piecrust. With so few ingredients, it seemed like something that I could attempt.

Mom sat across from me sipping her King Cole tea. For a moment, she looked at me as if she felt sad, as if I'd lost something or had been overlooked by a party giver.

"Well, you start with a pound of butter," she said.

Dad must have seen disappointment or perhaps confusion on my face, for he reached out and rubbed my hand, as if to say, *Don't worry.*

Being a good cook himself, he understood the *feel* of cooking, and he knew that it was a practiced art. His seasonal fried salmon and fried partridge would make today's admired chefs vote him king of the throwdown. Still, it was the searching and gathering of ingredients that truly inspired him. When he made his first money picking potatoes at the age of twelve, he took the train to the local town of Woodstock and then bought a pound of bologna, eating it all while sitting on a bench in front of the store.

MY YOUNGER BROTHER Aubrey and I often gathered with Dad, traveling the back roads to patronize farmers, gardeners, smokers, anglers, pick-
lers, and any number of experimental cooks. A favorite stop was an older
couple, Barry and Lillian McFarlane. They made salt pickles and headcheese from slaughtered pigs. Aubrey and I also loved the McFarlanes, because they had adopted two children, exactly our ages. Kevin and Carla.
Sometimes while Dad visited in their kitchen, we wandered through their
pumpkin patch or took turns sitting on their friendly Holstein Betty.

I often attended Carla's birthday dinners. Once, American chop suey
was served. I thought it one of the best things that I had ever eaten. Soon
after the party, Mom called Lillian to request the recipe.

Another time, returning to the car with headcheese, Dad lifted the
waxed paper that covered a glass dish and cut squares of the grayish gela-
tin with his jackknife for each of us. Neither a pâté nor a mousse, its cool
smoothness released a bounty of spices that melted in our mouths and
made us reach our hands out for more. I pondered the method. Had it been
whipped or stirred, folded or beaten? And what exactly was headcheese?
Images came to mind, but I never asked, knowing full well that Dad was an
organ man—liver, kidneys, heart, and gizzards. One of *his* many specialties
was cooking offal.

SOMETIMES IN OUR kitchen, I assisted with food tasks, helping Dad peel
the Sunday dinner vegetables. Grinning, he often said that no one could
turn a large Yukon Gold into a fingerling quicker than I could. Sometimes
I stirred custard while Mom quickly ran to do another task, but I was a
hesitant cook, even though I was encouraged. After all, a well-turned-out
coconut cake by my sister Linda warranted as much praise as a high exam
score, and when my brother Dana served omelets or his flaky biscuits, it
was as if he had won the winning goal at a hockey game.

Still, the home kitchen attitude was thankfully genderless. Girls could
barbecue steaks, and boys could whip up a soufflé. For a time, Aubrey and
I did a marching rendition of "I'm a Woman," he with a dishcloth tied like
a pirate's bandana. We'd gotten the idea from watching Cher and Raquel
Welch perform on *The Ed Sullivan Show*. My favorite line being "I can
make a dress out of a feedbag, and I can make a man out of you."

It was easy for me to perform in our kitchen, but the act of cooking made me nervous, even though Aubrey had already jumped in with gusto. Like the rest of my siblings, he seemed to have picked up cooking by osmosis.

Besides, if most recipes lived in Mom's head, where should *I* begin? With that large Bible-size book called *Joy of Cooking*? Or with something from the recipe box that had already been tested and then made by Mom, beautifully? How could I compete? I longed for my own recipes but did not have the gift of cooking invention.

Recently, I texted Aubrey to see what the first things were that he cooked. A restaurant owner and known cook himself, he immediately texted back: "Hot dogs canned beans sardine sandwiches egg in a hole dagwood sandwich. By the way, I'll never forget eating those God-awful cabbage rolls that you made."

LIKE DAGWOOD, AUBREY always had his evening forays to the refrigerator. The cabbage rolls recipe came from a newly arrived *Ladies' Home Journal* when I was seventeen. By then, I'd gotten over my nervousness about cooking. Of course, anything that had yet to be cooked was considered an experiment until tasted. Yet, we'd all enjoyed the cabbage rolls, even Dad, who never deemed anything with hamburger and tomatoes a favorite.

That night, Aubrey and our cousin Floyd came in late and found the leftover cabbage rolls in the fridge. They finished them off lickety-split and then both vomited for the rest of the night. Even milk toast, delivered the following morning on silver trays, could not restore them. My cabbage rolls took the blame, but it is quite possible that they may have earlier in the evening been visiting the test kitchen of libations.

Later, I would have my own rough night born of a kitchen experience. A night when I came home after trying some wacky tabacky with friends, Dad had a left a tall pot simmering on the back of the stove. From the aroma, I was expecting beef bones and herbs, but when I removed the cover, a giant cow's tongue appeared. I slammed the pot's cover down and jumped back in horror, covering my mouth and thinking of the lovely Holstein Betty.

Going forward, Aubrey would never reminisce about the cabbage rolls, without me adding the story of the simmering cow's tongue.

WHAT FINALLY STARTED me cooking was a delightfully-sized *Peanuts Cookbook* ordered from a Scholastic Book sale when I was ten years old. No bigger than a large greeting card with several pages, *Peanuts Cookbook* held so much promise that I teared up when my teacher delivered it to me. On the pink and green cover, Linus stood beneath a frying pan and utensils. His eyes were closed smugly, and he held a spatula behind his back. His apron said "The Chef Is In." On the back cover, Snoopy was kissing Charlie Brown, who was delivering a bowl of food that resembled a pile of entrails. Above, a caption read "All the world loves a good cook."

On my way home on the school bus, I read all the recipes and comic strips in my new cookbook. It began with a list of safety rules and then a recipe for Snoopy's Steak Tartare (for dogs and cats only). I pondered the "for dogs and cats only," since Aubrey had recently used ground raw beef tenderloin while creating a Dagwood for Dad. His idea for the Dagwood came from our brother George, who was married to a glam wife and had a very modern kitchen. *His* specialty was steak tartare. For the sandwich, Aubrey added the McFarlanes' salt pickles and a homemade mustardy mayonnaise that my mother often made for potato salad. He had ground the beef in a grinder that he fastened to our kitchen table. It was the grinder that Mom often used to make her healing soups.

Every recipe in the pink-paged *Peanuts Cookbook* appeared easy and doable: Beethoven's Green Beans with Bacon, Peppermint Patty's Prune Whip, Lucy's Lemon Lollipops, Franklin's Jam Tarts, Charlie Brown's Mother's Buttered Oven Potatoes, Peanuts' Peanut Brittle, Schroeder's Chocolate Sauce, Sally's Broiled Cheese Hot-Dog Sandwich, Linus' Lemon-Pineapple-Carrot Salad, Lucy's Lemon Squares, and Red Baron Root Beer.

I thought of starting with Lucy's Lemon Lollipops, but there was a stamped warning that made me shy away.

WARNING: LEMON EXTRACT CATCHES FIRE EASILY.

DO NOT USE NEAR STOVE.

So I decided on Lucy's Lemon Squares. The recipe looked easy and the cooking time short.

By dinnertime, Lucy's squares were cooled and ready for dessert. Everyone had seconds, and no adjustments were suggested. I felt smug with my parents' compliments. Over the next few days, I tried every recipe in my new cookbook, often asking Dad to pick up a list of ingredients during our breakfast together. After I had tested all the recipes, Dad chose Peanuts' Peanut Brittle as his favorite.

"Best brittle I've ever eaten," he said.

I thought: *The Chef Is In.*

HEARTBREAKINGLY, FOR MY siblings and me, our parents endured institutional cooking at the end of their lives, either due to hospitalization or a retirement home. Once, at Mom's retirement home, she was served a hot dog with fried lettuce. Not the wilted salad recipe one might find in a trendy food column, but more likely, the last-ditch attempt by a tired cook, of adding something green.

Within a week of that meal, my older sister, Doe, had moved our mother to her home. There, Mom sat in a comfy rocking chair, taking in my sister's glorious kitchen, and often serving as chief taste tester. Doe was the first graduate of Mom's kitchen, and she cooks most like Mom and Gram Corey. Like our mother, she warrants the status of food goddess.

AFTER ONE OF Dad's many cancer surgeries, he was served chicken à la king in his hospital room. Although we all cooked and brought things from home, every once in a while, Dad was enticed by a description on the hospital menu. I suppose it was as close to *gathering* wonderful ingredients as he could possibly get while bedbound.

Aubrey and I watched as Dad removed the silver dome on his tray, revealing a white glutinous mess of a stew. The decipherable ingredients were noodles and gray peas. Neither Aubrey nor I spoke, but I know that our hearts sank in unison, and then rose in fear that Dad might actually taste it. Finally, Dad said, grinning at us, "I guess I'll send this back to the king."

Within fifteen minutes, Aubrey returned to Dad's room with a large order of crisp fish 'n' chips from a nearby restaurant, aptly named The Whoa Daddy.

A few weeks later, we were all sitting at our family table celebrating Dad's recovery and enjoying fried calf's liver and onions, as well as homemade French fries, for lunch. George recounted then how he had eaten his first French fries while traveling with Dad through a nearby border town. He was seven years old. Dad had parked the car and told George to wait. Dad disappeared down an alley and then reappeared with French fries piled in a large cone shaped from newspaper. They sat together in the car eating and licking their salty fingers until they were finished, neither of them saying a word, but both feeling exalted.

Around the table, we each smiled and nodded. We knew the feelings that those moments held.

IF ONE SEES the cookbook *Joy of Cooking* from a distance, "Joy" is the only word one registers. And every synonym for the word can be experienced in a home where food is loved and shared: *delight, jubilation, triumph, glee, rejoicing, happiness, euphoria, bliss, ecstasy, rapture, exaltation.*

Our beloved parents are both gone now, yet the memory of their inviting kitchen and dedication to food lives on in each of our homes. For this, we seven siblings and all our children and grandchildren are thankful. Our parents taught us that a family kitchen is a place for everyone and that each of us have our own ribbon and part in the maypole dance.

RECIPE BOX
Lee Smith

M Y MOTHER'S RECIPE BOX sits on the windowsill in our North Carolina kitchen where my eyes fall on it twenty, maybe thirty times a day. I will never move it. An anachronism in my own modern kitchen, the battered box contains my mother's whole life story, in a way, with all its places and phases, all her hopes and the accommodations she made in the name of love, as I have done, as we all do. I can read it like a novel—for in fact, our recipes tell us everything about us: where we live, what we value, how we spend our time. Mama's recipe box is an odd green-gold in color. She "antiqued" it, then decoupaged it with domestic decals of the '50s. One depicts a rolling pin, a flour sifter, a vase of daisies, and a cheerful, curly-headed mom wearing a red bead necklace; another shows a skillet, a milk bottle, a syrup pitcher, three eggs, and a grinning dad in an apron.

Oh, who *are* these people? My father never touched a spatula in his life. My mother suffered from "bad nerves," also "nervous stomach." She lived mostly on milk toast herself, yet she never failed to produce a nutritious supper for my father and me, including all the five food groups, for she had long been a home economics teacher. Our perfect supper was ready every night at 6:30 p.m., the time a family *ought* to eat, in Mama's opinion, though my workaholic daddy never got home from the dime store until 8:00 or 9:00 p.m. at the earliest, despite his best intentions. Somewhere in that two-hour stretch, I would have been allowed to eat alone, *reading a book*—my favorite thing in the world. My mother would have had her milk toast. And when my father finally had his solitary supper, warmed to an un-recognizable crisp in the oven, he never failed to pronounce it "absolutely delicious—the best thing I've ever put in my mouth!" My mother never failed to believe him, to give him her beautiful, tremulous smile, wearing the Fire and Ice lipstick she'd hurriedly applied when she heard his car in the driveway. Well, they loved each other—two sweet, fragile people who carefully bore this great love like a large glass object, incredibly delicate, along life's path.

My mother's father had killed himself when she was only three, leaving a pile of debt and six children for my grandmother to raise alone on Chincoteague Island. Grandma Annie Marshall turned their big old Victorian home into a boardinghouse, and it was here in the boardinghouse kitchen that my mother had learned to cook. Her recipe box holds sixteen different recipes for oysters, including oyster stew, oyster fritters, oyster pie, scalloped oysters, and the biblical-sounding Balaam's oysters. Clams are prepared "every whichaway," as she would have put it. There's also planked shad, cooter pie, and Pine Bark Stew. Mr. Hop Biddle's Hush Puppies bear the notation "tossed to the hounds around the campfire to keep them quiet." Mama notes that the favorite breakfast at the boardinghouse was fried fish, cornmeal cakes, and "plenty of hot coffee." These cornmeal cakes remained her specialty from the time she was a little girl, barely able to reach the stove, until her death eighty-four years later in the mountains so far from her island home. I imagine her as a child, biting her bottom lip in concentration and wiping perspiration off her pretty little face as she flips those cornmeal cakes on the hot griddle. Later, I see her walking miles across the ice in winter, back to college on the mainland.

Her lofty aspirations were reflected in her recipes: Lady Baltimore Cake came from Cousin Nellie, who had "married well"; the hopeful Soiree Punch was contributed by my aunt Gay-Gay in Birmingham, Alabama, the very epitome of something Mama desperately wanted to attain. She wanted me to attain it, too, sending me down to Alabama every summer for Lady Lessons. The asparagus souffle recipe came from my elegant aunt Millie, who had married a northern steel executive who actually cooked dinner for us himself, wearing an apron. He produced a roast beef that was bright red in the middle; at first, I was embarrassed for him, but then it turned out he'd meant to do it that way all along; he thought red meat was good, apparently, and enjoyed wearing the apron.

Here are Mama's Bridge Club recipes, filed all together. My first idea of an elegant meal came from this bridge club, whose members met every Thursday at noon for lunch and bridge, rotating houses, for years and years until its members began to die or move to Florida. I can see Mama now, greeting her friends at the door in her favorite black-and-white polka dot dress. I sat on the top stair to watch them arrive. I loved the cut flowers, the silver, and the pink cloths on the tables, though it was clear to me even then that the way these ladies were was a way I'd never be.

The food my mama gave the bridge club was wonderful. They feasted upon molded pink salad, which melted on the tongue (back then I thought *all* salads were Jell-O salads); something called Chicken Crunch (cut-up chicken, mushroom soup, celery, water chestnuts, Chinese noodles) and Lime Angel Cloud. *All* the bridge lunch recipes required mushroom soup, Jell-O, Dream Whip, or pecans.

But the recipes Mama actually used most—these soft, weathered index cards covered with thumbprints and spatters—reflect her deep involvement with her husband's family and their Appalachian community: venison stew, Gaynor Owens's Soup Beans, Ava McClanahan's Apple Stack Cake, my grandmother's Methodist Church Supper Salad, and, my favorite, Fid's Funeral Meat Loaf. A ham was also good in the case of death, glazed with brown sugar and Coca-Cola. Mama's recipe for Salvation Cake had a Bible verse listed beside each ingredient (the almonds came from Genesis 43:11), and the only instruction given for baking was the cryptic Proverbs 23:14. Fat content was *never* a consideration. Biscuits called for lard, and chocolate velvet cake required one cup of mayonnaise. A hearty beef and cheese casserole was named "Husband's Delight."

I, too, have written out my life in recipes. As a young bride, I had eleven dessert recipes featuring Cool Whip as the main ingredient. Then came the hibachi and fondue period, then the quiche and crêpes phase, then pasta, and now it's the salsa years. Just this past Christmas, I made cranberry salsa. My mother would not have touched salsa—let alone sushi!—with a ten-foot pole. One time, when we all went out for bagels in Chapel Hill, she said, "This may taste good to someone who has never eaten a biscuit." Another thing she used to say is, "No matter what is wrong with you, a sausage biscuit will make you feel a whole lot better." I agree, though I have somehow ended up with a wonderful husband who eats rare meat, wears an apron himself upon occasion, and makes a terrific risotto. We share the cooking. I seldom have time to bake these days, but I still make Mama's Famous Loaf Bread upon occasion, simply because the smell of it baking takes me straight back to that warm kitchen where somebody was always visiting. I can still hear my mother's voice, punctuated by her infectious laugh, her conspiratorial "Now promise me you won't tell a soul. . . ."

On impulse, I reach for Mama's recipe box and take out one of the most wrinkled and smudged cards, Pimento Cheese, everybody's favorite, thinking, as always, that I really ought to get these recipes into the computer or at least copy them before they disintegrate completely. On this one, Mama has underlined Durkee's dressing, followed by a parenthesis: (The secret ingredient!) Though I would never consider leaving the Durkee's dressing out, I don't really believe it is the secret ingredient. The secret ingredient is love.

TAKE ANOTHER LITTLE
PIZZA MY HEART
Jennifer Finney Boylan

I HAD EVERYTHING I NEEDED—the sweet sausage, the grilled shrimp, the three kinds of cheese. The dough had been rising since midafternoon. All my spices were lined up, the sauces in the right bowls. I'd had a long time to prepare. You could say I'd been getting ready to make this pizza for twenty years.

My father left the Catholic Church when he was twelve. There's not much Catholic left in me, except for my fondness for ritual. And so, as my wife and I approached the date of the departure of our younger child for college, I thought long and hard about the proper way to mark the moment. We'd climb a nearby mountain, I thought, with the symbolic name of Tumbledown. We'd go out for lobsters and steamers. We'd head to the local Shakespeare theater and watch some Oscar Wilde.

But reality interceded. It rained the day we were going to hike Tumbledown; my children decided they wanted to go out with their friends instead of to the theater. When I'd hoped to go to the lobster pound, my son needed to go shopping and headed to the Maine Mall instead. And so, what with one thing and another, there wasn't time for any of the sacraments I'd so carefully imagined.

Instead we ate pizza.

Over the years, we've weathered the ordinary traumas of family life: friends moving away; the death of grandparents; my daughter Zai's concussion in a sledding accident. Later, Zai experienced the death of the television conservationist Steve Irwin as if she'd lost a beloved uncle. My son Sean, meanwhile, hated a teacher in fourth grade so much that there were some mornings when he lay in bed in his pajamas, in tears.

And yet, through it all, as my daughter likes to say, "We have always been held together with cheese."

Friday night had always been homemade pizza night. Some Fridays, teenagers kept coming through the door until I ran out of dough: lobster with fresh basil on grilled flatbread; andouille sausage with spinach; barbecued chicken with caramelized onions; a four-cheese car wreck of mozzarella, Romano, fontina, and Gorgonzola. There was even one called "Ring of Fire," a deep-dish containing jalapeno peppers and onion rings about which the less said the better.

I made my family pizzas when the dog died; on the night after the prom; on a day a Maine blizzard left us with snow up to the windowpanes and icicles as long as my arm.

Now, after twenty years, I was down to my last three pies.

My wife and I have long had differing attitudes about our children's spreading their wings. On the day that Zai first went off to kindergarten, I burst into tears and wailed, "We're losing her to the world!"

My wife smiled from ear to ear and said, "Yeah, I know!"

Now our positions had reversed. I was the one eager for the next phase of our lives, while my wife focused, sadly, on the way our family was about to change.

I put the pizza stone in the oven and heated it to 550. Then I fired up the outdoor grill. The first pie up was Meatzapalooza: local sweet sausage, pepperoni, bacon, and ham, with a red sauce, mozzarella, and shaved Parm. While that one was baking inside, I threw a dough on the outdoor grill and let it bubble up, then brushed the crust with olive oil and sprinkled it with garlic, kosher salt, cracked black pepper, and rosemary.

I went back inside and sliced up Meatzapalooza with a pizza wheel, threw some fresh basil on top, and brought it out on a cutting board. My wife popped open a bottle of prosecco.

As the kids got started with that one, I flipped the crust on the grill, let it brown, then added grilled shrimp basted in olive oil and garlic, and cilantro pesto.

They turned on *The Fellowship of the Ring* while I finished off the last pie (mushrooms and andouille). Bilbo was saying, "I regret to announce this is the end. I am going now. I bid you all a very fond farewell. Goodbye."

"This is good pizza," Sean said. My wife nodded. He'd be off to the University of Rochester a few days later, where he would study engineering and astrophysics. Zai, his sister, was starting her junior year at Vassar.

"To us," Zai said, and we all raised our glasses.

We sat there in the hot summer night, the windows open. Bilbo, on-screen, was off on his adventure, singing "The Road Goes Ever On." I looked at my family, my grown children, my wife, our two old dogs.

We were held together by a whole lot more than cheese.

ONE OF THE LUCKY ONES
Lyn Mikel Brown

I T'S NEARLY A YEAR into the pandemic. Our daughter is safe and living with her partner in Portland. My husband, Mark, and I are teaching
college courses in education remotely. We gardened until the ground froze,
and now we're inside painting walls and making dinners together. Our
dogs, so in love with being walked twice as often, have become clingy. Even
our judge-y cat has cozied up to our ever-present laps.

We attribute our contentment to the new digs. In June, we moved
to Eastport, a small island community closer to Canada, by water at least,
than the nearest US town. Through the summer, when COVID numbers
here aligned with New Brunswick's, our little pod of new friends hosted
socially distanced drinks, moving from deck to deck. On warm evenings,
our neighbor Ben serenaded us with "Good Night, Eileen" and "She'll Be
Comin' Round the Mountain" on his accordion.

It didn't last. The presidential election grabbed us by the heels, kicking
and screaming. The virus began spreading like milfoil in a Maine lake. Most
of our neighbors packed up and left for warmer climes. The rest of us chose
safety in distance. Aside from an irritated lunge for the radio off switch and
little fits of Twitter rage, we did just fine. Until my husband began laying
claim to my dinner salad.

It helps to know that I make the salad each night or actually two salads.
I make two separate bowls of salad. They are visibly different salads. No
mealy out-of-season tomatoes for me and nothing resembling a crouton.
As habit dictates, I put these two bowls of salad on a wooden table that
acts as a center island and, because he's the better cook, turn to other supportive roles like chopping vegetables or making rice. This one night, he
poured his balsamic vinaigrette on my salad. Oops. No worries, a simple

mistake. The next night, he did the same thing. Less okay, but fine. "Notice the tomatoes," I said. "This is not your salad." The third night, I moved my salad to the counter and, just to sharpen the point, put my bottle of red wine vinaigrette beside it. I left his salad in the usual spot. He avoided the island altogether, grabbed his dressing from the refrigerator, and put it on my salad. "What's with this?" I asked.

"Oh my God." He laughed. "I'm sorry."

I circled the air around his salad like Johnny in *Dirty Dancing*, announcing, "This is your salad. This is my salad. I don't eat yours; you don't eat mine. See the dressing? That's the clue." The next night, I put dressing on my salad, and like a dog pissing on his territory, he put his dressing on top of mine.

Out of the bowels of hell came a rage that surprised us both. "Why do you keep doing this?" I shouted.

"It was a mistake. I'm sorry."

"Once is a mistake. Twice, maybe. But this, this is deliberate."

"It's not deliberate. I just didn't think."

"No, this is not you not thinking. This is something else. What is going on here? Why are you doing this? What are you saying to me?"

My voice jumped an octave with each question. Our golden Lab inched closer, thinking this was a problem she could fix. Our hound, a better read of the emotional landscape, ran upstairs and hid in the closet. Like our dogs, we were in different places. He was here, in our kitchen, apologizing to his wild-eyed partner for a series of unintentional mistakes. I was back at my childhood dinner table living our nightly existential crisis, trying hard to make sense of an unpredictable world. I didn't know this at the time, of course. I just screamed and raged and stomped like a lunatic until I exhausted myself. I was a child. I was an adolescent. I was my father.

Did I say that I have food issues? Everyone in my family has food issues. As with any deep-seated trauma, it takes a village. A psychoanalyst would get rich unpacking the role of food in our emotional lives, explaining why we either ate our feelings or slopped them all over the table. Food was our associative language, the symptom of our psychological state, the manifestation of our doing and undoing. Resistance surfaced in the thud of a plate piled with hockey-puck burgers. Love took the form of Saturday night baked beans, corn bread, coleslaw. Ice cream was palliative care.

"Grief, when it comes, is nothing like we expect it to be," Joan Didion wrote in *The Year of Magical Thinking*, the memoir in which she tries to make sense of her fundamentally altered life after the sudden death of her husband. Mine was a family of sudden losses, all endured by children too young to grapple with the presence of absence, too little to bargain with the gods.

My mother was given away at birth—passed in shame from unwed to older married sister—and then, for years after, fought over. Her need for love was bottomless. Each Christmas she dove like a famished child into a coat box filled with her aunt's homemade candies—divinity fudge and peanut-butter balls and Needhams. Gifts of food. Beloved food. Freely given food. Wild blueberries and strawberries were "nature's little freebies," and we were sent into the fields and barrens to pick and rake. When it came to food, my father would say, our mother would take any given amount.

A gift received was also a gift withheld. "When do I get a vacation?" she asked to anyone within earshot as she cooked dinner night after night for an ungrateful family of six. In the absence of a response, she'd simply throw up her hands and walk away from the stove mid-meal, like she walked away from her damaged first marriage, my older brother and sister, then two and three years old, in tow. Their loss, like my mother's, without choice or explanation.

My father's father died when he was two. A few years before the Great Depression, with no income and four children to feed, his mother took in boarders, tried to sell Avon products to other poor women, and for a small fee made bread for the railroad station restaurant. As an adult, my father lost his temper when dinner was late. He insisted we leave at 3:30 p.m. for 5:00 p.m. church suppers, because the front of the line at the first sitting meant we didn't miss out on the best casseroles and pies. He was a natural story-teller, and the most vivid details he shared of his early life on the railroad, in the woods, on the river drives, were of food, a "charge of grub two men couldn't shake hands over," the taste of biscuits "thick and light as a feather and round as a coffee can," "big river drivin' cookies, molasses and sugar and gingerbread," and overflowing plates of bean-hole beans.

The thought of people alone, without enough food, brought him to tears. We never knew who would join us for holiday dinners until the last train left the station. A railroad engineer, he'd walk down to the station bunkhouse each Thanksgiving or Christmas day. Any lone straggler would grace our table. He drew the line at very few things. Eating chicken or "dirty dead birds," a reminder of his Depression-era childhood, was one of them. Waste was another.

In my moment of salad rage, I have no perspective. I'm not aware of my overreaction or my husband's apologies. I'm six, sitting amidst my undone family on a red Naugahyde padded chair at the Formica table tucked into the ell just off our galley kitchen. I'm watching a fight brew between my father and my older brother, so alike in their grief they are invisible to one another. My brother doesn't like his food to touch and a breech in the gravy boat he's made with his mashed potatoes is threatening the peas. My mother, lover of all food in whatever rebel form it takes, is defending her son's growing panic. I go quiet. My older sister looks nauseous and moves the food around on her plate. My younger brother becomes silly and loud. We all feel it. We each do the best we can. "Goddamn it!" my father suddenly shouts. He throws himself into a standing position, all imposing six-foot one-inch, 250 pounds of him, shoves his chair into the table, rattling the dishes, causing the gravy dam to burst, and walks out of the kitchen. My brother starts crying. We hear the door slam. "Jesus," my mother sighs, her lips in a tight thin line as she reaches over to help my brother rebuild his dam. My father, we all know, is marching down the hill to the American Legion to drink with the boys.

I have a therapist friend who links the body pathological to the body politic. We use our bodies, she theorizes, to speak the unspeakable and to channel our resistance to conditions we cannot control. *The Body Keeps the Score* is the title of a book on trauma. Our bodies know things. As a child, I didn't so much obsess about food as food was my means of obsession. I dreaded sleepover invitations, because I had no control over when and what I could eat. I was dieting in high school, anorexic in college, bulimic in graduate school. By sheer force of will, I made my body and my world predictable, orderly, without sudden movement. I left home, first emotionally, then physically. I lopped off old relationships the way I lopped off pounds. I scrubbed myself clean of all vestiges of my homely, working-class roots. My mother called me selfish, and I was. I went to what my mother called a la-de-da school and taught at a la-de-da college, and I lost myself.

These months of the pandemic, I'm in a lot of Facebook groups. Some, like Coronavirus Gallows Humor, offer a *Monty Python and the Holy Grail*–like release into absurdity. "Bring out your dead!" Increasingly, though, I'm lured to videos of lost or abandoned dogs. Over the course of a three-minute clip, they will be found emaciated on a beach or city street or abandoned house by some compassionate person who takes them home, washes, feeds, and nurtures them. Exposed ribs disappear, hair grows over reddened mange-infested skin. They learn to love, to play, to trust again. I wait for the happy ending. I want to believe it's this easy, this simple. But I know firsthand what comes of a potent stew of uncertainty and hunger. I know how loss morphs into the unrecognizable, the precarious. How it surprises and frightens. Starving children sit down at dinner tables decades later prepared for battle. Collateral damage.

As of this writing, the Maine CDC reports a record-high 814 cases of COVID-19. Fourteen more people have died. A person succumbs to the virus in the US every thirty seconds. Children are losing parents and grandparents. Thousands of families are lined up at food banks in their cars. The aftermath of this loss, this emptiness, this lack of control over lives and circumstances will be complicated and lasting. In her essay "Joining the Resistance: Psychology, Politics, Girls, and Women," Carol Gilligan writes, "The hallmarks of loss are idealization and rage and under the rage, immense sadness ('To want and want and not to have')." I know how this goes.

I don't mean to make my life a case study. I had it good, cushy even, compared to my parents, compared to those with empty stomachs now lined up in their cars. I had more than enough love and support and luck to ensure my body pathological landed softly here in an Eastport kitchen where the worst thing that happens is an existential crisis over salads. I'm just saying that there is a psychology of hunger, and our body politic is now bloated with grief. We will be excavating the rage and sadness from this for a very long time.

When Mark joined our family's Thanksgiving the first year of our marriage, he fell in love with the chaos, so unlike the quiet respectability of his own family. Everything about it—the way my father pushed a scotch into his hand and slapped him on the back as he came through the door; the small warm fragrant kitchen overcrowded with activity; the lace-covered table set in Friendly Village china and extended awkwardly into the living room with a card table to accommodate the grandchildren. The little bowls of homemade pickled beets, dilly beans, and bread and butter pickles, the twenty-pound turkey, the mounds of mashed potatoes and gravy. My mother's laughter, my father's booming voice and messy attempts at carving, the clatter of dishes, and the shoveling in of food. We were in that moment happy, the best versions of ourselves—messy, loud, full. We all knew it could change in an instant. But for that moment, it was everything.

SALAD DAYS

Patricia O'Donnell

I GREW UP SURROUNDED by fields of green, waving corn stalks. The backyard of our house in Iowa butted up against a cornfield, which stretched into another cornfield for miles. None of this corn was good for us, however; it was hard field corn, grown for cattle, not for humans.

We did buy fresh corn and watermelon in summer from the grocery store, but our other vegetables were pulled from the freezer in plastic bags with a picture of a happy green giant on them. My parents had saved money from my dad's factory job making metal parts, including bombs, to buy a clothing store in the small town of Parkersburg, Iowa. They poured their energy into making this business work. They worked long days, six days a week, and gardening was something they weren't interested in.

My mother had grown up the oldest girl of ten children on a farm far from town, where she worked hard. When she wasn't taking care of the younger children, she would help prepare food. She went outside to pump water from the well and carry it inside. She would pick and shuck beans; find wild gooseberries to make into pie; can pickles and tomatoes; pick cherries; kill, pluck, and roast chickens; bake bread; pound cabbage with a piece of wood attached to a broom stick handle for sauerkraut; and make blood pudding and headcheese. It wasn't until I was an adult that I learned that headcheese was not cheese, and blood pudding was not a sweet, red-tinged pudding.

After work, while my dad had a beer at Russ's Tavern, a few doors down from O'Donnell's Clothing, my mother came home to six hungry kids. She put dinner on the table as quickly as possible. In the 1950s, there were so many new, time-saving ways to keep and prepare food: in addition to bags of frozen vegetables, there were frozen hamburger patties, orange juice, and complete "TV dinners" in a box. On Fridays, the day of the week when we always ate fish, we would sometimes have shrimp, my favorite. It didn't seem strange to me that the shrimp was actually chopped up pieces formed into a shrimp shape, breaded, fried, frozen, and reheated. I didn't know it came any other way, and it tasted good dipped in the thick red shrimp sauce. Later, my parents bought a Radarange microwave oven, and dinner took even less time.

My family lived right across the street from Palmer's Groceries, and I would often be sent over to buy a loaf of bread. As I spread peanut butter on the white Wonder bread, my mother told me that bread like this was a delicacy when she was young, something they could rarely afford. They had to bake their own bread at home. I imagined it brown, aromatic, warm from the oven, with a crispy crust.

I didn't eat homemade bread until I dropped out of college in the '70s. I didn't know why I was in college, and living in a dorm was making me feel insane. I moved from Cedar Falls to Iowa City, where I took up with a group of student artists and poets from the famous Iowa Writers' Workshop and other dropouts like myself. I bought the *New York Times Natural Foods Cookbook* and pored over its recipes. No more TV dinners for me, no more shrimp shapes, no more institutional dormitory food. Later, I moved to San Francisco with one of the poets. Living in a tiny studio apartment, I tried making whole wheat bread, lentil soup, carob cookies, sprouted chick-pea salad, and other things I'd never had before. Some of the recipes turned out to be tasteless chores to eat, but some were delicious. I made an Indian recipe from the cookbook called Sweet Pellao. It consisted of brown rice with raisins, almonds, cinnamon, saffron, cardamom, butter, and brown sugar. I imagined blood pudding must be something like this.

The poet and I shared our studio apartment with dozens, maybe hundreds, of cockroaches. At night when I came into the dark kitchen and turned the light on, they scattered, disappearing. When I cooked and they came out onto the stove or countertop, the heavy paperback cookbook with the slick cover was the perfect weapon. I wiped it off after each murder, but eventually the stained, abused cover fell off. I strapped duct tape on to hold the book together. The cookbook graphics reflected the aesthetic to which I then aspired: a back-to-the-land, old-timey feel, a time when things were pure and genuine and simple.

Eventually, I broke up with the boyfriend and moved to a place by myself. After a few failed experiments at waitressing, I found a place that kept me on. I still could barely afford rent, so I stopped with the fancy recipes. The restaurant I worked at did not give us a free meal, but people left *so much* food on their plates. Before hauling them back to the dishwasher, I would take a bite here, a bite there, avoiding the places that had obviously been chewed. Lobster was my favorite; people would just give up, leaving tender meat in the shell, and melted butter still in the little dish. I would sometimes sneak stale bread rolls in my bag to take home, remembering Heidi, sent away from the mountain to stay with Clara in the city, stashing rolls in her closet to take home to Grandfather.

I was in San Francisco in 1974, the time of the Patty Hearst kidnapping. As is now well-known, a group calling itself the United Federated Forces of the Symbionese Liberation Army, or SLA, kidnapped the heiress from her apartment in Berkeley. Their demands for her release included boxes of free food to be distributed in sites across the Bay Area. Free food! I took a bus to a warehouse where I picked up a box, which had the SLA symbol on it. The food was welcomed, but as I put it in my little cupboard, I felt uneasy. In addition to the kidnapping, the group had killed a high school superintendent. I recall canned beans, white bread in a plastic wrapper, canned meat. Was I contributing to violence by eating it? I felt ashamed. I pulled off the SLA sticker to keep and thought about going back to college.

While working as a waitress, I had become hungry for real conversations about books and ideas. In time, I went back to the University of Northern Iowa and finished my degree in English, then my master's in English, an accomplishment I managed even though I'd become a single mother of two beautiful children. I told new acquaintances that I wasn't divorced; I'd just forgotten to get married. In love with books and with writing, I moved the children across the country so I could attend the MFA Program in Creative Writing in Amherst, Massachusetts. Coming home after an intense day of classes, teaching, and writing, I tried to make healthy fresh food, but it took so much time! And my children didn't like garlic and eggshell blended into their orange juice, no matter how healthy it was. I became familiar with fast food, as fast as I could make it. I understood my mother's desire for those moments of rest on the couch with her Pepsi. I confess that my young children learned to like frozen vegetables straight out of the bag, not even cooked. They were good for gums sore from teething, I told myself.

In the MFA program I met my future husband, Michael, and we moved to Maine, where I took a job at the University of Maine at Farmington, and he taught at Colby. We had a daughter together. The three children are grown now, having survived frozen vegetables and Hamburger Helper, and our old country farmhouse is quiet. Newly retired, and especially during the pandemic months, I have time to cook again. *The New York Times Natural Foods Cookbook* is still in my cupboard, the pages stained and their edges shredded, duct tape holding it all together. When pages fall out, I stick them back in. The old SLA sticker, the black seven-headed cobra on white, is stuck in its pages as a bookmark.

Now I make the recipe called Delicious Oatmeal Bread, and its crust is as crisp and fragrant as I remember. As I eat it, I remember the hungry, stressed young woman I was. I know that in Franklin County, where we live, there are people who hide their hunger, who miss meals, who sometimes have to choose between rent and dinner and sometimes don't have either. I will forgive the young woman I was in the 1970s for her scorn for frozen food, for fast food. And I will forgive her for taking food gained by violence; she was hungry, and everyone needs help sometimes, a bridge to carry them to a time of plenty.

AT THE TABLE
Kate Shaffer

I GREW UP IN a single-parent household, amid the stucco houses and smooth sidewalks of 1980s inland California. My siblings and I were a small, disparate band of adolescent pirates, in a constant state of mutiny against my mother and at odds with each other. Our home life was highly disciplined but fractured and shipwrecked, out-of-place in a sunny suburban neighborhood of two-parent families. The other parents were doctors and businessmen and real estate agents. Mom was a part-time grad student and full-time librarian. The others had green lawns, manicured weekly by the dads. We had what my mother called a rock garden, which we occasionally hosed down to remove the dust. They had back patios with a Weber and lawn furniture. We had a fenced-in forest of towering redwoods that served as my outdoor bedroom and leaked tannin-y needles over the neighbors' back lawns. They had fathers who barbecued on Saturdays and coached Little League baseball after work. We had a deadbeat dad and (briefly) a stepfather, who had the courtesy to leave us the dog and his beloved avocado tree, which never really took root among the redwoods.

I spent much of my adolescence setting booby traps for my older sister in our shared bedroom, stealthily avoiding my mother, or ditching my big brother at an event to which he was ordered to accompany me. Perhaps in an effort to instill some normalcy in a home life that seemed so often awry, mom insisted that every night, we eat dinner together.

It was torture. We were called to the table for a square but gag-inducing meal prepared by my mother as soon as she got home from work. Bony chicken breasts stewed in canned tomatoes. Boiled lima beans from the freezer. Leathery pork chops, iceberg lettuce, canned peas. And a Friday "meatloaf" made from the week's pulverized leftovers, forced into a bread pan and baked beyond recognition. And everything accompanied with jalapeño peppers (another legacy of the avocado-loving stepfather). When our plates were clean, and we were excused, my siblings and I were expected to clear the table, put away the leftovers, and wash the dishes. I resented this interruption to my daily life of misadventures. And I dreaded my mother's "cooking." But showing up for dinner was nonnegotiable. And to this day, I cannot remember a single occasion when any one of us dared not to.

I began to take my mother's place in the kitchen when I was eleven. Not because I had a change of heart about eating dinner together, but because in a plot to escape mealtime, I had suddenly declared myself a vegetarian. The emphatic announcement, which came to me in a spontaneous revelation one night over cube steak and stewed jalapeños, was received by my older brother and sister with raucous exclamations of betrayal. Mom sipped her wine, calmly insisted that I finish my dinner, and gave me leave to become a vegetarian tomorrow.

Over the next few weeks, my mother brought home cookbooks from the library—*The Vegetarian Epicure*, *Diet for a Small Planet*—and fresh produce from the grocery store. When she came home from work, she poured herself a glass of wine and left the kitchen. Her message was clear: if I was going to be a vegetarian, then I would learn to cook.

And so I did.

And while the vegetarianism didn't last, the lessons I learned from those first cookbooks did. Wash, chop, prepare with intention.

I eventually spent my Saturdays at the library with my mother, foraging the shelves for more lessons—Julia Child, Jeff Smith, Irma Rombauer, Fannie Farmer. I made grocery lists for my mother that included things like Gruyère, bok choy, arborio, and saffron. At fifteen, after my brother and sister had left home and it was just the two of us, I took over the shopping altogether.

For most of my adult life, I have thought of my mother's cooking—her hatred, really, of the kitchen—as one of the many ways she failed us as a parent. It sounds petty, I know. But as a tender-spirited girl, I craved hugs, a kind guiding hand, hot chocolate, and comfort. Instead, I received harsh discipline, reference books, silent lessons, and . . . well . . . jalapeños. You get the picture.

And yet, I have had a beautiful, varied, adventurous career in food. Half a lifetime of feeding strangers, friends, and family alike. A love—a need (perhaps much like my mother)—of calling people to the table.

And lately I've realized that the very best memories from my childhood were from events that took place at mealtime. My brother cracking jokes that had me spraying milk out of my nose. My ecstatic delight for a fondue party on my tenth birthday. My family's dubious and hilarious reception of my first all-vegetarian dinner. And the unexpected affection and pride I felt when they created a French café in our living room for my prom night.

The dinner table and the requirement to be there gave me a reason to learn how to cook. I learned the ways of butter, broth, and salt. I learned from those things, not only how to make food taste good but also how to feed a hunger that my mother could not.

I came to our family meals a wild thing, resentful and unguided. But I left having made those meals my own with purpose and a path. Whether by accident or design, I see that my mother gave me these gifts. She gave them selflessly and without ego. All I had to do in return was show up at the table.

SATURDAY BREAKFASTS
Susan Sterling

I ONCE BELIEVED THAT family rituals were inevitably passed on from generation to generation, like old photographs, treasured books, half-secret family recipes. If we take our children to the beach in winter or serve waffles for Sunday supper, it is because we did these activities when we were small. Many of us, even those of us with difficult childhoods, have an unconscious loyalty to the past and the way things were done then, and we discover the surprising strength of these loyalties when we become parents and have to negotiate the shape of celebrations.

Eventually, though, I had to qualify this theory because of Saturday mornings.

Neither my husband nor I ever went out for breakfast when we were children; we weren't even passionate breakfast eaters when we met. But two years into our marriage, eating breakfast out on Saturday mornings became an essential part of our life together.

That year, we became friends with another couple who, like us, had recently moved to Maine and who looked for unusual things to do each weekend, activities they couldn't do in New York City, where they'd grown up—attend a Lebanese church supper, for example, or a Franco-American dance. One Saturday morning, they suggested we meet for breakfast at a café in Oakland, a town so small and untraveled that, at the time, there had never been a single traffic light within its borders. For our friends, the café was a one-time discovery, but for my husband and me, it was a revelation.

We liked the drive, which took us along Messalonskee Stream from the town of Waterville, where we lived, to Oakland, through a landscape that shifted evocatively with the seasons—red maples in the fall, snowmobile tracks across winter fields, fog creeping in from the river in the spring. The café, the Coffee Pot, was unpretentious. From the outside, it resembled a converted railway car, while inside it was just one room with three booths, three or four tables, eight stools at the counter, and a grill. Even when the café was redecorated with new red-and-white checked curtains and plastic plants hanging on the walls, it remained stubbornly itself: a diner that catered mainly to local residents, to policemen on their breaks, electrical repairmen, housewives, and the occasional college professor.

While the Coffee Pot had a proper menu, most customers ordered one of the specials that were listed each week on a chalkboard. My husband and I always ordered "the No. 1," which consisted of two eggs, toast, and, depending on the week, ham, sausage, or bacon. Al, the cook and owner, was a wonderful baker, and once we discovered his cinnamon rolls, we asked for them instead of toast. After we had been coming and ordering the same breakfast for a while, we became known, and the waitress Jane would put our order on the grill when she saw us getting out of our car.

When our son, Greg, was born, there was no question but that Saturday mornings at the Coffee Pot were to be part of his life. We set his infant seat on our table and fed him baby cereal that we brought from home. He became something of a regular, too, and if Jane wasn't busy, she would whisk him off to greet the other customers.

The Coffee Pot was the kind of restaurant where you saw the same people week after week. Rarely did we learn names, but we knew where people worked, exchanged comments on the weather, and worried about one older couple when they didn't show up for a couple of weeks. (Jane didn't know their names either and confessed that she and Al referred to them by their standard order: Blueberry Muffin and Bacon.)

Saturday breakfasts assumed such a place in our life that in the three separate years when we lived away from Maine, we searched, with varying degrees of success, for a substitute café. It had to be a certain sort of place: where the local paper is left out on the counter and the eggs are done just the way you like them, where the waitresses and waiters are friendly and efficient, where the cook may come out and ask how the muffins were this morning. Only one year, when we lived in England, did we have to forego our Saturday routine: the English never go out for breakfast. Restaurants open for lunch, and the noted English breakfast of tomatoes, bacon, eggs, grilled mushrooms, and cold toast is one you find only in hotels.

One summer, we came back from our vacation to find that the Coffee Pot had been sold. Al had become tired of finding a crowd waiting at the door when he arrived at 5 a.m.; he wanted to play golf on the weekends. Under the new ownership, the cinnamon rolls burned. The Coffee Pot was sold yet again and reopened under a new name.

Sometime later, we discovered that Al had bought the Open Hearth Café in Waterville, down the road from one of the paper mills. It was what we had been looking for during the previous months of Saturdays, and we started to go there. As at the Coffee Pot, there was a bulletin board on one wall where customers could post their cards and advertise their trades—snowplowing, carpentry, accounting.

Here, too, the menu hung on a nail next to the table, and the specials were listed on a chalkboard near the kitchen. Sometimes there were more elaborate offerings. The weekend San Francisco played in the Super Bowl, the café offered a "49ers Special"—four eggs and nine strips of bacon. Again, we fell into conversations with people whose names we didn't know, exchanged friendly greetings, bits of advice. Everyone knew our kids, and when one of them spent the night with a friend, questions were asked.

Our children indulged us in these conversations and made intricate drawings on the red-and-white paper place mats when they finished before us. Will they continue this tradition with their own families? Perhaps, perhaps not. They weren't always thrilled to be putting on their boots on a rainy spring morning and would sometimes rather have stayed home in their pajamas. Yet Saturday breakfasts had become an expected item in the rhythm of their week, like music lessons, riding the school bus, and family dinners in the kitchen. They understood that it was time that we had set aside for the four of us to be together.

When she was six, I overhead my daughter, Erica, now a mother herself, explaining all this to a friend. The friend suggested they play together that weekend, and Erica indicated that anytime later in the day would be fine. "Saturday mornings," she explained cheerfully, "we *always* go out to breakfast."

TAJ
Alana Dao

I N SUGAR LAND, Texas, the land of megachurches and sprawling suburbs, a Hindu temple was erected in the early aughts. BAPS Shri Swaminarayan Mandir is situated in Fort Bend County. Major media outlets like
the *New York Times* often bring up Fort Bend County when talking about
what the future of America should look like: an oasis of diversity and mul-
tiethnic communities residing at peace.

Built of Turkish limestone and Italian marble that was hand carved by
over 2,000 artisans in India, BAPS Shri Swaminarayan Mandir is representative of its own kind of diversity. Constructed according to guidelines
outlined in ancient Hindu scripture, the temple, with its white-stone cur-
vature and red flags beckoning from the top, is heart-stoppingly beautiful
and, in many ways, miraculous; its limestone and marble were shipped to
Houston in 150 containers. One hundred seventy-five volunteers from
India fitted the pieces together in tongue-and-groove fashion, like a three-
dimensional jigsaw puzzle. The entire structure does not contain a single
piece of iron or steel.

The mandir is a stone's throw from my childhood home in Sugar Land,
and my family would regularly have tea in the community center that also
sold dry goods and items for worship like bells and incense. After I moved
to the East Coast, when I was eighteen, my family and I would visit the
mandir whenever we were back in Texas. My mother always bought extra
boxes of sweets from the mandir, so I would later have cashew burfi or
cardamom-scented dried fruit rolls on snowy days in Maine.

CONTRARY TO COMMON misconceptions of a Texan childhood (no,
I did not ride a horse to school), much of my childhood reflected what

it meant to live among so many different ethnic communities, under the waving red flags of the mandir. Our weekend routine was breakfast burritos at Soliz across from the local high school, Asian grocery shopping for Chinese vegetables with my mother, and a stop for afternoon chai and samosas at the mandir's community center.

Yet despite this diversity, questions marking my racial difference arose. I am visibly Asian of some variety. (Which variety people love to guess.) And growing up, I was asked on more than one occasion if I ate fried rice for dinner every night. I didn't. I ate dal and chapatis, rajma and raita to combat the chilis.

This was because during the week, I attended a very white and very conservative parochial school in another county, and there was nobody to pick me up after school. So my mother, who worked full time in real estate administration, pored over the school directory, looking for families to carpool with.

One day, the sweet Indian family who would be our savior invited us over for tea to work out the details. The mother served us milky chai and spicy chaat. Over time, my carpool mom saw that cooking dinner was probably beyond my mom on some nights—after all, my mother often picked me up well after dark—and so began a routine. If it was getting dark, I'd eat with the family, and if my mother was on time, I would be ready by the door with a glass Pyrex full of dal for when we got home. At some point, my mom ended up coming in, and we had dinner together a few times a week, our noses running as we grew accustomed to the spice and heat level.

When my carpool mom had visitors from India, she always pulled out all the stops, making more labor-intensive foods, including Southern Indian delights like dosa, a crispy crepe with any number of fillings, and beloved Indian street foods, like pav bhaji, a soft sandwich made with vegetable curry and rolls so buttery that my fingers would leave stains on the family's glass coffee table. Other treats: crunchy sev, puffed puri, and (my favorite) chaat, an umbrella term for a large array of snacks, typically made with fried dough, eaten with a variety of other snacks, all smothered with sauces, chutney, and/or yogurt.

I CAN'T REPLICATE these foods myself, but I have found a placeholder at Taj, an Indian restaurant near where I now live in Maine. The restaurant is presumably named after the Taj Mahal in India, which was constructed in the 1600s by Mughal emperor Shah Jahan, in memory of his wife, Mumtaz

Mahal, who died in childbirth. Now considered one of the Seven Wonders of the World, the Taj Mahal represents magnificence and beauty but also love, loss, and memory.

"My" Taj is located in a strip mall near the Maine Mall in South Portland, where it sits next to a hardware store and in front of a nondenominational Christian church that boasts a full-service community center and indoor soccer field—a combination that reminds me of Houston, where there is no zoning and a strip club will sit next to a Seventh-day Adventist church. Ranging from Indo-Chinese specialties like Hakka noodles to Northern and Southern Indian specialties, Taj's menu is representative of cultures melding together being touted as progress. In fact, people have been eating this way for ages now. Nothing is ever a monolith.

IN TIMES OF UPHEAVAL, I have noticed my tastes regress. When I was pregnant with my first child, all I wanted was my mom's vegetable soup, Chinese tomato egg, and chaat. Three years later, in 2016, when I became pregnant for a second time, everything fell apart. As the political climate contracted, so did my workplace. I was bullied for being pregnant, discriminated against for being Asian, and everything I thought was steady became unsteady. During the pandemic, in a year when my entire family stayed home, my taste buds shrank even further. I needed to be reminded of love and steadfastness.

In particular, I craved dosa. Taj was the only place I could think of to go, but dosa at Taj could be unreliable. Good when the grandmother of the family who made them was in Maine, unavailable when she went to visit India.

I turned to samosa chaat. A samosa is a samosa, but a samosa chaat shakes everything up. It is a samosa quartered and topped with sev, chickpeas, cilantro, and tamarind chutneys, chopped tomatoes, or diced red onion.

Chaat, in its simplest definition, is just an array of basic ingredients that create a contrast in textures and flavors when together: spicy, creamy, crunchy, tangy. Crispy bits atop a soft samosa, dunking savory donuts into a sauce-like broth, and experiencing a full range of flavors and textures in small bites feels like making something out of nothing, a way to make something feel whole. Chaat—like the mandir, like Sugar Land, like me—combines many things.

When my second daughter arrived, things were irretrievably broken at work, and it was my own mother who helped put me back together. While she could not tell me how to make a dosa, all that time she spent working in an office while I was eating chaat at somebody else's house paid off. She told me how to navigate banal details like healthcare and how to draft a polite resignation letter, so I could leave a piece of myself that no longer fit, breaking things apart in order to move forward.

Chaat, and by extension, assembling something greater than the sum of the parts, makes me think back to the mandir at home. All those snapped-together pieces of marble and limestone make me think of the ways in which I have pieced myself together, or back together, so many times and for so many reasons. I think of all our own tongues and grooves and how they can fit together. Perhaps not as smoothly as with the Taj Mahal, but whether it is a restaurant in a strip mall or a Wonder of this World, we are all at once greater and more whole than we ever thought possible.

MY GRANDMOTHER'S KITCHEN
Marilyn Moss

I N 1940, WHEN I was born in Bellepointe, West Virginia, both my mother and father were working: Mom, the youngest woman to be teaching in one-room schools in Appalachia. Dad, a civil engineer who drove large road-building equipment for the State of West Virginia. I was left with my maternal grandparents from my first months into my ninth year, during which time my parents divorced and my father died. I called my grandparents Mom and Dad Nash.

We lived in Elgood. The town, atop an Appalachian mountain, consisted of a US post office window in the general store, my grandparents' house, a school, and a church. I was the sole child in town and had friends only when school was in session. Kids were bused in from the hollers and other mountains. A couple of older boys who lived further from town would occasionally come by to play cowboys and Indians.

Without close friends, I enjoyed hanging out in my grandmother's modest kitchen. A large wood cookstove, which was never without a fire in the firebox, occupied most of the room. A small kitchen table doubled for food preparation and eating. A cupboard and an iron sink with a hand pump competed for space. We stored food in the root cellar or the icehouse. After the arrival of electricity, we got a refrigerator, which we stored on the screened-in porch.

Outside of a manual meat grinder, a butter churn, and a breadboard to work dough for biscuits and piecrusts, Mom Nash didn't have cooking tools to ease the life of a cook and hasten meal preparation. Sometime, though, in those first nine years of my life, running water, along with an aluminum sink with faucets, magically materialized.

Mom Nash eventually accepted a Sears and Roebuck electric cook-stove. She resisted for a long time. She didn't trust the fancy stove. "I jes' know it won't make good biscuits," she said. And I agreed. The wood cook-stove was better. Later in life, I had one of my own in Maine, as well as a fancy gas stove.

In the cold Appalachian winters, her kitchen was the warmest in the house. A coal-burning pot-bellied stove in the dining room provided what heat it could for the rest of the two-story old wood house. The most warmth, though, emanated from Mom Nash herself, always ready to give me a big hug. The aroma of her biscuits, cornbread, roasts, pies, soups, stews, and casseroles pervaded every room.

I loved the way she would get up early, bathe, and put on a clean dress, earrings and necklace, then add a flower-patterned starched apron, freshly washed and ironed, over her dress. Her brown and gray hair, short in small curls with a perm, was combed and neat. Her nylon stockings rolled down with the garters to her ankles, were all ready to pull up. Her best shoes side-by-side on the floor, waiting for her swollen feet to slide into them.

"Mom Nash, are you goin' somewhere today?"

"I jes' wanna' be ready to hitch a ride if someone stops by on their way to Princeton." She didn't drive.

Up by pre-dawn, Mom Nash would be stoking the fire and starting breakfast with the tantalizing smell of bacon in the cast-iron skillet, sifting up through the heat register in my bedroom over the kitchen. As I entered the kitchen, I would hear the sizzle of fresh eggs frying. Shortly after, Mom Nash would grab a hot pad and reach into the oven to pull out a pan of steaming golden biscuits.

If I came downstairs earlier, she greeted me with, "MarilynRae, go wash yer hands. Time to help make biscuits." By the time I was six or seven, I shared the morning chores with my uncle. I helped milk the cows and gather eggs. He and I would occasionally shoot two or three squirrels to add to breakfast. My father had taught me to shoot a .22 rifle when I was six.

Mom Nash would sit me on books piled on a chair to watch her knead the dough. She would give me a small piece with which to imitate the movements of her flour-covered, rough farm hands. I loved the feel of the dough as I kneaded, watching and feeling it take a breath, rising back up after I pushed it down. She handed the dented round tin cutter to me to cut out the pieces from the flattened dough. Then she gently picked up each perfect shape, as one would a jewel, dipping it lightly in the flour and placing each in her buttered round pan. When I got older, she allowed me to do this delicate step.

I didn't stray far from the kitchen until she brought the biscuits out of the oven. Seeing them puffed up and golden never ceased to amaze me. Mom Nash slathered two halves with her homemade butter and huckleberry jam. The biscuit was gone by the time she'd poured a glass of milk. "Don't put so much in yer mouth at once or you'll choke. 'Member? Opal Thompson's boy, Eugene? He got a piece of potato stuck in his throat and died right thar.'"

"Yes, ma'm," I managed to say. "Please may I have another one?"

I learned to make biscuits, pies, cakes, cookies. Fry bacon, eggs, squirrel, pork roasts, and chicken. To chop off the heads of chickens, pick out their feathers, and truss them for roasting. I helped gather vegetables from the garden and pick fruit from our trees and bushes and prepare them for her canning cellar.

Mom Nash made most of my clothes from flower-printed seed bags. She canned our food for winter and stored apples and potatoes in the cellar. Dad Nash butchered pigs around Thanksgiving. This provided meat for a year. Mom Nash canned sausage and spareribs. She cured ham and bacon in the smoke house, rendered lard on the stove and stored it in jars. She made jams and fillings for pies from wild blackberries and huckleberries.

My grandparents always shared whatever they had. During the Depression, the Nash household had sheltered and fed those who were needier. My mother said this generous behavior rubbed off on me in a big way. She claims that on many occasions, and much to her dismay given her own meager income, I would take off my sweater or coat and give it to a coatless classmate or invite classmates for dinner and to stay for the night.

The Nash farmstead was mostly self-sustaining and, by most standards, impoverished. I did not realize this at the time. I remember only riches—a generous, warm, and loving environment, delicious meals prepared from our large garden. We had cows, pigs, sheep, chickens, turkeys, and fruit trees. Farm smells can still transport me back to the haying fields or the cow barn or the pig barn or the chicken house or the rich garden soil.

All this was in the early 1940s, the war years. In our area, hunger plagued most households, even though subsistence farming helped. The Depression popped up at every dinner discussion. Talk about the failing lumber industry, the mines producing too much coal, and the textile mills closing down.

Mom Nash spent endless hours preparing the familiar and treasured Southern dishes for Sunday dinners, served at 1:00 p.m. She prepared a lot, never quite sure who would show up, but always had enough. The core group included Mom and Dad Nash, my aunts and uncles with their families, and me. Sometimes my mother, when she was teaching in a one-room school in West Virginia, would also come. On occasion, Mom Nash invited the preacher of the day, contingent on whether she liked his sermon or not. Or our neighbors Lottie and Luther. She might extend an impromptu invitation to someone at that morning's church service or someone who lived alone and looked in need of a good meal. People varied. The food and preparation did not.

Mom Nash started on Saturday, cutting off the heads of two or three of our chickens. I picked off the feathers as the chickens soaked in cold water. In summer, she harvested fresh tomatoes, carrots, potatoes, collards, green beans, onions, cabbage, shell beans, corn, spinach, peas, and cucumbers. She baked pies filled with fruit from the orchard. In the fall or winter or early spring, she used some of these same items from her canning and root cellar. Mason jars glistened on the wooden shelves lining the cellar walls, trophies of colorful vegetables and fruits from her fatiguing summer and fall work. Wooden bins were filled with hay-cradled apples, potatoes, squashes, and onions.

At 4:00 a.m. on Sunday mornings, Mom Nash got out of bed, put on her Sunday-go-to-church dress, necklace, and earrings. She slipped on an apron and headed to the kitchen to prepare the remaining dishes before she left for church. At the service, when the preacher had conferred the last prayer, Mom Nash would quickly shake hands with the preacher, then make her exit back to her kitchen to serve the feast for all who came.

LOCAVORE

Sandy Oliver

THE RASPBERRY HAD planted itself in the crotch of a large, very old tree next to the Italianate house where we waited for the realtor to show up. Since it was August, the reddish-pink berries on it were ripe, and I reached up, picked off the ripest, and popped them into my mouth. Those berries were the first island-grown food I ate.

After another year had passed, we found a house, barn, and several acres of land to buy. Another seven would pass before we came to occupy it year-round; meanwhile, during summer visits there were more raspberries and blueberries to eat, and clams and mussels to collect and cook. We moved in over Memorial Day weekend, rejoicing in rhubarb that grew in the yard, a relic from Adrianna Bunker, who occupied the house in the last half of the 1800s and for first two decades of the 1900s. We planted a garden and that first summer ate our first meal consisting of island-grown food, locavores long before that word existed. New potatoes, mussels, salad, and raspberries for dessert with cream from off-island.

So started over thirty years of gardening and foraging island food. For a while, there were pigs rooting up a large section of the back and chickens scratching and pecking the margins, finding things I cannot even see, and laying eggs notable for their brilliant yolks. In the fall, there were wild grapes to gather and apples from ancient trees planted by long-gone sea captains, fishermen, shipbuilders, and the caretakers for summer residents who came by steamer for August in grand cottages.

Conventional wisdom is that a garden needs five years to show what it will do, and that certainly seems to be true. Each year offers slightly different weather. Insects infest, disappear for a while, return in different numbers. Viruses invade, wipe out whole crops, while other years, plants fight them off. A good gardener rotates crops; enriches the soil by replacing organic material, amending with minerals, making the space inviting for worms—called "cows of the soil" for their rich castings—and welcomes pollinators with wildly flowering herbs and perennials to corners and edges. Without them we do not eat.

I've yet to fail to be amazed at how much relatively little space will provide. For years, 2,000 square feet made us self-sufficient in potatoes, onions, carrots, beets, garlic, cabbage, broccoli, cauliflower, fresh corn, a few tomatoes, eggplants and peppers, summer and winter squashes, bushels of lettuce, spinach, kale, green beans, and cucumbers. Adding another 6,500 square feet meant peaches, strawberries, enough corn to freeze, storage beans of several sorts that had room to grow in quantity for baked beans all winter, and a hoop house where we could be certain of ripe tomatoes enough to can a year's supply of sauce. I sell and share produce with my island neighbors.

I won't pretend that growing this quantity is easy. The gardens howl for my attention from June well into October. And as my seventh decade progresses, I ponder a retrenchment to the old self-sufficient days and think about when I might not be able to garden at all even.

The problem is that the garden, this property, is now a material part of me, and my very body answers the call of the soil here. Apparently, our bones regenerate about every ten years, so my femur and little finger and kneecap have been remade about three times in part from the very soil I occupy, never mind my muscles, nerves, and all my other tissues. I am literally this island together with bits of the mainland, California, or Iowa, and maybe even Greece.

I am my garden, and it has been a blessing, worth seeking.

LIES AND ENGLISH MUFFINS

Sarah Braunstein

M Y FATHER TAUGHT me that when you can't sleep, when your mind is too busy to rest, the thing to do isn't to toss and turn but to get up and make yourself an English muffin. This, my father says, is the best medicine for nighttime distress of any kind. After that, you'll sleep. And it's true—it works. It could be toast or tea or cereal or a glass of milk, but because my father said it was an English muffin, that will always be my platonic midnight snack.

As a girl, I found the English muffins were also a way to come down after a family fight, a tenderness afforded me in light of an upset. I would be allowed up past bedtime to eat when I wasn't supposed to, just me and my father at a dim table, the others asleep. Generally, this was reparation for whatever disaster had befallen the evening. I frankly can't remember what most of the yelling was about. Small conflicts, white lies, failures to obey. The negotiations of ordinary family life could become—sometimes, not all the time—hours of chaotic arguing, booming, righteous monologues. Afterward, my father could not apologize to me for his rage—the English muffin was as close as he got, and I took it.

My father is beloved by many for his irreverent, playful, quick wit. He is charismatic and sentimental and funny and warm. There is a darker side, too, as so often there is with men of his era—born smack in the middle of the last century. His jaw, when he got angry, made a terrible clicking sound. He shouted. He squared his body, lifted his shoulders, his eyes fierce and focused.

He would describe himself as passionate. I can't disagree, but it's more complex than that. He couldn't be cruel to us, he argued. He loved us too much.

He showed us with food. When I was six, he wrote a recipe in verse—a poem called "Sweet Sarah's Cheesecake"—which begins: "The first part of the recipe is surely a must, for what's a cheesecake without a crust?" And it includes the tender couplet: "Then a little more sugar, for sweetness, like daughters. You'll need to use a full cup and three quarters."

We got seconds of whatever we wanted. Sometimes there was Sara Lee pound cake, those silky, buttery slices, cut generously. Always a sprinkle of nutmeg on our Christmas eggnog. Always egg-roll appetizers, wonton soup. Always English muffins for sleepless nights, waiting for us in the freezer.

A FEW DAYS after the November 2020 election—when it was clear to the free world, if not its leader, that Biden would become the next president—one of my brothers called me. He said our father was taking Trump's incipient defeat hard.

"He voted for him again? He really did that?"

"Yep," said my brother with a sad sigh. He said our father was listening to right-wing blowhards and talking about dead people on voter rolls.

I was in my car during this conversation, sitting in a nearly empty parking lot on the Portland harbor, looking out at Casco Bay, the low winter sky. I was chewing gum, one piece after the next, mercilessly, until my jaw hurt, and listening to CNN on satellite radio.

This was our father? My brother and I shared a stunned rage. Our father, the man who commanded us never to lie, who demanded decency at all costs. Wasn't that *why* he yelled? To ensure that we followed rules: that we were just and good and honorable? The experience of our childhood, its punitive culture, had been in service to this truth.

Sometimes I feel compassion for my father and for all people deluded by their own certainties. And sometimes I don't.

IN IOWA CITY, 1998, when I was twenty-two, I happened to look out the window and see a mail truck go by, driven by an older mailman, a white-haired Iowan eating an ice cream cone. That was all, a mailman eating a soft-serve ice cream, and I remember thinking: *We're all just people trying to get by.* It was an obvious, sad, simple thought, but it hit me deeply. I still think about this mailman regularly—a grown man licking an ice cream cone on a spring day, twisting it to keep it from dripping on his hand. When I am angry at my father, sometimes this mailman springs to mind, a kind of sentimental shorthand.

Watching men indulge in crappy food or sweets or their mother's food—the dopamine foods—makes me feel tenderly toward them. Something in me softens when I see a problematic man submitting to an appetite. He is vulnerable, at the mercy of a need. Watching my father eat a milk chocolate bar, seeing him burrow in, can sometimes bring me to tears.

MY HUSBAND TOLD me about a theater technique: When an actor is struggling to appear natural on stage, to relax into convincing personhood, a smart director might have them eat something. Put an apple in his hand. One can't eat inauthentically. One can't eat in bad faith.

That's why it always comes back to the table. Problems arise and are solved there. With the food we must share, the food that says sorry. We have no choice but to eat with our authentic selves. My father is quite generous with food. When I heard a press report, early on in the presidency, that Trump got *two* scoops of ice cream and his guests got only one, I thought, "Well, that's not my father." He would never give himself more ice cream than his guests. If there was only enough ice cream for his kids, he'd contentedly go without.

MY FATHER TELLS a funny story—how his Italian American mother once asked him, as an adult, what he'd like her to cook for his upcoming visit. "Anything at all," he told her. "Lasagna, spaghetti, baked ziti, veal parmesan . . . ?" He listed his favorites, meaning: *You choose.* Meaning: *You can't go wrong, Mom. I love it all.* When he got there, he discovered she had made every single thing he'd listed. The table was full, steaming platters, everything. She'd been cooking for days, since she hung up the phone.

Evidently she was a yeller too, a woman who raged, who raged and cooked. My father says she had a terrible temper, but she was only ever sweet to me. A big, effusive woman with a Brooklyn accent who once gave me a tiny porcelain boot. She died before I could understand what made her cook that much, what kind of rage it was. I don't want to ask my father. I do not prefer to hear his version. What I want from him is her recipes.

I FELT SUCH empathy for the Iowa City mailman with his ice cream cone. Sometimes I even felt empathy for Trump—not when I think of him as an adult, but as a boy, who just wanted his extra scoop of ice cream and whatever solace it brought him. Though perhaps all this ice cream empathy would be better directed inward. Maybe I should give my *own* child self an ice cream cone. Or maybe I should say what *I* want, which isn't ice cream or an English muffin but quite a simple thing, so simple I never asked for it: an apology.

MEASURING LIVES
Margery Irvine

U NLIKE PRUFROCK, the women in my family measured out our lives not with coffee spoons but with rolling pins and mixing bowls. I don't think that made us any different from most of the women of our generations, when fast food was an oxymoron, when takeout was light years away, and when freezer compartments were so frost-coated that all they had room for were ice cubes. Dinner meant everyone in the family around the table, seven nights a week, grandparents included on the weekends. My life falls neatly into two parts: the years when my grandmother and mother cooked for me and then the almost-sixty years when I did the cooking.

My dad's mother lived with my parents, my younger brother, and me. Her husband had died of influenza in 1918, when my dad was three, and Grandma Ida lived forever after with whatever relative would have her. So she never had her own kitchen, which might explain why she was such a dreadful cook. Her hamburgers, hockey pucks; her calves' liver, shoe leather; but her potted lambs' tongues, sublime.

My maternal grandmother was the cook who provided us with the yardstick I still use: "These sugar cookies are good, but not as good as Grandma Edith's."

Edith's parents came to the US from Germany; a Lutheran, Edith caused a scandal in both families when she married Joseph Alderman, a Jew whose mother had come from Russia as a young woman. For Sunday dinner, you were just as likely to get sauerbraten as you were to sit down to a bowl of chicken soup with matzo balls. And let me tell you, those matzo balls could have floated out of the soup, risen to the ceiling, and danced the hora. Her blintzes were the thinnest and tenderest; all the fat disappeared on her roast duck, leaving just crispy skin; her custards silky smooth; her pastry flaky. And she never took shortcuts.

She creamed butter and sugar with a wooden spoon in a yellow mixing bowl; she chopped by hand; she'd sooner poison you than feed you a potato pancake that had been warming in the oven instead of coming straight from the cast-iron pan to your plate.

Nothing, of course, ever went to waste. Nor did it go into countertop compost bins. Nope, you carried those watermelon rinds home in your pockets and then Grandma transformed them into crunchy, sweet pickles.

Edith was proud of her cooking and disdainful of anyone who didn't give food the time and attention it deserved. She made jelly using a muslin bag tied to a broomstick suspended on two chair backs. The cooked fruit went into the bag, and the jelly slowly dripped out, before it was poured into jelly glasses (sealed, of course, with melted paraffin wax). Now, some cooks might get fed up watching the drip, drip, dripping. Some cooks might squeeze that jelly bag, but those cooks wouldn't have had jelly you could see through, jelly as clear as the window glass she polished that very morning, while the jelly dripped.

Before it went into the jelly bag, the fruit and sugar cooked a long, long time, until they reached the jelling point. Some cooks, like Edith's best friend, Stella, might use powdered pectin to hurry the process, but then you'd risk having Edith tell her granddaughter, "Stella Hecht is a very nice person. But she uses pectin."

My mother never did quite measure up to Edith as a cook, but she worked outside the home as soon as my brother and I were in school. When she had the time, though, she'd spend hours making eggplant parmigiana (the kind where every paper-thin slice of eggplant is fried separately) and huge pots of vichyssoise, which we'd eat during the week when she got home too late to cook. Mom liked to try different things, recipes she cut out of magazines and newspapers (I have them now), some of which were . . . odd. There were her flounder fillets wrapped around dill pickles and served with mustard sauce, or salmon rolls using Bisquick and served with cream of celery soup sauce. (Actually, that one was pretty good.) Once she found out you liked something, you'd see it on your plate for the next six months. Acorn squash. Smoked haddock in cheese sauce. Criss-cross meat loaf. (That would be with the cheese slices on top.) And my brother swears she sent him to school with Taylor Pork Roll sandwiches every day of grades four, five, and six.

Always in a hurry to get dinner on the table, Mom depended on her stove-top pressure cooker, the single most frightening object in the apartment. Nobody wanted to be in the kitchen when that baby was rocking and rolling on the stove; steam hissed, the little button danced up and down, the whole stove swayed.

Mom's triumph, made on weekends, when she had plenty of time, was a meal she learned from Edith, when Edith had her German toque on. She'd roast a fresh ham (not easy to get), make dark brown gravy with the drippings (gravy for the mashed potatoes, of course), and an *einbrenn* ("burn once") sauerkraut that had us licking our plates. For the latter, she'd "burn once" the onions in pork fat, add a few big cans of sauerkraut, a pig's knuckle, and a can or two of water. And then she'd just cook the mixture for hours. After eating the sauerkraut, my dad's cousin Herbert said that his belly button was about to pop off and take flight around the dining room.

By the time I was in high school, I was cooking dinner, so Mom wouldn't have to when she got home. I enjoyed it, but mostly I loved my father's comment on everything I ever served him (and this lasted until he died): "This is the best [you fill in the blank] I've ever tasted."

Married young, I moved seamlessly from my mother's kitchen into my own. And just as Edith learned to cook blintzes and matzo balls from her Jewish in-laws, I picked up Scottish recipes from mine. I've been making my mother-in-law's shortbread for almost sixty years, and her "mealy puddin'" (an oatmeal stuffing for chicken and turkey) is on every Thanksgiving table today, not only mine but also on my children's and nephews'.

My own cooking was influenced by having to feed five children and, fortunately, by the largesse of a farm and garden. With the help of an annual MOFGA (Maine Organic Farmers and Gardeners Association) apprentice, my first husband and I, and all the children, raised chickens, turkeys, rabbits, goats, beef cattle, milk cows, and pigs. Oh, and bees and earthworms. Our acre of garden gave us vegetables all year—fresh from June to November, canned and frozen the rest of the year.

By today's standards, I suppose our food pyramid was upside-down, and, in fact, today one of my children is a vegetarian, one avoids dairy and wheat, and one has an advanced degree in Cooking with Kale. We never had to deal with picky eaters when they were young, though, and pretty much anything on their plates was their favorite.

My mother, visiting from her city apartment, used to shake her head at the way we lived. I'm sure she wondered why, with a supermarket so close, we chose to pay with our sweat for everything on the table. The garden: days on end of rototilling, planting, weeding, thinning, staking, and then harvesting. The animals: every morning, every night, throwing down hay from the loft, filling water buckets and feed troughs, and milking milking milking.

My grandmother, had she lived long enough to visit, would have been equally befuddled. My life had become so different from theirs. It's sometimes hard to see the ties that bind us. Any time I feel separated from the kitchens of my mother and grandmother, though, and therefore from them, I need look no further than the beat-up notebook on my shelf. Here are the recipes that they both clipped and taped or wrote out by hand. My grandmother's fresh pig's tongue; her lemon cake pudding; her crullers and corn oysters. My mother's chopped liver and chocolate ice box cake. Her crab cakes. Her apple fritters.

The three of us shared a belief that with food came love and laughter. I wish I could tell them that my children and grandchildren use their own rolling pins and mixing bowls to measure their lives. They embrace what I embraced to feel a connection to the past.

MEMORABLE MEALS
Carl Little

F ROM EARLY ON, my mother, Patsy Little, was the architect of memorable family repasts. While my father, Jack Little, made a mean slumgullion and eggs "any mook" (my way of saying "without gooey stuff"), my mother created the Chinese dumplings (*jiaozi*), Swedish meatballs, borscht, and manicotti that are the makings of family legend.

The labor-intensive dumplings owed their inspiration to my grandfather, Lester Knox Little, who had been Inspector General of Customs in China, and my father, who had spent time in Shanghai when he was young. Thanks to them, the family menu leaned a bit to Chinese, with the pork-filled dumplings as the *pièce de can't résistance.*

I vaguely remember my mother rolling out the dough and twisting the dumplings into their odd, almost origami shapes. With five children and a husband, there was a lot of stuffing and pinching. While it never felt like it was every child for her- or himself when it came to dinner, some of us were swifter than others to ask for seconds.

The recipe for the Swedish meatballs with their brilliant dill accent may have come from my godmother, Inger Hagen. A survivor of the Nazi invasion of Norway, Inger was one of the most self-reliant people I ever met—and she loved food. Among other Scandinavian delicacies, she turned us on to Norwegian goat cheese. Seated at her breakfast table in Alford, Massachusetts, we would slice the light-brown block onto homemade bread and sigh as we ate, taking our time with each forkful, dividing up the roughly round balls of meat into halves and quarters to make them last longer.

The borscht most certainly owed its place in my mother's culinary repertoire to Katherine "Katia" Alexeieff. A longtime faculty member at Manhattanville College—she taught Russian—Katia was among my mother's closest friends. In spring, she offered a remarkable Russian Easter spread at her home in Sea Cliff, New York, which featured all manner of sweets, pickled things, and old-country specialties.

I hated beets, but my mother's borscht recipe somehow cooked the unpleasant taste out of those deep-red roots and gave them the appearance of boiled potatoes. I wielded my spoon with eagerness and added generous portions of sour cream.

And the manicotti: Perhaps the greatest meal of all and the one with the most associations. In my late teens, I'd get stoned if I knew manicotti was on the menu—the pot enhanced the appetite. My brother John and I, and sometimes a couple of our friends, would appear at the table all smiles, eyes gleaming, almost sighing for what lay ahead, the wonder and aroma of ricotta cheese, tomato sauce, pasta shells, etc.

At the time, my parents were headed toward the end of an increasingly bitter marriage, the tension in the household palpable. I can see my mother bearing the dish from the oven, her mittened hands grasping the Pyrex. And for some reason, I picture my father in the next room watching Olympic ice skaters, exclaiming at successful triple Salchows.

In retrospect, that image of my parents seems a bit simplistic, but it's how I remember them: my mother, angry and suffering; my father, seemingly oblivious in front of the television. They divorced a few years later, much to everyone's relief. You might say the manicotti helped us survive those sometimes trying times, providing a savory escape.

Neither I nor my siblings (to my knowledge) make any of my mother's dishes today, which is a shame. They are a part of our shared past and any one of them, prepared properly, would provoke a Proustian reaction, swiftly return us to a crowded table and tender, if sometimes troubled, times.

Of course, new great meals have arrived to take their place, along with the loved ones who make them—my wife, my children, my siblings and their spouses, family friends. A supreme chick-pea curry topped with hot mango chutney, cilantro-accented fish tacos, over-easy eggs on an everything bagel—these and other offerings are the delectable foundation of future memories.

TEN-YEAR CHILI
Lewis Robinson

THE SUMMER BEFORE my sophomore year at Middlebury, I worked on campus driving the college's recycling truck, picking up blue plastic bins full of paper from the language schools and the school of English, Breadloaf. I lived in a '70s-era dorm room that, during July and August, felt like the inside of a pizza oven. I didn't have the meal plan, so I made a lot of peanut-butter and jelly sandwiches.

At the end of that summer, I drove to see my parents in Bethlehem, New Hampshire, where my dad was the head of the White Mountain School. They lived in campus housing—for most of my childhood we'd lived in campus housing—but that summer, they'd decided to build a small house in the middle of the woods, in the tiny nearby town of Lyman, because they wanted to have a place of their own.

It was obvious to me that the house-building project was a last-ditch effort to save their marriage. Right after I'd graduated from high school, they'd separated, but now they were temporarily back together. Building a house in an idyllic setting gave them something new to pour their hearts into. Over the course of a few weekends, my brother, sister, and I helped them with the project, erecting the framed walls, pounding nails.

The next fall, I took a Shakespeare class taught by the nature writer John Elder, who focused on the Bard's reverent and precise observations of the natural world. I joined the Mountain Club and was soon hiking every weekend in the Green Mountains and Adirondacks and more and more surrounded myself with earnest people who chose not to wear deodorant. What I ate in the dining hall: Grape-Nuts, ricotta-stuffed shells, iceberg lettuce, deli meats, Ben & Jerry's. When I was growing up, my dad's refrain was *food is fuel*, and I took after him. I wasn't one to linger during meals or care at all about nutrition. On our trips into the mountains, we stuck to mac and cheese.

Once the Lyman house was built, the vibe out there pleased me as a burgeoning nature boy: exposed wood beams, woodstove, pine tongue-and-groove walls, windows looking out at the hillside, and the brook running through. It would surely be the family's hearth for years and years.

Within months of finishing the house, though, my parents told us they were splitting up for good. We cried but weren't surprised. I felt resigned to this outcome and actually somewhat relieved. They'd tried to salvage their marriage for years. Now, they'd built a beautiful little house together in the woods, but that hadn't worked either.

My mom moved to western Massachusetts, and my dad poured himself into his work at school, so the little house remained mostly empty. My brother and I built a sweat lodge down the hill from the house by the brook. It was a crude tent-like structure, ribs made from saplings staked into the earth, and covered with tarps, with a fire pit nearby where we could heat rocks, which would then heat the sweat lodge. Our own little house, just for us and untouchable.

And once we'd built the sweat lodge, my brother and I decided the next logical step was to host a New Year's Eve party for our college friends. We drank too much and shivered in the sweat lodge; we hadn't quite figured out how to keep the structure from leaking heat, and some of the rocks exploded in the fire. Also, we hadn't planned for food. We ate what we found in the house: cereal and cans of corned-beef hash.

But we'd established a tradition. Our parents, who in the coming years would move from state to state, marrying other people, had less claim on us.

YEAR TWO, WE built a better sweat lodge, found rocks that wouldn't explode, invited people we wanted to sweat naked next to. There were many more people at the party, much more booze, and because of this, we needed to plan meals. I still didn't know how to cook, but I figured chili would be an easy enough way to feed the drunken group. I dumped a bunch of canned beans and tomatoes and browned meat in a pot and heated it up. It was awful but it didn't kill us.

The years went by, and the party kept growing. My sister started college, and she and her raucous friends joined the mix. How did the party veterans describe it to the newcomers? *Middle of nowhere dance party, naked sweat lodge.* I was beginning to understand my responsibility as chili chef:

the food needed to be good enough, enticing enough, that no one would get alcohol poisoning. This meant I had to start the chili early. Soften up the beans, cook them and the tomatoes with the right blend of chili powder, garlic, and salt for hours and hours. Adding bacon and pork to the hamburger gave it good depth. Dark chocolate too. I offered a vegetarian option, which at first just seemed like glorified minestrone soup, but it got better because I was determined not to disappoint my sister's friends.

As the chili improved and diversified, so did the party. My brother would get things started at sunset by wrapping an old T-shirt around a crowbar, dipping it in motor oil, and setting it on fire, then marching down the hill to the fire like a post-apocalyptic Olympian. Waves of people rolled in and out of the sweat lodge, some of them so hot they broke a hole in the frozen brook and dunked their heads. To give the party the all-night energy it deserved, the dehydrated sweat-lodgers got some chili on board before the dance party started. Chug that cheap tequila too fast on an empty stomach—no matter how good the music is—and you might end up passed out in a boot closet or crashing a plastic toboggan at full-speed without any clothes on and badly abrading your nether regions.

Often, during that ten-year stretch of post-divorce New Year's Eve parties, I was the last person to go to sleep. The dance floor—every inch of it—was always covered with sleeping bodies, some of them in sleeping bags, others just looking like they'd been dropped from the sky.

At the last of our parties, nearly twenty years ago now, I tiptoed around the house in my tighty-whities with a couch cushion tucked under my arm, looking for a place to crash. I wandered into the kitchen, peered into the two titanic chili vats, now empty, and curled up right there at the base of the stove. The revelers had been nourished—by the chili and by heading deep into the woods and sweating together. In a few short hours we'd all be waking up at the same time, like a family, ready to start a new year.

RECLAIMING THE BODY
Gregory Brown

WHEN I WAS younger, I felt surrounded by giants. They were broad, tall, and thick. I remember kitchen chairs creaking under hulking older cousins. Bodies completely filling doorways. Cars sinking into their springs. Trips to the big and tall sections of department stores.

As a kid, I just kept getting bigger too. Everyone in my family did. We ate, and we fed each other, doing so together and with joy when we were happy. And we ate and fed ourselves, sometimes in the dark hours of the night, sometimes far beyond the point of being full, with a certain desperation, looking to replace sadness with fullness, when we were alone and distressed.

By the time I was sixteen, I was six and a half feet tall and weighed three hundred and fifty pounds. I felt like I was buried in my own body. I had become one of the giants.

I hid from the world. I dropped out of school and turned to smoking pot (which I secretly hated), computers (better), and books (way better) to escape. It felt so much better to be anywhere other than in my body. The cycle was vicious, though: the larger I got, the more I hated myself, and the harder I was on myself, the more I ate to cope with my disappointment and to punish myself for being so fat.

What was worse, suffering from the kind of mind-body disconnect that's so common to depression, I didn't exactly understand how I had gotten so big. Not only did I feel *huge*, but I felt completely out of control of my own body, attacked by food, attacked by genetics, betrayed.

Around 2000, as I was turning eighteen, I began to walk, and walking, I have no doubt, saved my life. Within two years, I'd lost more than one hundred pounds and was no longer clinically depressed. The same pleasure I had found in food, which was often the pleasure of distraction from something unpleasant in my life, I found in the observational nature of walking, which allowed me to go as slowly or quickly as I wanted, any-where I wanted, and provided seemingly endless discoveries once I learned to slow my mind and really pay attention—the way deep water sounds as it shifts under the surface of a frozen river, how sun light falls through an interlaced canopy of maple leaves versus oak leaves, how a body changes smell with each step as it collects sweat.

I know how this might sound: take your food trauma and funnel it into a different obsession, or a different practice at least. Get your body moving and all will be better. It's the talk of life coaches, trainers, and gurus ped-dling pat answers and easily packaged personal reinventions. While it's true that motion does amazing things to our bodies and minds, body shame and depression are not easy-to-fix issues. There may be no harder change than behavioral change, which requires us to disrupt ingrained habits, while simultaneously making space for new, unfamiliar actions.

The truth is there's a certain privilege in being able to achieve three hundred and fifty pounds of body mass at sixteen, even if that achievement was made largely through cheap food, processed food, quick and fast food, the kind of food that runs through the brain like a shot of dopamine-releasing lightning and was easy to come by for us, a family often strapped for cash and always strapped for time, which also excelled at traditional Maine country cooking—baked haddocks, pot roasts, fish chowders, cakes, donuts, pies, pies, and more pies.

Remembering myself twenty years ago, when my own toxic relation-ship to food seemed insurmountable, I'm amazed to be where I am now: healthy, active, comfortable (most days) in my body and with my weight. More importantly: empowered in my relationship with food.

MY FAMILY HAS stayed shockingly close to Penobscot County and Waldo County. It seemed to me as a kid that we'd always just kind of been there. I marveled at the aunt who managed to leave Maine and head for Califor-nia or the distant cousin who was travelling in Europe. In an increasingly mobile civilization, we stayed put. I resented it then. Later, I realized how preposterous and special it was to be able to stake that much permanence, that much known geographic history, to one's past.

WHEN I DECIDE to call my great aunt Marise in Carmel, Maine, and tell
her I want to talk about our family's relationship to food, she doesn't seem
surprised, even though it's been years since we last spoke.

"Well," she says, "we like to eat, don't we? And to feed people too."

Yes, I think. *Perhaps too much*, I stop short of saying.

We compare notes on who lives where now. Who's married to who.
Who has a new baby, a new dog, a new house, a new truck, a new garden
plot, or pretty much a new *anything*.

Marise is eighty-three and the youngest of three sisters. Her sister,
Charlene, my grandmother, died in 2009. Her other sister, Betty, the oldest,
died in 2015. Our conversation turns to the Homestead Restaurant and
the Homestead Dairy Bar in Unity, Maine, which Betty owned for many
years and where everyone in the family worked.

Here are two nuggets of wisdom about running country food establishments in rural Maine that I gleaned as a child.

One, enact the following hiring and firing policy. *Give them a chance.
Then, the minute you hear them swear, fire them on the spot.* Say what? Who
doesn't swear while working in a restaurant for fuckssake? *If they can't control
their emotions and find a better way to express their displeasure, well, then, they're
going to end up getting into it with a customer.* So, the firing test isn't about
profanity exactly, or Puritanical censorship, but an ability to be resilient,
adaptable, self-controlled, and customer-focused, according to family logic
at least.

Two, when you own an ice cream stand, the best place to keep the
money isn't in a safe (talk about obvious) but in the microwave. *People don't
look in a microwave at an ice cream stand*, goes another quip of oddly illogical
family logic. Unless you're my sister and me, at four and eight years of age,
stuck hanging around inside a tiny ice cream stand watching the people
outside actually eat ice cream, bored as sand as our mother talks to her
aunt. You start messing around with everything in sight, obviously opening
the microwave door because it has a button, and what kid doesn't love to
push a button? Then you watch as huge piles of cash spill out all over the
place, causing a sudden and delightful panic in the ice cream stand as all the
adults simultaneously scramble to collect the scattered bills and scold you
for touching what doesn't need touching.

For Marise and me, it's impossible to talk about the joys of food (the
huge and tumultuous family gatherings at her house) and the joys of service (for my family, running a country diner was as much an act of love as

a money-making endeavor) without also addressing the high human cost of food—the diabetes, the heart disease, the heart attacks, the obesity, the alcoholism, the food addiction. Tales of too many people in our family lost far too soon because food consumed them. Tales of too many people struggling to "get their weight under control," "eat better," "decrease their portions," "cut out the salt and fat" so they could stay here with us longer.

It took years to change my relationship to food from one of instant emotional gratification followed by self-castigation to something richer. These days my wife, daughter, and I grow our own food. We frequent community gardens. We prepare food with others when possible. We embrace ritual in hopes of being more mindful. It feels like a return to something very old, generations old.

My aunt tells me people used to come to the restaurant not just to be fed, but to be loved. She tells me she's glad I've found that in food too.

While I'm happy as well, I can't explain to her that it's not that simple, that everything isn't entirely *fixed*.

Once you become a giant, you don't ever stop feeling giant. Even though my life is now one of slow food, and I am no longer the three-hundred-and-fifty-pound teenager I once was, I still feel "too large" much of the time. My intellectual self can identify this as dysmorphia. But when has the embodied self ever cared about what the intellect knows? I am often shocked when I see a photo of myself and note how much the giant has actually shrunk.

AFTER GETTING OFF the phone with Marise, I head into the woods near my house to walk, thinking about how there's pleasure, and potentially danger, in being alone with a thing.

While we were often together with food in my family, we were often alone as well. When sad, distraught, or struggling to find hope, the pattern for many of us was to eat. I think about how being less alone with food—not going downstairs in the middle of the night to eat more ice cream, not opening a new bag of chips while watching television, not having another beer while reading—can save a life.

What if those people in my family who lost their battle with food had had more support around food addiction and dependence? What if instead of feeding them more, arguably encouraging a pattern of overconsumption, we had paid more attention to what they were going through? What if instead of saying, "Come eat something," we had asked,

"How are you *feeling*?" What if they had had fewer moments alone with their distress and more moments with an objective witness or, even better yet, a supporting, loving witness?

I wonder how their lives might be different. I wonder if they would still be here for me to call as well.

COVID'S MOVEABLE FEAST
Caitlin Shetterly

> It was always Paris and you
> changed as it changed.
> —ERNEST HEMINGWAY

WE BEGAN WITH a croque-monsieur. A simple, hot, bubbly, cheesy sandwich retrieved by my palate from dusty memories of cafés and Gauloises cigarettes and black *express* in tiny cups.

It was March of 2020. COVID had descended. Our boys were home. We were *all* home. *All* the time. Back in February, in a moment of uncharacteristic prescience, my worst-case-scenario thinking had paid off: I had thought, "Yeah, our kids are coming out of school any day now." Over two weeks, I cleaned our entire, rambling pre–Civil War money pit while the kids were in school. Then, one stormy evening at dinner, as February turned to sleet-and-brown-snow March, I turned to my two boys, ages eleven and five, and tried to sound casual: "So, guys . . . if we were to take you out of school, or school just somehow stopped, say, and we had to homeschool, what would you want to study? Just for a few weeks?"

My eleven-year-old son, Marsden, paused his recitation of his favorite lines from the "Taco Town" skit on *Saturday Night Live*.

"Huh?" His eyes tried focusing on the extraterrestrial that had replaced his mother.

My youngest son, Levin, piped up. "Egypt," he said, and then, "mummies." Mars had another suggestion: "How about French?" he asked.

Ah, French. A language that I once spoke fluently. Before going to Brown, I took a gap year in Paris to study French language and culture at the Sorbonne. At Brown, I became a French language teaching assistant my sophomore year and then went on to study French poetry. I went back to Paris one more time in 1998, with my dad.

But as of 2020, I hadn't strung together more than ten French words since that last trip. French had become a forgotten and lost part of my story, as the many selves I once were sloughed off, leaving only the one enormous, engulfing role of *maman*.

"OK," I said. "Great ideas." When lockdown began, we dove into Egypt and mummies immediately and decided to commit to a "French Friday" for language study.

WHEN THAT FIRST Friday rolled around, after an ersatz on-the-fly French lesson, it occurred to me that the kids and I should make something French for lunch. Rooting around the fridge showed me that I had bread and smoky turkey bacon and cheese.

"OK, so there's this sandwich," I explained. "Maybe we can make it? It's got bread and cheese and ham . . . but . . . I think we can use this turkey bacon. Here's a photo of one; it's called a croque monsieur, which I think means Crunchy Mister. Or maybe it's Mister Crunch. One of those two! *Bof!*"

"Crunchy Mister! Mister Crunch! *Bof!*" hooted Lev.

Both kids could agree that it looked mighty tasty. Too late, I realized that béchamel was involved, and we were already out of *lait*.

I scanned the fridge. Hmmm. No milk, but I had yogurt. And butter.

"Mars," I said, "can you find the Calvados in the cupboard over there? I think we can make something with yogurt and butter and Calvados."

Lev, on the other hand, was busily pulling every bag of flour onto the counter and reaching for an old bag of marshmallows. "*Non, non,*" I scolded. "*Assieds-toi!* Sit down. In a minute you can cut the bacon."

Quickly, Marsden and I whisked together the butter, Calvados, and some brown rice flour over low heat. As he stirred, I scooped in the cream top of the yogurt. He kept whisking. It was getting thick. I ground up some pepper in the mortar and pestle and added that and some salt.

It needed nutmeg. I called Levin for the task.

Grating *noix de muscade* is a very special and favorite chore in our house. Even Lev, at five, understands that to make an unctuous Bolognese, a transcendent creamed spinach, or a sublime apple pie, the tiniest hint—never too much—of nutmeg is the secret. He arrived with his chest puffed out with importance, clutching the grater and the little acorn-shaped spice. *Râper, râper, râper.*

"*Parfait!*" I exclaimed.

I tasted it. Then we all tasted it. "*Ajouter du sel,*" I said. We added salt. Hmmm. "Oh, I know. A bay leaf." I threw that in. "And Parm." I added some grated Parmesan, because who had Gruyére lying around in their *frigo* on March 20 of 2020?

"*Ajouter de beurre,*" I told Mars. He regarded me for a long second. I stared back.

"Oh, I know . . . butter?" he asked.

"*Oui.*"

"Jeez, why didn't you say so?"

We all tasted it again. "Wow," Mars said. It was delicious. Tangy and cheesy and warm and savory, with the tiniest hint of Calvados.

Then, he asked, "Is that what béchamel is supposed to taste like, Mama?"

"Pretty darn close," I said, pretty darn amazed.

Finalement, we had two sandwiches slathered with béchamel and stuffed to the gills with thick slices of bacon and a deceptively Gruyére-like Parmesan and cheddar cheese mixture. We popped them into the oven and waited. It felt like hours.

Well, cooking with one's children *toujours* feels like hours. And when they are hungry, it feels like *les années. Mais, enfin,* the sandwiches got melty and golden brown, and the smell in the house was cheesy and aromatic.

THERE WAS ONLY enough for two. As our children ate, saying, "Oh God, this is the best sandwich ever," my husband and I hovered like hungry dogs, lucky enough for the piece of crust our youngest threw us to split.

But, oh, the joy on their two faces!

From that Friday forward, for a year-and still-counting, French class became language plus a full-family cooking class. We've made a *tarte Tatin;* croissants that made the house smell like a real patisserie, palmiers, clafoutis, crepes, sole meunière, *bifteck haché, salade niçoise, gougères, mousse au chocolat, soufflé aux fraises,* chicken roasted with forty cloves of garlic, pissaladière, steak-frites, and *pan bagnat* for a picnic at Morse Mountain.

And each Friday, in the chaos of flour going everywhere, my kids snatching spoons from each other and yelling, some tears of frustration of my own, and four rumbling bellies, we have found a few minutes to laugh and, eventually, to sit down to eat something unexpectedly wonderful. Admittedly, a glass of Bordeaux became de rigueur for the grownups.

With that glass in my hand, and *les bougies* flickering from the center of the dining table and radiating a warm glow into the afternoon gloam, I've found myself, week after week, in the momentary silence of my children devouring something delicious and new and interesting, going back in time using the portkeys of my nose and taste buds. First, I wander into the pâtisserie around the corner from my light-filled apartment in the Fourteenth Arrondissement, ironically on the Avenue du Maine, the same name as my home state. My apartment had balconies all around and louvered doors from which I could step outside high above the avenue. Watching my family eat on Friday afternoons, I could almost feel the weight of two warm baguettes for dinner in my arms, and I could smell their yeasty, crusty fragrance, and taste the sweet pastry *choquette* I had bought to tide me over on the cold walk home, that Parisian wind cutting right through my stylish dark wool coat. In the approximate quiet of "mms" and chewing from my boys, I could remember the roseate face of the butcher at the Sunday street market not a five minutes' walk from my apartment, who sold me a *dinde* for Thanksgiving that year; I thought of the time my friend Nils taught me to make *mousse au chocolat* in his apartment and the time another friend, Luce, taught me how to use crème fraîche in, well, everything. I'll never forget standing next to the actor Daniel Auteuil at a café bar as we both drank our morning *express* together, our shoulders touching; or the *chocolat chaud* delivered in a bowl at Café de Flore, making me feel like a spoiled child, and over in the corner sat Kristin Scott Thomas drinking a modest tisane; or the cobblestone and falafel smell of the Marais; or reading—uninterrupted—(something I can't even imagine now with two young children) for entire afternoons at the Bibliothèque Sainte-Geneviève, the brass lights on the long wooden tables casting golden orbs onto ancient texts. Finally, I find myself entering the sculpture garden of the Rodin museum, which I did at least once a week to draw or, sometimes, to just sit on a bench, and a feeling of bliss and peace comes over me, once again.

"Paris," as the great writer once wrote, "is a moveable feast." I just didn't know that it could be resurrected for me quite like this, despite the loud bumps and bangs of two energetic boys, as we all sheltered in place. Without their even knowing it, my kids were giving me back a part of myself, long forgotten. And I was accepting it, like *une boisson* of cool water on a hot day.

THE GREAT PERSIAN PALATE
INVASION OF 1988
Desi Van Til

THOUGH THERE WERE probably some hidden pockets of back-to-
the landers growing their own arugula, culturing heritage sourdough,
or making confit from their own ducks, my rural Western Maine town in
the late 1980s was a food desert. Rich in lakes and streams, yes, effusive
with scented pine forest and perennial flowers, awash with precipitation,
absolutely . . . but provocative cuisine found no purchase. This was well
before the gourmet revolution rolled through the country with thick-
paged cookbooks of full-color, well-lit food photography; it predates the
expansion of the "ethnic" section of the local Shop n' Save to more than
just Ortega taco shells and Top Ramen.

If there was a gourmet scene in my hometown, it was happening so
far underground that you wouldn't catch a whiff from under the door. It
wasn't happening in the two restaurants downtown that abided by the holy
trinity of protein, veggie, and starch, starting with the ever-present cold roll
and foil-wrapped butter packet. It wasn't happening in any number of the
grease-forward pizza parlors, the Irving truck stop on R27, or the diner to
which you considered bringing your own silverware, though these were
hallowed grounds for birthday dinners, late-night onion rings, or dense
blueberry pancakes, respectively. Fine dining was something people did in
movies; sushi was a preposterous concept we heard about from a piece on
Tom Brokaw's *Nightly News*—and openly mocked.

NOR WAS IT happening in my childhood home: it wasn't in the water
and it certainly wasn't in the fridge. I was raised by parents for whom food
wasn't a frontier to be discovered but a well-trodden commute that took

us past the familiar scenery of iceberg lettuce, broiled chicken, boxed rice pilaf, and broccoli or spinach, which generally entered the house as frozen rectangular pucks. There were grilled burgers and all-beef dogs for summer cookouts, and fruit salads that I thought were quite fancy (even fancier than the one that came from a can, with a maraschino cherry masquerading as legitimate food, drowning as it was in high-fructose corn syrup). My mom would hand Dad the melon baller and the tacit assignment to disembowel honeydew, cantaloupe, and watermelon, and my father employed his economist's mind to maximize the number of marble-sized satellites that could be rendered from each spheroid mothership. And though my parents tried year and year again to coax beefsteak tomatoes out of their rocky soil, it was always a race against the frost, and one they rarely won. I don't mean to condemn the people who loved, raised, and kept me fed; rather to explain the somewhat anodyne food scene of my childhood before Iran came to town and changed the landscape of our appetites.

VARIETY MAY BE a crucial spice in most people's pantry, but my father, both enthusiast and satisficer, could happily devour the same good meal every day for a year before it occurred to him to try something different. When I was a kid, my dad would routinely eat a pair of scrambled eggs for breakfast, a turkey sandwich for lunch, and chicken breast slathered with "curry sauce" (his mixture of curry powder and mayonnaise) for dinner, along with a late-night bowl of cereal to accompany Jay Leno's monologue. But when he whipped up a meal, he went for it. His PB&Js were my favorites because he laid it on obscenely thick, taking down a quarter of a jar of jam per sandwich. When he doctored up my Cream of Wheat on cold winter mornings, he'd plop a massive hunk of butter (or, more likely, margarine) on the peak of the gentle white slope, echoing *Close Encounters of the Third Kind*. The melting puddle would stream down the sides like magma, before he dusted it liberally with white sugar and cinnamon. If we had company, my father would concoct a decadent batch of "Littlefield Dip" appetizer, origin unknown, though probably invented by a corporate chef for the American Cheese Association: a semi-solid, savory amalgam starring cream cheese, cheddar cheese, and pimentos. It was served in a ceramic jar used only for this purpose, and in concert with buttery Town House crackers. I would scrutinize our guests like a hawk, wanting to clock the exact moment they took their first bite, waiting for their appreciation, as if I could take credit for their pleasure. I can hear my young, eager voice asking, "Do you like it?" just as readily as I can hear my mother warning my father, brother, and me to lay off and leave some for the guests.

MY FATHER IS a lifelong teetotaler who even at age seventy-five has yet to let a sip of wine pass through his lips. Instead, he guzzled *getorkum*—his homemade elixir of grape, orange, and pineapple juices, made from tubes of frozen concentrate mixed in a plastic pitcher, served on the rocks. Once in a while, he'd order *getorkum* at restaurants when a server asked what he'd like to drink, gently pushing back on the assumption that booze is the only legitimate beverage. It was an earth-shattering moment when I learned that *getork* (familiar usage) was Van Til–generated vernacular, an inside joke for his siblings and old high school pals. And here I thought it was just a Latin synonym for juice.

Like his own mother, whose tastes and gratitude were shaped by the Great Depression, my father was hyperbolic with his praise for any food he was enjoying. His penchant for exaggeration made him easy to cook for years later when I blossomed into an insufferable food snob. He never once seemed disappointed when I cooked for him, and always asked, "So Des, what's this dish called?" as if everything I made was so extraordinary that it deserved a title or a pithy descriptor after a colon. I felt bad deflating his expectations with "Grilled chicken?"

Meanwhile my mother donned the mantle of prolific baker, known in town not only for the quality of her blueberry breads, cream cheese brownies, and chocolate chip cookies, but for their prodigious quantity. She baked for our teachers, doctors, dentists, students, soccer coaches, and theater directors, the plow guy and the butcher. If I heard the oven turn on, I'd ask, "Do I have a doctor's appointment tomorrow?" She baked often into the night, at times despite herself, frequently through exhaustion. She baked birthday cakes from a box but made chocolate buttercream frosting from scratch, my parents tag-teaming the decoration of elaborate sheet-cakes for all special occasions. Even with my father's atrocious chicken-scratch handwriting, unperfected as he'd skipped third grade, he was always entrusted with the pastry bag, my mother shying away from the high-stakes pressure of putting food-colored frosting on chocolate veneer. The joint effort of cake production that put my parents squarely on the same team may be another reason, besides the obvious, that I still love cake.

But though she was more confident as a baker of confections, if too intimidated by yeast to attempt bread, my mother was never as sure-footed as a chef and would rarely stray from recipes she knew through muscle memory, from cooking with her mother. Rosetta Blumetti, a name almost too cinematic to be true, was a Long Island Roman Catholic with a classic *Sopranos* accent, a cigarette in one hand and her race-track picks in the other. Grandma Rosie's gravy—my mom's tether to the island she left behind—was what we happily ate on every holiday, most birthdays, and once even on Thanksgiving when mom didn't want to deal with turkey in an infuriatingly spastic oven. Served atop various incarnations of pasta, tomato "gravy" was pre-soccer-game, carbo-charging, post-skiing comfort food, and the easiest way to feed a crowd when, years later, my big brother brought home friends from Colby, ravenous for home cooking. Sometimes sweet Italian sausages or chicken thighs floated through her sauce like icebergs, the majority lurking under the surface, but there were always pulpy, perfect meatballs, made with the bedrock pair of spices and the single herb that were on permanent rotation in our kitchen: onion powder, garlic powder, and fresh parsley. It was only when cooking stuffed manicotti would my mom's long since eradicated Lon-Giland accent resurface; cheeses were called "muzza-rell" or "rigott," the final vowels inexplicably vanishing into a *Goodfellas* abyss.

The times my mother dared step outside her culinary comfort zone were for dishes that came out of regional cookbooks with plastic ring spines, or off 3" × 5" index cards from her tin box of hand-copied recipes, shared and borrowed. We owned a copy of *Joy of Cooking*—text-dense and used primarily as a reference book or a booster seat, but not exactly inspirational. Non-Italian dinners took the shape of things like summer-squash casserole, tuna-noodle casserole, or anything upon which a can of cream of mushroom soup could be reasonably deployed. At least once there was a successful foray into fine French cooking in which chicken breast was stuffed with sliced ham and Swiss, then breaded and baked until gooey. This attempt to make chicken cordon bleu was a triumph of home-cooking sophistication, rarely repeated, because who needs to climb Everest twice? Mostly, our dinners were the simplest, most economical way from point hungry to point sated, accompanied by several glasses of milk, and occasionally, if my mom hadn't already given them all away, a chocolate chipper.

MY HOMETOWN IN the '80s matched the rice that nestled up to our proteins. The diversity I experienced was almost all 2-D via the Huxtables and the *Fresh Prince*. I grew up steeped in the myth of color blindness, oblivious to the systemic racism that festered well beyond the end of Jim Crow, and I had no firsthand experience contextualizing my whiteness. I believed racism was wrong but felt isolated from the experience of non-white, and even non-Christian, Americans. But then, at the end of that Reaganomic decade, having only lived in Maine a couple of years, having moved ourselves north from suburban Boston, my father was tasked with steering the hiring committee to expand the University of Maine-Farmington's Economics and Finance Department by precisely one. They chose a boisterous Iranian scholar named Waleck Dalpour, fresh on the academic job market and eager to take a full-time, tenure-track position at a public liberal arts college. Waleck, his wife, Nahid, and their toddler son had been living in Colorado, where Waleck had just completed a post-doc degree. Just a few years before, when Nahid was still in Tehran and sepa-rated by a blue Atlantic and a green card, Waleck and Nahid got married via a three-way phone call, looking at framed photographs of each other. But now he would live the American dream—moving his young family to Farmington to teach Americans about money.

If my dad was in charge of the search, my mom was the unofficial head of the welcoming committee. I should note that my New York born-and-bred mother had never intended to move to the wilds of Maine; the exigencies of academia, my father's love of privacy, and his frontier men-tality brought our family to the wooded desert. Donning blaze orange in November, learning to decode the r-optional accent, heartily accepting buckets of live smelts and fresh venison as welcome gifts, and settling into the isolation of rural living were all things my mother came to own when a family from farther afield, who had even more drastic adjustments to make, moved to town. Suddenly, she was not the most alienated in this outpost; she became a relative expert. I remember how we'd listen to Tim Sample and *Burt & I* comedy on cassette tapes, getting in on the joke mere mo-ments before explaining this distinct regional humor to our new Iranian friends.

My parents immediately invited their family to our home for the inevi-table rigatoni and meatballs. Our guests revealed themselves to be irrepress-ibly lovable people: open-hearted, ebullient, generous. Nahid was humble and subversively hilarious; Waleck, outrageous and playfully argumentative. I was taken with their sing-song Farsi accents and the gentle way Nahid squealed when hugging me, singing "How *are* you?" like the opening bars of a musical. I was fascinated hearing them speak to their adorable son, or to each other in quick marital asides, in their mellifluous mother tongue. Waleck warmly interrogated me about every aspect of my young American life while peppering me with impish dad jokes, cheeky even in a second language. They instantly treated the four of us like family, as if our friendship was predestined. To this day, both of them call me Desi Jooni, a Farsi term of endearment; I've never heard either of them say my name without this loving epithet. Uncle Waleck, as he was soon dubbed, would never simply speak my new diminutive but, rather, sing "Desi Jooni" to the tune of "Na na na na/hey hey hey/goodbye," as if I had been granted a bespoke Persian battle cry. (Ask me if I liked it when he sang that fever pitch from the sidelines of high school soccer games, and I can honestly answer yes.) From the time that I was little, Waleck made me an oft-repeated promise that were I ever to earn a PhD, in any subject, he would buy me a real Persian rug. For a ten-year-old, this abstraction didn't hold massive incentive, but I will confess there have been moments on more than one occasion, when I felt either at sea in my career or dissatisfied with my floor coverings, that I would wonder if that doctorate wouldn't be such a bad idea after all.

IT DIDN'T TAKE LONG until our new friends reciprocated our dinner invitation and thus began the shift both in my palate and my worldview. The first time we went to their lakeside rental house a few towns over, we crossed their threshold and an exotic blend of fragrances wrapped us up like sheets fresh from the dryer. The warm scent was pervasive, assertive, like another guest in the room that required introduction, an invisible entity taking up space. The spiced aroma stoked curiosity but gave us no information; it was giving a lost traveler a blank map. But there, on a buffet table behind Nahid, was its source. A panoply of different platters and bowls, their contents concealed beneath turned-over dishes, crowded the table so there was hardly room to admire the intricate tablecloth, stitched with golden thread. We took off our coats, admired their scenic view, but the elephants in the room sat just over there, stewing. There was no reason to wait, dinner was ready, and Nahid casually removed the covers one by one, a gustatory strip-tease revealing . . . well? We weren't quite sure. The unveiling didn't solve the mystery, but the quantity and variety of foods was gob-smacking. It was as if Nahid had opened a Persian speakeasy restaurant between the mechanic's and the redemption center. I saw my parents look at each other baffled. How did one woman possibly make all these different foods? Did she start cooking last week? Where did she find these far-flung spices? Who else was coming to dinner? If she didn't expect more company, did that mean they ate like this all the time? I could also sense a shadow of anxiety pass over my mother's beaming smile: What if it was too spicy, or worse, what if she just didn't like it? How could we ever offend the largesse of our friends' hospitality? My parents effusively thanked Nahid for the feast before they even took a first bite, and she waved away their astonishment in sing-song dismissal. She lilted, "It was nuuut-ing."

At last, my father could ask enthusiastically, "Does this dish have a name?" and get a satisfying reply. It was *ghorneh sabzi*! It was *bademjan*! It was *koofteh* and *fesenjoon*! Served alongside the ever-present *tahdig*. And what were they? Here, chicken and lamb *khoresh*, or braised stews, over there, eggplant dishes with dried lime and onions, and beef kebabs with sumac, and Persian meatballs with prunes and split peas. These were served always and forever alongside the fluffiest basmati rice, miraculously one part air to two parts grain, dappled with saffron bloomed in water, with the coveted crispy yellow bottom. They were mouthwatering, complex and utterly foreign to our heretofore unchallenged tastebuds. We were a family who had never eaten even Americanized Indian food. Who had little to no experience with the staples of spice blends from the Middle East and South Asia. Hummus hadn't even hit local grocery stores yet. If I'm honest about it, I'm sure that at first I played it safe, protecting my sheltered palate, sticking with saffron rice and *koofteh*, but over time it became easy to eat more adventurously; all of it was succulent goodness. It would take years for me to be able to identify the cumins and cardamoms, the turmerics and gingers, the fenugreeks and pomegranate molasses that went into the symphony of Persian dishes that we would devour with regularity in their home, departing Western Maine and taking flight, by dint of our tongues, to Tehran. We had been invited to an oasis, and we never turned back.

RAUCOUS, HIGH-DECIBEL MEALS at Nahid and Waleck's became a staple of my parents' slender social life. Frequently some sporting event on the TV simmered in the background, Waleck a rabid Broncos fan, while the foreground soundtrack was a spirited din, rife with political discussion among the grown-ups, often about the history and consequences of the Iranian revolution and the role of the Ayatollahs, the Shah, the Shia, and the Sunni. These were words and concepts as foreign to me as the *gheymeh* and *aash*, but gradually, those phrases and ideas were normalized, too, and what was once just a thin outline on a map in a clutch of desert nations whose names—at best—I had memorized in sixth-grade geography, Iran began to take on texture and relief. It suddenly bubbled over with voices, opinions, nicknames, laughter, faces, and flavors. Waleck mischievously taught us to refer to the bathroom as "the Shah's office"; we had inside jokes in this family too.

This also became my first exposure to the Muslim faith. We would all joyfully celebrate the end of Ramadan at Eid al-Fitr and toast to their New Year of Nowruz in spring. I was awed by the nature of their fast, much more draconian than what was required of me during Lent. I learned about the rugs for Nahid's thrice daily prayers toward Mecca and the hijab that she would wear when she returned to Iran, now that the Ayatollah was in power and instituting Islamic law. I saw firsthand how being apart from her birth family was a source of steady tears and how wrenching it was (and is) for immigrant families to stretch their love across oceans, continents, time zones, phone lines. I could sense her anticipation when planning that annual pilgrimage home to reunite with her family for months at a time, making sure her children got to know their aunties, uncles, and grandmother. When Nahid returned to Maine, her heart may have been conflicted, but her suitcase was plump full of a year's worth of spices. I witnessed the paradox of one family's assimilation, holding fast to their Muslim identities, while making room for the customs and facets of new ones. We celebrated Christmas with them, too, eating Persian delights beside their artificial Christmas tree, Nahid and Waleck adamant that their American children participate in this culturally essential holiday, never wanting them to feel other, or less than.

OUR FRIENDS, HAVING located the way life should be, put down Maine roots, and bought a house on a quiet village street. Not long after, they filled it by having a second child—a gorgeous little girl whose name translates to "rare gemstone." We all eagerly anticipated and celebrated the baby's arrival, our collective family gaining a new member in a symmetrical arrangement for each of us: older brother, younger sister. Their new home, like our own, was a modest cape, and when we eight dined together, there wasn't enough room to seat us all at the kitchen table, so we squeezed into their living room, perched on the overstuffed sofas and armchairs that bore a new upholstery seemingly every time we ate. It was as if the old fabric matched last month's *fesenjoon* and needed to be updated for this current menu. I recall several meals in which we'd take our first satisfying bites, my father would find a new grandiloquent way to praise the food, and then my mother, concentrating hard on the flavors, would ask what was different . . . and Nahid would point to the curtains. Since she had given up her career as a civil engineer in Tehran, Nahid put her mechanical acumen to a different use as the go-to area seamstress. Nearly every dress I wore to a high school prom or winter semi-formal was sewn by her adept hands, pinned to fit me when we were there gorging ourselves on Persian delights. I was young enough that I could still wear the dress even if the fitting was after dinner, and I was naive enough to think that everyone had a worldly craftswoman tailor them bespoke prom gowns. Our desert didn't have many places to go dress shopping either, but there were always the brimming fabric aisles at Jo-Ann's or Marden's in Waterville, and the good fortune that if I could draw a decent enough picture, Nahid could make it manifest.

OVER THE COURSE of my childhood, this deep connection to my Iranian family became part of my identity—and my taste. No longer daunted by the likes of turmeric and saffron, I realize that when I cook with these spices now, I'm not transported to the Iran of my mind's eye but rather to a white suburban house in the foothills of Western Maine. Those flavors that were an integral part of my upbringing, the blend of black teas served with a cardamom date cookie, are my own madeleine transporting me to a place when borders were swallowed and erased. We were charged with welcoming them to Maine, to give them a toehold in their new community—the only Persian family for hundreds of square miles. In return, they threw their doors open wide, their intoxicating foods welcomed us in, nourished us, gave us a delicious excuse to sit around a table—or perch on sofas—and become a meaningful and steady part of each other's lives.

As a college student years later, I would periodically pass through New York's Penn Station to and from school. I would grab my pre-boarding snacks from one of the station bodegas (knowing the year, it was likely some vanilla Snackwell cookies and a peach Snapple). Once, an older woman working the register delivered my total with a strong Farsi accent. I lit up with recognition and asked her, like the friendly rube that I was, if she was Persian? She gave me a skeptical, exhausted look: why is this perky, blonde stranger interrogating me about my ethnicity? But she asserted that she was originally from Iran, and I exploded with excitement, putting my hand over my heart, telling her that my best family friends in Maine were also from Iran, and that her accent felt like home. She smiled broadly, a little bemused, and gave me my change. I went on my way, not realizing until years later that it wasn't such an astonishing coincidence to run into a Farsi speaker in Manhattan. Still, whenever I encounter someone of Persian descent, I find myself drawn to them warmly, nostalgically, and tend to act overly familiar. They can't tell from the outside, but I'm actually one of them. And I realize my job now is to make sure my children know how to cook both sorts of meatballs: Grandma Rosie's—and Great Auntie Nahid's.

COOKING IS COMMUNITY
Margaret Hathaway

I N EARLY 2020, every morning began the same way. At 5 a.m., I padded downstairs in heavy wool socks, navigating the hall and stairs in the
dark so as not to wake my husband and daughters, or our dog, Banjo, who
would whine and want to go out. I turned up the heat as I passed the dining room thermostat, pausing for a moment to listen for the whoosh of the
furnace and the syncopated tick of steam through the pipes. In the kitchen,
I turned on the lights and put on a kettle, measuring coffee into the French
press. While the water heated, I crossed through the dining room into my
office and opened my laptop. As email loaded, I felt a familiar rush of
adrenaline: whose recipes would arrive this morning?

The jumble of voices coming from my inbox were replying to an invitation to submit favorite recipes to the *Maine Bicentennial Community Cookbook*, a project that I was working on with my husband, Karl. The previous
spring, Karl, a Maine native, had stumbled across the *Maine Jubilee Cookbook*,
a sesquicentennial community cookbook that came out the year he was
born. That book, a spiral-bound collection with a hand-drawn cover, originally cost three dollars and came in a little cardboard box for storage. Its six
hundred recipes, chosen by the editors from three times as many entries, are
a treasury of buttery pound cakes and flaky pie crusts, rich wild game, and
iridescent fish caught in Maine's fresh streams and brackish coastal waters.
These are New England classics, underscored by frugality, leaning heavily
on British traditions and French Canadian influences and avoiding strong
spices and flavors; recipes call for cayenne pepper by the grain, not the
teaspoon. An artifact of its time, the sesquicentennial cookbook presents a
vision of Maine that celebrates local flavors but is somewhat parochial in its
depictions. State pride can read as arrogance—if Maine is life "the way it

should be," how pitiable are those beyond the borders. Having moved here with Karl two decades ago—we say that he imported me—this book bears little resemblance to the state I've come to love.

Karl and I are frequent collaborators: I work with words; he, with images. When he discovered the sesquicentennial book, we had just finished putting together a compilation cookbook, *The New Portland, Maine, Chef's Table*. I had collected and edited the recipes from chefs around town, and Karl, a photographer by training, shot profiles of the contributors, their spaces, and their food. Working with the bounty of Maine, these cooks spice liberally and weave together flavors and cooking techniques from around the world. In the recipes I'd gathered for that project, native cod was paired with Chinese fermented sausage, wild game was topped with bright North African chermoula sauce, and locally milled buckwheat and cornmeal were baked into dairy- and gluten-free pound cake with olive oil and pistachios. Fifty years after the *Maine Jubilee Cookbook's* publication, the state's wide-ranging and much celebrated food landscape would be unrecognizable to its editors.

The *Maine Bicentennial Community Cookbook*, as we conceived of it, would be an answer to the sesquicentennial book. What are people cooking in Maine today? We envisioned a diverse and inclusive snapshot of home cooking around the state, a celebratory peek into kitchens in all sixteen counties, representing cooks from all backgrounds. Young and old, lifelong Mainers and those, like me, "from away," lovers of Yankee staples and keto-friendly experiments: all would be welcome to submit stories and recipes for the book.

A true community cookbook, we learned from our friend Don Lindgren, a historian and antiquarian book dealer who owns the largest collection of Maine community cookbooks in the world, is described by three characteristics: the community can be defined, the recipes are drawn from that community, and a charitable component brings proceeds from the book back to a project within the community. In the case of the *Maine Bicentennial Community Cookbook*, our community was the state of Maine, our recipes were drawn from people around the state, and we determined that two dollars from each book sold would go to organizations fighting hunger and food insecurity in the state. We would work with local professionals to design and proofread; Islandport Press, a publisher in Yarmouth, would distribute the book; and the project would be funded through pre-sales and ads, which would be scattered through the pages. Don would provide an introduction to community cookbooks for the front of the book, and we would include five essays from scholars and activists about Maine's food heritage. Governor Janet Mills would provide the foreword.

We reached through every media channel we could find to put out a call for recipes, and by January of 2020, each morning began with a fresh batch.

"My father, Thomas W. Easton, b. 1921, d. 1987, was a Colby professor who, among many other things, wrote a number of short essays on the way things were done in his boyhood. . . . Years ago I gathered them all together for the family, under his title, 'The Way It Was.'"

"We have compiled three Foss Family Favorites Cookbook. My Uncle Paul designed each of three covers. In the family, we refer to them by their color—blue (1982)—red (1988)—yellow (1995). This is the dedication in the red Foss Family Favorites: To the Five Foss Family Girls: It is from you that we have learned the true meaning of family. Your loyalty is unquestionable, your love is unbreakable, and your spirit of family is inspirational."

The sharing of food—on a plate or in recipe form—invites intimacy, and it is impossible to divorce a beloved family recipe from the people who love it. From the beginning, the recipes we collected were far from being simple formulas for a dish or a drink. Each was accompanied by a note, sometimes a story about the person who'd made it, sometimes a memory of an earlier time, sometimes a history of a specific community in Maine. We received scans of recipe cards, wedding photos, and obituaries. Each morning, we pored over church bulletins, illustrated place cards, and long letters written in spidery hands on lined notebook paper. Unprompted, Senator Susan Collins emailed us her mother's blueberry muffin recipe. We received memoirs—finished and un—and copies of family cookbooks. A retired grade-school teacher invited us for tea and cake at her home, where she shared class cookbooks that her students had compiled and let us copy a recipe that her fourth graders had received in 1984 from then vice president George H. W. Bush. From three branches of a single family with particularly wide spreading Maine roots, we received three photos of the same matriarch: as a corsaged bride at her engagement party, in a sweater vest and wide '70s lapels as a home economics teacher in middle age, and now, in old age, bowing her head to consult a hand-written recipe through thick glasses. Her hair changed over the years, but the smile was the same.

"No one who cooks cooks alone," wrote Laurie Colwin in her classic food memoir *Home Cooking*. "Even at her most solitary, a cook in the kitchen is surrounded by generations of cooks past, the advice and menus of cooks present, the wisdom of cookbook writers." The truth of this observation was demonstrated in every recipe that came in. Long dead ancestors were summoned with each turn of kneaded dough. Restaurants that had burnt to the ground half a century ago shimmered back to life, their kitchens bustling once more to turn out dessert cups of Indian pudding and cut-glass bowls of cheese dip. The margins of old cookbooks were a palimpsest, their thin pages stained and folded at odd angles, traces of ink and pencil vying for primacy.

A few months into our project, we were in love with every family we met. Our printing budget was shot as we added sixteen pages, then another sixteen, and another. Karl and I began to talk about families as if we knew them. One story, of a father's failure to bag a deer for his five daughters during a lean, Depression-era Thanksgiving, moved me to tears so heavy they gathered into choking sobs.

Like the matriarchs of the stories we received, I became protective of traditions and recipes and of the people who'd submitted them. In early February, when we assembled a group of local food writers to help with initial edits of the materials that had come in, I found myself feeling personally hurt by *any* critique of *any* submission. Even the most pedestrian dishes were perfect to me and were under my guard. Though the writers' notes were totally warranted, they seemed critical of my new friends, these strangers who had invited me into their kitchens. I wanted to keep them all in, to tell every story.

Of course, not every recipe could be included, and not every recipe should've been. There were some that were missing steps or ingredients, others that came on notecards too faded to read. There were duplicates of dishes whose recipes were so similar that we depended on the accompanying story to decide which to include. Some called for ingredients that would be hard for a contemporary cook to track down: oleo, dried sea moss, neck scrag. (In these cases, we offered substitutions, when possible.) Some seemed so archaically muted in their seasonings that we wondered if they would appeal to modern taste buds.

As we moved forward in time, to recipes submitted by recent immigrants or created to appeal to contemporary tastes, flavors grew bolder, and seasonings branched out to include bunched cilantro, garam masala, and white miso paste. A pie called for a concentrated reduction of Moxie soda, while a vegan cake incorporated chia seeds and unsweetened coconut yogurt. Categorizing the recipes and striking the right balance between offerings became a puzzle that we worked each day to solve. We shifted donuts between the bread and dessert sections, before finally sorting them and beans into their own dedicated chapters. We pruned abundant recipes for molasses cookies and whoopie pies to just a few and chose between two Brazilian lobster stews. By early March, Karl and I had a rough draft of the book completed and were working around the clock, editing recipes and images, filling omissions in each chapter with recipes from Don's historic community cookbooks, and trying to make space for latecomers whose recipes seemed too wonderful to leave out.

And then came the global pandemic.

"The amounts for this recipe are completely dependent on how many people you're serving! Adjust amount so that each person gets some of everything they want."

"Whenever we went to visit Grandma and Grandpa, this meal, with ployes, was always on the table. It tastes like a hug from my grandparents."

Each time I read a new recipe, I imagine who I would serve it to. Flipping through any of my favorite cookbooks, I plan a party in my head. Maybe it's just a cozy family dinner for me, Karl, and our three girls. Or maybe I've found a dish I'm sure my father-in-law would love: something with ginger, or dark chocolate, or lamb. No cooked cereal or seared fish for my mother-in-law, but always an extra serving of mashed turnips for our youngest, Sadie. I know people by their tastes, and I express my love by honoring them. I would no more serve my mother red meat than I would force blue cheese on my middle daughter, Beatrice, or bananas on my eldest, Charlotte. I find great satisfaction in the planning, the consultation of cookbooks, the note-taking and menu arrangement. Assembling a successful meal is a puzzle, much like putting together a book. It's an essentially optimistic act that begins with an amorphous idea and settles into a tangible thing. It's no wonder that I enjoy doing both.

In a larger sense, bigger than a meal or the contents of a single book, cookbooks hold comfort. They contain story and history, the flavors of childhood and possibility, with instructions for success. Their heft gives weight to our cravings—for love, community, stability. Even now, when our iPad charges on a wall mount in the kitchen, Karl and I turn to cookbooks for recipes and reference. We love the tactile feel of them, the weight in our hands as they fall open to favorite recipes, their pages loosened by use. We love their design, so clearly dating the book, the trim size and page organization shifting over decades. And, of course, we love the contents, the spattered recipes triggering memories of seasons past, dishes tried, and meals shared. Tucked in the cookbooks on our shelves are place cards drawn by our daughters, dated index cards planning holiday menus from the past two decades, and notes on favorite meals, dashed quickly onto scraps of Karl's old letterhead from *Time* magazine. Inscriptions, marginalia, and the collected ephemera that spill from their pages trace the trajectory of our lives. How often do I find solace in a sheaf of cookie recipes, carefully copied out in my grandmother's flowery handwriting? Or in the recipe for my favorite oatmeal bread from childhood, its page marked by the Valentine I gave to my mother in second grade?

As the pandemic set in and our family locked down, the cookbook I spent the most time with was the one we were finishing. If I had felt protective of this community before, the spread of the coronavirus and all the changes it wrought on our world magnified that feeling exponentially. I worried about elderly contributors and wondered how families were holding up. When I had questions about their contributions, I began each email with concern. One recipe, Leah's Fried Rice with Lobster, originated with a Bowdoin professor, Leah (Ya) Zuo, who comes from Wuhan, China. Though I didn't know her at all, I found myself obsessing over the health of Professor Zuo's extended family.

With the world in such disarray, it was a gift to be working on a project that felt so full of connections. That fearful feeling of confused dread that took over each day—should we be washing the outsides of our groceries? where can we find more latex gloves? is it worthwhile to spend $40 on a two-pound brick of yeast? (answer: yes)—abated when I lost myself in work on the cookbook. Despite our isolation, as we closed our farm to visitors and quarantined with our children, my community was expanded to include each contributor to the book, these new people I cared about, strangers but also intimate familiars. In so many stories in the *Maine*

Bicentennial Community Cookbook, hard times are looked on, through the distance of years, with nostalgia and even pride. The voices that began in my inbox as a cacophony settled into a chorus of encouragement: we've done hard things and we can do them again. Stories of resilience—through illness, war, displacement, and hunger—made me resilient.

As the months of the pandemic wore on, the book was published, if slightly behind schedule. In-person events and bicentennial celebrations were canceled, though the brave new world of Zoom made it possible to hold cook-alongs and give presentations about the project. Since the cookbook was one of the few bicentennial projects that had come to fruition—so much had been canceled or postponed—we received more media attention than we'd expected. The book was nominated for some regional awards and went into multiple printings. A second volume was then planned for release. Six months after publication, we were able to distribute more than $14,000 to organizations fighting hunger in Maine.

As it went out into the world, the book developed a life outside of us: a Methodist minister from a small Down East town cooked her way through the entire book and blogged about each recipe. Maine Farmland Trust, a farming conservation organization, gave the book as a prize for a summer scavenger hunt. A realtor bought a copy for each new house he sold. The community formed between its covers spun into more communities, off the page.

In the first pages of the cookbook, I began my editor's note: "This is a book about people." As strongly as I feel about recipes, we didn't test all that came in. Partly it was a question of time constraints, and partly it was trust that people were sending us their best. Most of all, we were as interested in the contributors as we were in their food. But as the pressure of deadlines receded, curiosity took hold, and we started cooking. We have yet to meet a recipe that didn't turn out beautifully. Perfect Popovers really are just that: perfect, and they've replaced our old recipe, which I'd made for years. Claptrap, a creamy mash of carrots, potatoes, and rutabagas, is a deceptively simple side dish that all three of our girls love. Chicken "Cuniglio," mujuddarah, red flannel hash, and squash rolls have started popping up on our family table. Cooking is community, and each of these recipes brings the stories and histories of other families into my own. Every time I open the *Maine Bicentennial Community Cookbook*, whether I'm making Somali sambusas, baked yellow-eye beans, Representative Chellie Pingree's roast chicken with apples, or simple corned hake, I am met with friends.

AFTERWORD
Debra Spark

I N MY LATE twenties and early thirties, I worked as a freelance editor for a variety of publishing houses around Boston. One day, I called the managing editor at one of my bigger employers and asked her to give me as many assignments as possible. The reason? My sister had just died at the age of twenty-six.

I have always liked to distract myself from pain with work.

This made Deborah Joy Corey's pandemic-era request that I help co-edit her anthology *Breaking Bread* an absolute gift. That the work was for a good cause was another plus.

Deborah and I met in Boston when we were both young writers. The first time I saw her, she had a large, silky, colorful scarf wrapped around her head, do-rag style. Her (quite handsome) husband was by her side. I thought, "Wow, she looks like a model, and he looks like a rock star."

Turns out, Deborah *had* worked as a model, and her husband *had* spent a lot of time with rock stars, on account of his then-business. They seemed too glamorous for me, but I quickly learned, through their incredible warmth to both me and my sister, what good and loving people they were. At some point, back when my sister was struggling with breast cancer, I had split the world into two: those who came through for you in times of trouble and those who didn't.

Deborah came through.

That she quietly turned that quality into a nonprofit fighting hunger was something I didn't even know (or fully grasp) until I got involved with this project. Nor did I understand how much a part of her daily life Blue Angel was, until emails were zooming from my house in North Yarmouth, Maine, to hers in Castine. I'd send her an edited essay for her to review, and she'd send back a "will read after I drop off this shipment of food" message. Or she'd send the essay back later that very day because one of her beloved daughters had done a food run for her, and she had a little extra time for editing.

Coming up with the idea for this collection—imagining a fun project with both serious and lighthearted essays about food—is another way that Deborah has come through and allowed others, through their contributions here or simply through their purchase of this book, to be in the camp of those who help. Thank you all.

About the Editors

DEBORAH JOY COREY is the author of three award-winning books, *Losing Eddie*, *The Skating Pond*, and *Settling Twice*. Many of her short stories have been anthologized, and she is the recipient of numerous awards, including Books in Canada Best Novel Award, the David Adams Richards Prize for Fiction, the "Elle's Lettres" Readers Prize, and the NPR Selected Shorts Prize. She is the founder and director of Blue Angel, for which she created this anthology, *Breaking Bread*. Born and raised in Canada, she now lives in Maine.

DEBRA SPARK is the author of six works of fiction, including (most recently) *Unknown Caller*, *The Pretty Girl*, and *Good for the Jews*. Her other books include two collections of essays on fiction writing and the anthology *20 Under 30*. Spark is the recipient of a National Endowment for the Arts fellowship, a Bunting Institute fellowship from Radcliffe College, a Wisconsin Institute Fellowship, the Michigan Literary Fiction Prize, and the John Zacharis/*Ploughshares* award for best first book. She is a professor at Colby College and teaches in the MFA Program for Writers at Warren Wilson College.

About the Contributors

KIFAH ABDULLA is the author of the memoir *Mountains Without Peaks* and the poetry book *Dead Still Dream*. Originally from Baghdad, Iraq, he is also a visual artist, performer, and teacher.

GABRIELA ACERO ditched plans of going to law school and instead worked in New York City restaurants for years. Now, she and her partner, Derek Richard, live in Camden, Maine, where they opened their first restaurant, wolfpeach, inspired by the decadence of New York and the simplicity of home.

JENNY BICKS is an award-winning television and film writer. Her credits include *Sex and the City* and the film *The Greatest Showman*. Her new series, *Welcome to Flatch*, premiered in March 2022 on Fox.

JENNIFER FINNEY BOYLAN, author of sixteen books, is the Anna Quindlen Writer-in-Residence at Barnard College of Columbia University and a trustee of PEN America. She is a contributing opinion writer for the *New York Times*, where her columns have appeared since 2007.

SARAH BRAUNSTEIN's fiction has appeared in the *New Yorker*, *Playboy*, and the *Harvard Review*. She is the author of the novel *The Sweet Relief of Missing Children* and winner of the Maine Book Award and the Rona Jaffe Writers' Award. She teaches at Colby College.

GREGORY BROWN is the author of the novel *The Lowering Days*. His stories have appeared in *Tin House*, the *Alaska Quarterly Review*, *Epoch*, and other magazines. A graduate of the Iowa Writers' Workshop, he lives with his family and a mess of dogs who believe the kitchen is completely theirs.

LYN MIKEL BROWN is a professor of education at Colby College and the author of six books, including her most recent, *Powered by Girl: A Field Guide for Supporting Youth Activists*.

JANE BROX's fifth book, *Silence*, was selected as an Editor's Choice by the *New York Times Book Review*. Her work has appeared in many journals and anthologies, including the *American Scholar*, *Best American Essays*, the *Boston Globe Sunday Magazine*, the *Georgia Review*, and NewYorker.com.

KATE CHRISTENSEN is the author of seven novels, including *The Great Man*, which won the 2008 PEN/Faulkner Award for fiction, and two food-centric memoirs, *Blue Plate Special* and *How to Cook a Moose*, which won the 2016 Maine Literary Award for Memoir.

MELISSA COLEMAN is the author of the best-selling memoir *This Life Is in Your Hands*. As a travel writer based in Freeport, Maine, her work has appeared in the *New York Times*, the *Boston Globe*, *Travel Weekly*, and *National Geographic Traveler*.

SUSAN CONLEY is the author of five critically acclaimed books. She is a fourth-generation Mainer who grew up in a rural town near the Kennebec River, and she writes about questions of women's power and class and belonging.

MARTIN CONTE is a high school English teacher and cofounder of the Unsafe Space Writing workshop and the *Thieves & Liars* underground graduate literary journal at the University of Maine. When he's not ushering students through poetry and fiction, he's playing steel-pan music, cold-water swimming, and flower gardening.

STEPHANIE COTSIRILOS is an author, a lawyer, and a performing artist whose songs and scripts were produced in New York. Her novella *My Xanthi* was published in 2021, and in the same year, she was the inaugural Krant Fellow at the Storyknife Writers Retreat in Alaska.

HAL CROWTHER is the author of *An Infuriating American: The Incendiary Arts of H. L. Mencken* and five essay collections, including *Freedom Fighters and Hellraisers*, which won the IPA gold medal for nonfiction in 2019.

RON CURRIE's writing has been translated into fifteen languages and has won the New York Public Library Young Lions Award, the Metcalf Award from the American Academy of Arts and Letters, the Alex Award from the American Library Association, and the Pushcart Prize.

Born and raised in Texas and Hong Kong, ALANA DAO now lives and works in Maine. A graduate of Smith College and the School of the Art Institute of Chicago, her work explores food, culture, and identity.

ANNE ELLIOTT's short stories can be found in *Story*, *A Public Space*, *Crab Orchard Review*, *Ploughshares Solos*, *Witness*, *Hobart*, and *Bellevue Literary Review*, and in her collection *The Artstars*. She is a graduate of the MFA Program for Writers at Warren Wilson College.

GIBSON FAY-LeBLANC is the author of two books, including *Deke Dangle Dive*, and his poems have appeared recently in *Poetry Northwest* and *Orion*. He directed the Telling Room from 2006 to 2011 and now serves as executive director of the Maine Writers & Publishers Alliance.

RICHARD FORD is a novelist, a story writer, and an essayist. His work has received many international and US prizes, among these the Pulitzer Prize and the 2019 Library of Congress Prize for American Fiction.

ALICE BINGHAM GORMAN's essays and short stories have been published in *Vogue*, *Oprah Magazine*, the *Louisville Review*, and others. Her first novel, *Valeria Vose*, was published in 2018.

ARIELLE GREENBERG is the author of five books of poetry and three books of creative nonfiction. She is the originator of the feminist literary theory the Gurlesque, and a second edition of her co-edited anthology on that subject is forthcoming.

PEGGY GRODINSKY is the food and books editor at the *Portland Press Herald*. Previously, she was executive editor of the Boston-based *Cook's Country* magazine (America's Test Kitchen), and she lived in Texas for several years, writing about food for the *Houston Chronicle*.

JASON GRUNDSTROM-WHITNEY, adopted son of Joan M. Dana, Bear Clan Mother of the Passamaquoddy, is a poet, a musician, an activist, a wilderness lover, a substance counselor, and a husband, father, and grandfather. He is the author of *Bear, Coyote, Raven* and *Blues of the Lost Places*.

KATHY GUNST is a James Beard Award–winning food journalist. She is the resident chef for NPR's *Here and Now* and the author of sixteen cookbooks.

MYRONN HARDY is the author of five books of poems, most recently, *Radioactive Starlings*. His poems have appeared in the *New York Times Magazine*, *Ploughshares*, *The Baffler*, and elsewhere. He teaches at Bates College.

MARGARET HATHAWAY is the author of six books on food and farming, including the memoir *The Year of the Goat* and the *Maine Bicentennial Community Cookbook*. She lives with her family on Ten Apple Farm, a homestead and agritourism business in southern Maine.

SHONNA MILLIKEN HUMPHREY wrote the novel *Show Me Good Land* and the memoir *Dirt Roads and Diner Pie*. Her essays have appeared in the *New York Times*, *The Atlantic*, *Salon*, and *Down East Magazine*. Her most recent book, *Gin*, is part of Bloomsbury's Object Lessons series.

MARGERY IRVINE has made the trip from Brooklyn, New York, to Brooklin, Maine. She teaches a class in narrative nonfiction at the University of Maine and has written essays for newspapers and Maine Public Radio.

Published in many journals, magazines, and anthologies, ANNALIESE JAKIMIDES's prose and poetry have also been broadcast on Maine Public and NPR. After years on a dirt road in Mt. Chase, Maine, population 160, she now lives in downtown Bangor.

REZA JALALI has taught at the University of Southern Maine. He is the author of a children's book, a play about women in Iran, and a collection of short stories. He is also the co-author of *Dear Maine: The Trials and Triumphs of Maine's 21st Century Immigrants*.

NANCY HARMON JENKINS is a food writer, a food historian, and an authority on the Mediterranean diet and olive oil. A Maine native, she divides her time between Camden and her Tuscan olive farm.

SUSAN KENNEY is the author of five novels, including *In Another Country* and *Sailing*. Her essays, short stories, and reviews have appeared in *Epoch*, the *Hudson Review*, *Redbook*, the *New York Times Book Review*, the *Boston Globe*, and *Down East Magazine*.

STUART KESTENBAUM is the author of six collections of poems, most recently *Things Seemed to Be Breaking* and a collection of essays, *The View from Here*. He served as Maine's poet laureate from 2016 to 2021.

LILY KING is the author of five novels, most recently *Euphoria* and *Writers & Lovers*, and a short story collection, *Five Tuesdays in Winter*. She has been awarded the Kirkus Award and the New England Book Award, and has been a finalist for the National Book Critics Circle Award.

A number-one *New York Times* best-selling author of eight novels, including *The Exiles*, *Orphan Train*, and *A Piece of the World*, CHRISTINA BAKER KLINE is published in forty countries.

JONATHAN and DESMOND LETHEM are members of the same family. Jonathan, a recipient of the 2005 MacArthur Fellowship, has published twelve novels, including *Motherless Brooklyn*, *Fortress of Solitude*, and, most recently, *The Arrest*. Desmond is a sixth grader.

MICHELE LEVESQUE has a BFA from the Nova Scotia College of Art and Design and an MFA from the California College of the Arts. She is the chef and owner of the acclaimed El El Frijoles in Sargentville, Maine.

A native New Yorker, CARL LITTLE moved to Maine in 1989. He is the former communications manager at the Maine Community Foundation. He is the author of numerous art books and reviews for *Hyperallergic*, *Art New England*, and other publications.

DONNA LORING is a Penobscot Indian Tribal Elder, a Vietnam veteran, an author, a playwright, and a radio host on *Wabanaki Windows*, WERU.org. She holds an honorary doctorate from the University of Maine at Orono and received the Courage Is Contagious Award from the Maine School of Law.

WESLEY MCNAIR has written eleven volumes of poetry, including the 2022 collection *Late Wonders: New & Selected Poems*.

SUSAN MINOT grew up in Manchester-by-the-Sea, Massachusetts. She writes fiction, nonfiction, poetry, plays, and screenplays. Her most recent story collection, *Why I Don't Write and Other Stories*, is her eighth book.

GENEVIEVE (G. A.) MORGAN is a writer and the fiction/memoir editor at Islandport Press. She is the author of The Five Stones trilogy, as well as several nonfiction titles, including *Undecided: Navigating Life and Learning After High School*. She writes extensively about food, health, and nutrition, despite her shockingly limited culinary skills.

MARILYN MOSS is the author of *Bill Moss: Fabric Artist & Designer*, as well as numerous articles. She is currently at work on "Barefoot to Boardroom," the story of Moss Inc., the company she cofounded.

PATRICIA O'DONNELL is a professor emerita of creative writing at the University of Maine at Farmington. Her work has appeared in the *New Yorker* and elsewhere, and she is the author of three books of fiction and one memoir.

SANDY OLIVER is a food writer and food historian writing weekly for *Bangor Daily News* and regularly for *Working Waterfront*, plus other Maine publications. The author of several food histories, her *Maine Home Cooking* was published by Down East Books.

ELIZABETH PEAVEY is the author of three books, countless print columns and features, and the celebrated one-woman show *My Mother's Clothes Are Not My Mother*. She has helped people craft and share their stories for nearly thirty years.

CATHIE PELLETIER has published twelve novels, two of which became television films. She cowrote *Proving Einstein Right*, with physicist S. James Gates Jr., a National Medal of Science recipient. Her most recent work is *Northeaster, the Maine Snowstorm of 1952*.

MARY E. PLOUFFE, PhD, is a clinical psychologist and writer of essays, creative nonfiction, and opinion pieces that view culture through a psychological lens.

KIMBERLY RIDLEY is a science writer, an essayist, a contributing editor to *Down East Magazine*, and the author of nonfiction nature books for children, including *The Secret Pool*. Her new book for adults is *Wild Design: Nature's Architects*.

LEWIS ROBINSON is the author of the story collection *Officer Friendly* and the novel *Water Dogs*. He teaches at the University of Maine at Farmington.

ROXANA ROBINSON has written ten books and is a Guggenheim and National Endowment for the Arts fellow. Her work has appeared in the *New Yorker, The Atlantic*, and elsewhere. A former president of the Authors Guild, she teaches in the Hunter MFA Program.

BILL ROORBACH's newest book is *Lucky Turtle*. Other works of fiction include *The Girl of the Lake*, *The Remedy for Love*, and *Life Among Giants*, and works of nonfiction include *Summers with Juliet*, *Into Woods*, and *Temple Stream*.

KATE RUSSO is an artist and writer who has an MFA from the Slade School of Fine Art and exhibits in both the UK and US. Her debut novel, *Super Host*, was published in 2021.

RICHARD RUSSO is the author of nine novels, two collections of short stories, a memoir, a book of essays, and several produced screenplays. His novel *Empire Falls* won the 2002 Pulitzer Prize.

MELISSA SENATE has written more than thirty novels, primarily in the romance genre. Her debut, *See Jane Date*, was adapted into a TV movie. Melissa lives in the small coastal town of Yarmouth, Maine.

KATE SHAFFER is the founder of the award-winning confectionery Ragged Coast Chocolates. She has authored three cookbooks: *Desserted: Recipes and Tales from an Island Chocolatier*, *Chocolate for Beginners*, and *The Maine Farm Table Cookbook*.

CAITLIN SHETTERLY is the author of three books of nonfiction—*Fault Lines*, *Made for You and Me*, and *Modified*—and the upcoming novel *Pete & Alice in Maine*. When she isn't entertaining her children or chopping up vegetables for a mirepoix, she is writing or working as editor in chief for Frenchly.com.

BRIAN SHUFF is the coauthor of *About Grief*. He teaches at Thomas College in Waterville and contributes regularly to *Décor Maine*.

LEE SMITH's many books include *Fair and Tender Ladies*; *The Last Girls*; her recent novella, *Blue Marlin*; and *Dimestore*, a collection of personal essays. Winner of many awards, she lives in North Carolina and Maine with husband Hal Crowther.

MAUREEN STANTON's memoir, *Body Leaping Backward: Memoir of a Delinquent Girlhood*, received the 2020 Maine Literary Award, and her book *Killer Stuff and Tons of Money* won a 2012 Massachusetts Book Award.

SUSAN STERLING is the author of the novel *Dancing in the Kitchen*. Her stories and essays have appeared in the *Best American Sports Writing*, the *New York Times*, *Witness*, and other literary journals.

KEVIN ST. JARRE is the author of seven novels, including *Celestine*, *The Twin*, and *Absence of Grace*. His writing has appeared in journals such as *Story* and *Solstice Literary Magazine*. A native of Madawaska, Maine, he now lives on the coast.

Tattooer, classicist, and writer, PHUC TRAN is the author of the acclaimed memoir *Sigh, Gone: A Misfit's Memoir of Great Books, Punk Rock*, and *The Fight to Fit In*.

JUSTIN TUSSING is the author of two novels, *Vexation Lullaby* and *The Best People in the World*. He teaches creative writing at the University of Southern Maine, where he directs the Stonecoast MFA and Stonecoast Summer Writers' Conference.

A native of Farmington, DESI VAN TIL worked in LA film production on such movies as *13 Going on 30* before turning to screenwriting. She wrote the romantic dramedy *Tumbledown*, set in her hometown.

KAREN WATTERSON is a freelance writer, a former food editor, and the author of *Sweet on Maine*, a blog about the sweet life in the state of Maine. She can most often be found in the kitchen baking with chocolate or walking her dog, Maple.

TANYA WHITON's writing has recently been featured in *Collateral, Cut-Bank, Fanzine, Cincinnati Review*, and *Beer & Weed Magazine*. She is the cowriter and an associate producer of the documentary feature *The Zen Speaker: Breaking the Silence*.

GEORGIA WILLIAMINA ZILDJIAN is a playwright, writer, and theater practitioner living and working in Downeast Maine.

Credits

"Take Another Little Pizza My Heart," by Jennifer Finney Boylan, originally appeared, under a different title, in the *New York Times*, August 27, 2014. It appears here by permission of the author.

"Father, Forgive Me," by Hal Crowther, originally appeared in *Cathedrals of Kudzu: A Personal Landscape of the South* (Baton Rouge: Louisiana State University Press, 2000).

"My Mother, the Lunch Lady," by Ron Currie, originally appeared in *Maine Women Magazine*, April 2019.

"A Suitcase of Tomatoes," by Christina Baker Kline, originally appeared in *Edible Jersey*, August 31, 2017.

"The Zen of Fiddleheads," by Cathie Pelletier, originally appeared in *Yankee*, May–June 2022.

"Saturday Breakfasts," by Susan Sterling, originally appeared in the *Christian Science Monitor*, April 8, 1990.

FOR THEIR HELP WITH THIS VOLUME, warm thanks to Gibson Fay-LeBlanc for help identifying writers to contact, to Molly McGrath for her writing coaching and advocacy for one of the authors in the volume, to our agents Jennifer Carlson and Eleanor Jackson for their thoughts and advice, and to Georgia Williamina Zildjian for her skills as editor, scribe, and tech assistant.